Palgrave Studies in Literature, Culture and Economics

Series Editors
Paul Crosthwaite
School of Literatures, Languages & Culture
University of Edinburgh
Edinburgh, UK

Peter Knight
Department of English and American Studies
University of Manchester
Manchester, UK

Nicky Marsh
Department of English
University of Southampton
Southampton, UK

This series showcases some of the most intellectually adventurous work being done in the broad field of the economic humanities, putting it in dialogue with developments in heterodox economic theory, economic sociology, critical finance studies and the history of capitalism. It starts from the conviction that literary and cultural studies can provide vital theoretical insights into economics. The series will include historical studies as well as contemporary ones, as a much-needed counterweight to the tendency within economics to concentrate solely on the present and to ignore potential lessons from history. The series also recognizes that the poetics of economics and finance is an increasingly central concern across a wide range of fields of literary study, from Shakespeare to Dickens to the financial thriller. In doing so it builds on the scholarship that has been identified as the 'new economic criticism', but moves beyond it by bringing a more politically and historically sharpened focus to that earlier work.

More information about this series at
http://www.palgrave.com/gp/series/15745

Neil Cocks
Editor

Questioning Ayn Rand

Subjectivity, Political Economy, and the Arts

Editor
Neil Cocks
University of Reading
Reading, UK

Palgrave Studies in Literature, Culture and Economics
ISBN 978-3-030-53072-3   ISBN 978-3-030-53073-0   (eBook)
https://doi.org/10.1007/978-3-030-53073-0

This Palgrave Macmillan imprint is published by the registered company Springer Nature Switzerland AG
The registered company address is: Gewerbestrasse 11, 6330 Cham, Switzerland

CONTENTS

NOTES ON CONTRIBUTORS

Neil Cocks is a lecturer in the Department of English Literature at the University of Reading, UK. He has authored two books previously for Palgrave: *The Peripheral Child in Nineteenth Century Literature and its Criticism* (2014) and *Higher Education Discourse and Deconstruction* (2018).

Jerome Cox-Strong is due to begin a Ph.D. in English and American Studies at The University of Manchester in 2021, researching dystopia and the child. As a researcher and activist, he also holds a particular interest in pedagogy and Higher Education.

Jan De Vos is author of, amongst others *Psychologisation in Times of Globalisation* (Routledge, 2012) and *The Metamorphoses of the Brain. Neurologisation and Its Discontents* (Palgrave, 2016). His most recent book is *The Digitalisation of (Inter)Subjectivity. A Psi-critique of the Digital Death Drive* (Routledge, 2020).

Lisa Downing is Professor of French Discourses of Sexuality at the University of Birmingham, UK. She is the author of a raft of publications including, most recently, *Selfish Women* (Routledge, 2019).

Bonnie McGill gained her doctorate at the Graduate Centre for International Research in Childhood: Literature, Media and Culture (CIRCL) at The University of Reading. She has an ongoing interest in constructions of time, and is currently researching time in relation to ideas of mathematical infinity.

Ian Parker is a psychoanalyst and Marxist active in Manchester, UK, whose latest books are *Psychoanalysis, Clinic and Context* (Routledge, 2019) and *Psychology Through Critical Auto-Ethnography* (Routledge, 2020).

Stephen Thomson is a lecturer in English Literature at The University of Reading. His broad research focus is on ways in which ideas and anxieties of modernity are played out in literary narratives of the nineteenth and twentieth centuries, and his recent publications include work on Derrida and Descartes (*Oxford Literary Review*, 2017) and Agamben and gender (*Textual Practice*, 2020).

Kristina West is an Independent Scholar and member of the Emerson Society. She has two books forthcoming with Palgrave: *Louisa May Alcott and the Textual Child* (2020) and *Reading the Salem Witch Child* (2020).

LIST OF FIGURES

Chapter 6

CHAPTER 1

Introduction: Uncanny Rand

Neil Cocks

1 DIVISIVE RAND

In 2018, I organised a conference on the work of Ayn Rand, the controversial and popular novelist, founder of the philosophical movement of Objectivism, and cheerleader for unrestrained capitalism. As far as I know, this was the first conference to approach its subject from a perspective consistently and explicitly resistant to her ideology. This fact still surprises me. Since her death in 1982, Rand's influence has only grown. One might think that the result of having possibly the most famous twentieth-century American theorist of the right top bestseller lists, receive praise from powerful politicians and business leaders, and gain endorsements from weighty academic tomes, would be a substantial counterattack from progressive or left-leaning academics.[1]

Is this reluctance to discuss Rand due to her work being figured as morally and politically irredeemable? Perhaps. This is the author of *The Virtue Or Selfishness*, who argued for child labour, idolised the child-killer William Hickman, and described Native Americans as 'savages' (Rand 1974).[2] I think this is not the whole of it, however, as her output is also

N. Cocks (✉)
University of Reading, Reading, UK

© The Author(s) 2020
N. Cocks (ed.), *Questioning Ayn Rand*,
Palgrave Studies in Literature, Culture and Economics,
https://doi.org/10.1007/978-3-030-53073-0_1

considered by many to be vulgar, confused, and, well, just a bit *silly*. Her classic novel, *Atlas Shrugged*, turns on the invention of what is fundamentally a perpetual motion device, after all. It also praises artistic refinement despite climaxing in a speech by its hero, extolling the virtues of Rand's own Objectivist philosophy, that goes on (and on) for sixty uninterrupted pages. Taking *Atlas Shrugged* seriously is not without its risks, therefore, as it might result in some fellow theorists being less inclined to afford one the same privilege.

Rand's writing divided opinion from the moment it encountered a significant audience, and a stubborn resolve to ignore or ridicule the work has long been established as an acceptable critical response. Desperate to escape deprivations in communist Russia, the 21-year-old Rand travelled to America in 1926, gained some success as a scriptwriter in Hollywood, and, 10 years later, a Broadway play and her first novel met with modest sales and some positive reviews. It was with the publication of *The Fountainhead* in 1943, however, that Rand began to gain widespread recognition. The novel concerns an architect successfully pursuing his personal vision in a world hostile to individualism and self-reliance. It was not well publicised, and did not instantly find a readership, but within a year it entered the bestseller lists, largely through word of mouth, was made into a film in 1949, and by 1956 had sold 70,000 copies. *The Fountainhead* met with derision as well as praise, with one particularly unimpressed critic concluding that 'anyone who is taken in by it deserves a stern lecture on paper rationing'.[3] The film version was savagely reviewed: 'incredibly stupid'; 'the silliest picture of the year'.[4] *Atlas Shrugged* was published 14 years after *The Fountainhead*, and follows a group of business leaders as they prove their worth to society at large, and ultimately turn a profit, by going on strike. It was even more successful and divisive than her previous work, with the fiercest criticism coming from thinkers on the right, shocked by Rand's unapologetic celebration of selfishness and sexuality. In a notorious review, conservative commentator Whittaker Chambers initially describes 'a remarkably silly book', but ends with a far darker assessment: 'From almost any page of *Atlas Shrugged* a voice can be heard, from painful necessity, commanding: "To a gas chamber—go!"' (Chambers 1957). Rand was dismayed by this reception, retreated from public life for a while, and abandoned the novel as her preferred form of expression. When she re-emerged, it was as a writer of non-fiction and public speaker, publishing her own periodicals and releasing several collections of essays.[5] All of Rand's writing, fictional or not, consistently champions her philosophy of Objectivism, which she summed up in the following terms: '(1) Metaphysics: Objective Reality; (2) Epistemology: Reason; (3) Ethics: Self-Interest; (4) Politics: Capitalism' (Rand 1988, 343). If Rand's work is rejected by some because of its violence or absurdity, it is arguably the starkness of her worldview evidenced here that is the greatest contribution to the polarisation of critical responses.

2 ACADEMIC RAND

Despite the initial rejection of Objectivist literature by conservative thinkers, Rand and her followers exercise a profound influence on the contemporary right, not only in America, but across the world, and since the 1970s, critical commentary on Rand has been produced largely by uncritical defenders of her work. Recently, however, unswerving adherence to Objectivist philosophical principles has, in some quarters, been replaced by more nuanced and scholarly assessments. Most significant here, perhaps, is *Goddess of the Market* by Jennifer Burns, an academic biography published by Oxford University Press in 2009. Burns is sympathetic to Rand, but offers a rich and detailed history that very much departs from the parochialism that characterises much of what passes for scholarship in the field. Despite this, it is instructive that Burns' work, and that of other comparable figures such as Anne C. Heller, is often taken as a politically neutral assessment of Objectivism. Roderick Long calls Burns' text 'even-handed', Elaine Showalter describes it as a 'dispassionate intellectual history', and, in a recent monograph on Rand and Posthumanism, Ben Murnane praises its 'nonpartisan' approach (Long 2001; Showalter quoted in Burns 2017; Murnane 2018, 4). It could be argued that such reviews do little more than establish what their authors regard as politically unmarked. *The Goddess of the Market* rejects the critical view that Rand is a 'right-wing extremist', for example, and resists also the argument that her work is racist: for Burns, although Rand 'opposed the 1964 Civil Rights Act, a litmus test of liberal acceptability', she was not 'truly prejudiced' (Burns 2009, 205).[6]

Something of a connection can be made here to *The Journal of Ayn Rand Studies*, the main source of academic work on Objectivism, which also makes the claim for neutrality, encouraging those who would both criticise and celebrate Rand to contribute articles. The journal has done much to legitimise the study of Objectivism by encouraging scholarship from academics opposed to it, and has received strong disapproval from some Objectivists for this (Glenn 2007). If it can thus be applauded for encouraging genuine academic debate, one could also understand its work in a more critical sense: by bringing in recognised, mainstream academic voices, the journal grants legitimacy to the work of down-the-line Objectivists. Instead of being taken as limited, inward-looking works, Objectivist texts are reframed as both entirely equal and a necessary counter to those of established academics. Significantly, in relation to claims of neutrality, *The Journal of Ayn Rand Studies* was created and initially edited by Chris Matthew Sciabarra, arguably the most successful contemporary academic promoter of Objectivist thought, Stephen Cox, editor of *Liberty* magazine, and R. W. Bradford, who, although critical of aspects of Rand's philosophy, was also a libertarian.[7] Although these academics may offer divergent opinions, they do so from within a specific—and to those on the outside, rather niche—tradition of political thought. It is my understanding, then, that texts that claim neutrality on Rand more usually end up endorsing and normalising at least some of her ideas, and it follows that the approach taken by this present book is *one of critique*.

Although the response to Objectivism from left-leaning or progressive commentators has often been amused indifference or horrified recoil, the chapters that follow are not the first to question Rand's ideas in detail. Many individual articles in *The Journal of Ayn Rand Studies* do offer pointed criticism from positions not aligned with libertarianism or Objectivism, the most celebrated of these perhaps being Slavoj Žižek's 'The Actuality of Ayn Rand', a work that is analysed at length within the opening chapters of this present book (Žižek 2002). Arguably, the initial, path-breaking engagement occurs in the 1970s, however, when feminist scholars such as Susan Brownmiller offer brief yet reasonably detailed responses to *The Fountainhead* and *Atlas Shrugged*. Brownmiller takes issue with the gender politics forwarded by these texts, and figures Rand as 'a traitor to her own sex', not least because of her ambivalent attitudes to rape (Brownmiller 1999).[8] More recent feminist work, although strongly critiquing Rand's patriarchal worldview, moves on from wholesale rejection, seeing in these novels also a subversive potential: Rand's heroines enjoy sex with multiple partners, and suffer no repercussions for this, while her 'libertarian rages against the strictures of family, church, and state appeal to many LGBT readers' (Duggan 2019, 11).[9] In 1999, a number of such responses were collected in *Feminist Interpretations of Ayn Rand*. Despite this, the text does not offer a sustained critique of Rand's work, and the majority of the essays included are in support of Rand, with many of them coming from a straightforward Objectivist standpoint. The work is edited once again by Sciabarra, this time joined by Mimi Gladstein, another prominent defender of Objectivism.[10]

More recently, a growing understanding of the urgency of engaging in detail with Rand's ideas has resulted in a number of particularly astute responses from critics outside the field of Ayn Rand Studies, in texts not edited by scholars with a declared allegiance to Randian ideas, nor even with any investment in wider libertarian or Republican narratives. I am thinking here especially of Myka Tucker-Abramson engaging Rand to locate the origins of neoliberalism in mid-century 'urban renewal projects', Andrew Hoberek's related account of *Atlas Shrugged*, mental labour and changes to middle-class employment, and Sarah Comyn offering an exacting reading of differences between the Objectivist model of 'economic man' and that to be read in the work of Friedrich Hayek. It was not until 2019, however, with the publication of Lisa Duggan's *Mean Girl: Ayn Rand and the Culture of Greed*, that this more independent and critical approach became, for the first time, the single focus of a major academic book.[11]

3   MEAN RAND

With *Mean Girl*, Duggan offers an account of the rise of neoliberalism in the twentieth century, told through a history of Rand's life and work. In its initial chapters, the book charts the subtle shifts in Rand's politics: her unhappy formative years in Russia; the move to America, and her work as a screenwriter; the subsequent, transformative experience of discussing anti-New Deal politics and freedom of opportunity with New York intellectuals; her time as a hawkish 'cold-warrior'; the emergence of a small, youthful, and rather claustrophobic group, led by Nathaniel and Barbara Branden, dedicated to promoting Randian ideas; the writing of her two most celebrated novels; her public promotion of purportedly free-market economics in the mid-1960s and 1970s, endorsement of politicians understood to be in pursuit of the same, and the support this garnered from conservative youth groups and libertarians; the recognition she received from The Republican Party during her final years.

As Duggan argues, this last was achieved through Rand's influence on the development of neoliberalism, the 'decidedly planned version of "laissez-faire" capitalism' that emerged in the 1970s to become, from Ronald Reagan's presidency onwards, the dominant force in American politics (Duggan 2019, 81).[12] Rand's novels can be understood to offer an early and seductive articulation of the values of what would become known as 'disaster capitalism': the destruction of a range of economic safeguards is engineered, and the 'privatization of public services, deregulation of corporate operations, and erosion of consumer and workplace protections' is forwarded as a remedy for the chaos that ensues, with this whole process increasingly and violently pushed beyond western borders as part of a global 'civilising' project.[13]

Because neoliberalism combines its utopian commitment to individual freedom with shadowy economic interventionism, it could be argued that it significantly strays from strict Objectivist principles. As I will argue below, however, the radical independence promoted by Rand and her followers always requires a frame, shaping hand, or guarantee, and thus, in one sense, neoliberal steerage demonstrates fidelity to the Randian worldview. In any case, as Duggan concludes, this notion of a dominant right-wing discourse citing Objectivism as an influence even as it diverges from it sets something of a template for subsequent operations: in a move vital for neoliberal expansion, Rand's disciple Alan Greenspan dropped his investment in the gold standard, central to Objectivist economics, shortly before becoming the Chairman of the Federal Reserve; Donald Trump cites Rand as an influence, yet his cronyism, corruption, and willingness to intervene in business matters sets him up as a typical *Atlas Shrugged* villain; Republican Rand devotees such as Paul Ryan embrace the religion she hated; Silicon Valley entrepreneurs may cite Rand as an influence, but they exemplify the libertarianism she consistently disparaged for its failure to strictly adhere to principles of 'reason'; if the post-crash resurgence of faith in Randian economics indicates the extent to which the bizarre logic of her 'shock doctrine' has gained a kind of intuitive sense, it is an acceptance that is achieved only through a widespread recognition of 'the flaw' in those economic theories. For Duggan, Rand 'stood alongside rather than within the neoliberal project', a positioning, it can be claimed, that is repeated wherever Objectivism encounters a major body of twenty-first-century right-wing thought (Duggan 2019, 87–88). Rand's influence, for Duggan, cannot be traced back to any particular formulation within her work, nor even any specific set of ideas, but is identifiable instead in society's general direction of travel: 'We are in the midst of a major global, political, economic, social, and cultural transition [...] the unifying threads are meanness and greed, and the spirit of the whole hodgepodge is Ayn Rand' (xiii).

4   PURE RAND

While I share Duggan's understanding of this history, and her scepticism towards Objectivism, the chapters included in this present book take a slightly different approach to questioning Rand's work. One advantage of an edited collection is that it enables multidisciplinary perspectives on the work of a multidisciplinary writer. Rand was interested not only in economic policy and the near-future dystopian novel, but also, for example, architecture, aesthetics, epistemology, popular fiction, and tap-dancing. This book is designed to respond to at least some of the fields that drew her attention, with work on subjects as diverse as Civil Rights, Romanticism, and psychoanalysis. Our interest is in their specificity, and, for reasons that will become clear, each of the following chapters attends closely to the detail of the discourse it engages.

Secondly, the multidisciplinary approaches to Objectivism in this book share a concern with the theoretical implications of two connected ideas that are taken to be central to the Randian project, and that lead us to the detailed reading of her texts: purity and revelation.

Considering the former, we might begin with one of Rand's most cele-brated formulations: that the philosophy of Objectivism is based on 'the concept of man as a heroic being, with his own happiness as the moral purpose of his life, with productive achievement as his noblest activity, and reason as his only absolute' (Afterward to Rand 1957).[14] 'Man'—and it is generally 'man' with Rand—can acquire certain knowledge of the world through rational enquiry, and use this knowledge to transform his envi-ronment and achieve his desires. He may compete with others but never come into conflict with them, so long as they too are thinking rationally. Such thought necessitates a shared understanding of the world, and a consistent need to embark upon transformative projects in order to meet one's desires within it. It follows from this that Objectivism draws a clear line between productive members of society and others whose influence is only destructive. On the one hand there are heroic wealth producers, the factory owners, inventors, and transport tycoons whose companies invariably bear their name, and the good workers who help actualise the vision of these captains of industry through diligent labour. On the other there are the 'second handers' who redistribute this hard-earned wealth, and the undeserving poor who ungratefully receive it. The hatred for this latter group is absolute: they are 'parasites', 'moochers', 'looters'. In part, such a Manichean worldview is justified in Rand's writing through the claim that these corrupt individuals cannot generate wealth themselves precisely because their thinking is unfocused and irrational. They lack the clarity of mind that is the single quality worthy of respect. The flip side of this is that those who do possess clarity of mind will not identify any ethical nuance in those they are set against because such subtleties oppose the form of thinking that is the condition of their success. Rand claims as the central tenet of her philosophy a law of non-contradiction, 'A = A'.[15] The Objectivist faith in this law can be understood to be vital to both its reactionary identity politics and its claimed adherence to laissez-faire economics: for the Objectivist, any analysis of society must be rooted in a notion of a hard-impacted subject. The Randian self is singular and independent. It is authentically free to choose, and its choice cannot be compromised by inconsistency and division. Likewise, this self must choose between stable objects, untouched by any perspective upon them. What we have termed 'Randian purity' is, then, that of subject and object seemingly divested of any 'other', free from influence, and liberated from any wider organising structures; not only does no one tell the Objectivist what to do, there is no requirement for such an individual to explain to anyone else what she is doing. As Sarah Comyn has argued, it is an understanding that, again, might seem to place Randian thought against wider trends in the neoliberalism she influenced (Comyn 2018). In Philip Mirowski's phrase, neoliberalism promotes not the secure individual but 'The Incredible Disappearing Agent': its subject is fractured, dispersed, and irrational. Within contemporary neoliberal theory, rationality and self-realisation dwell not with the subject, but the market, figured as a flawless and 'uniquely omnipotent information processor' (Mirowski 2013, 59, 141).

Because the Randian is supposed to act gloriously alone, she must, of course, be understood to be independent of any discursive frame imposed upon her. What matters is her ability to stay true to herself and to reason, not whatever opinions others might have of her. One difficulty with this idea, and with an unproblematic distinction between Randian and neoliberal subjects, can be introduced, however, if we consider the manner in which Rand's novels are narrated. These are not first person texts: when Randian heroes think and act, they do so through the frame of an external perspective ('[Howard] Roark knew that the last act of kindness he could offer was to claim no bond', etc. [Rand (1943, 723)]). What is of interest to a number of the chapters in this present book is the way this perspective compromises the Objectivist commitment to a hard-impacted self. The seemingly radically independent subject, neither touched by nor employing neoliberal manipulation, is not independent of others in Rand's fiction, but constituted precisely through an additional perspective.

For Rand, the ability of a third person narration to constitute an independent hero in this way is, no doubt, attributable to the universality of reason, as introduced above. If all Objectivists follow reason, then a reasoned perspective on the Randian hero will turn on the same truths as that offered by a heroic, first person narrative. To suggest that a first and third point of view are fundamentally the same is, however, indicative of an instrumentalist understanding of literature: for Rand, the precise language of a given text, including whatever point of view it establishes, has no shaping influence on its meaning, and any compromises to the self that it introduces can therefore be ignored. Instead, language is there to realise a prior, individual vision: literary 'style' is, in Objectivist terms, 'only a means to an end, the means of telling a story', with the 'revelatory power' of literature being its ability to 'express [...], fundamentally, under all its lesser aspects [...]: "*This* is life as *I* see it"' (Rand 1975, 24, 88).[16] It is for this reason that I would question Whittaker Chamber's attack on *Atlas Shrugged*, as quoted previously: for Chambers, what is damning about the novel is not any of its specific textual formulations, but instead a 'voice' that can be heard to command the same thing over and over from 'almost every page'. However powerful this description might be, it pins its critique on the idea of a singular, unified, and idealised message, a move to transcend textual difference that repeats at least one aspect of the Objectivist philosophy it sets itself against. Counter to this, it is my contention that the precise terms of Objectivist texts are not incidental to whatever ideology they espouse. Analysing Objectivist ideology necessitates taking seriously what could all too easily be dismissed as its merely revelatory, and thus secondary, aspect. There is an interest in this present book in returning to Objectivist texts something of the excess of meaning they deny; that part of language that is not *useful*. Rand famously claimed that she could 'give *the reason for every word* and every punctuation mark in *Atlas Shrugged*' (Rand 2000, 4). But what, I would ask, of the meaning beyond reason? Or, to put it another way, what possibilities of reading are opened up if one thinks of Rand's writing as literary, rather than simply purposeful or functional?

5   Uncanny Rand

With the notion of Randian purity introduced, a further connected issue can be understood to come to light. If all the chapters in this book, in different ways and to different extents, offer a critique of Randian politics, they also focus on the uncomfortable meeting points between such politics and their own political commitments. It is the contention of this book that this is as it should be. As I argue in my own chapters, those on the left who would simply dismiss Rand, understanding her to be a horrible monstrosity forever set apart, are in danger of repeating the very divisive politics she supports.[17] Those following such a line of argument will end up wedded to an ethics of purity, and as Jacqueline Rose argues in a short essay in *The Guardian*, published on Donald Trump's elevation to the Presidency, that is, especially perhaps at the present time, a very difficult arrangement to maintain:

> There is a problem with the tendency among those of us opposed to Trump to disparage his supporters as mere bigots – misogynists, racists, 'deplorables' in Clinton's unfortunate expression – even if, or especially if, somewhere that also feels true. This tendency makes the mistake of claiming possession of the house of reason, as if no ugly thought or hateful impulse has ever entered our own hearts and minds. It makes a false claim of innocence […] After all, it is the rhetoric of innocence – only the other is to blame, we have done nothing – that gives licence to kill, as we have seen so starkly since the US wars against Afghanistan and Iraq were set off in response to 9/11. […] At the very moment we galvanise politically, we must remain as vigilant of ourselves as of everyone else. Otherwise, before we know where we are, we will simply have joined in the murderous rhetoric of hatred. (Rose 2016)

It is not that there are no differences between, for example, a politics that engages in the necessity of the social and Rand's own commitment to a discrete and selfish subject, but rather that any argument that furthers these differences from a point of political purity will find itself caught in a most disruptive and damaging iteration. One difference between Randian ideas and the criticism of them forwarded by the contributors to this book is that the latter can tolerate the notion that it might not be entirely pure, might, at some stage, be touched by its other. Rand, in contrast, is no champion of the dialectic.[18]

With this in mind, my argument that there is an unaccountable excess to Randian texts that can be returned to them can be further refined: I take the following chapters to suggest that there is something *uncanny* about Rand.[19] It might come as a surprise that the Freudian term is understood in relation to Objectivism, as it opposes the stability of self-identity promoted in that philosophy. Approached in another way, however, it may seem wholly right that the uncanny should find itself caught up in such a problematisation of seemingly secure divisions between methodological approaches. As Freud suggests in his 1919 text on the subject, although the 'German word "unheimlich" is the opposite of "heimlich" ["homely"], "heimisch" ["native"]', and therefore 'we are tempted to conclude that what is "uncanny" is frightening precisely because it is *not* known and familiar', '[s]omething has to be added to what is novel and familiar in order to make it uncanny',[20] and this results in the following difficulty:

> This addition turns out to be the very term 'the uncanny' has been positioned against: as Freud works through various definitions, he finds that 'amongst its different shades of meaning the word "heimlich" exhibits one which is identical with its opposite, "unheimlich"'. What is *heimlich* thus comes to be *unheimlich*, and Freud's mission to locate the 'definite form' of the experience results, at the very point of success, in an acknowledgement of the impossibility of the enterprise. Native to 'the uncanny' is all that is of necessity most foreign. (Freud quoted in Cocks 2016, 364)

In framing 'the uncanny' in terms of Objectivism, we are first of all interested in the extent to which Randian discourse is necessarily compromised by its other. Thus, for example, in his chapter Jan De Vos charts the moves by which Randian anti-psychology always finds itself appealing to the psychological; Lisa Downing returns the gendered subject to the universality of Objectivist narratives; Kristina West reintroduces the constitutive figure of the child to a literature that is widely thought to ignore it; my first chapter emphasises the unacknowledged textuality that Rand's arguments require. Indeed, one of our central approaches is to set up a dialogue between Rand and other writers, situating her work in contexts that are unexpected, but also drawing out what, for example, is Marxist or Emersonian about Rand. In returning these 'dangerous supplements' to Rand's texts, we are not only disrupting the secure binaries on which they depend, but are also engaged in a project of making strange what can too easily become a familiar body of work.[21] In bringing to light what is unhomely in Rand, we are suggesting not only that those committed to Objectivism need to revaluate their key texts, but that declared progressive or radical-left critics of the movement also need to address their own assumptions about this polarising body of work. This does not necessarily entail an understanding of this work as equal to its criticism, nor an endorsement of a purportedly non-partisan approach, but, instead, a critique that engages its own limits and dangers.

It is here also that we might return to the majority of previous scholarship on Rand and identify a difference between this and our own work. As I have suggested, often the more sophisticated academic responses to Rand are premised either on a careful contrasting of her ideas with wider Objectivist, libertarian, and conservative discourse, or an equally careful comparison of Objectivist thought and wider, established philosophical positions. Both approaches have the advantage of resisting a reductive reading of Objectivist thought.[22] In my understanding, however, this promotion of complexity comes at a price, as the process of making strange, as introduced above, is not encouraged. By drawing out what is uncanny in the words of Rand and her followers, the following chapters trouble the kind of criticism that sets itself the task of choosing between secure philosophical standpoints. Such positions are compromised within our reading of them, with Objectivist texts understood to say more and less than their arguments require, and never wholly removable from their philosophical others. In the nine chapters that follow, A is never quite A.

6   THE CHAPTERS

Although this book is purposefully designed so that its central concerns can be followed across all of the chapters, I have divided these into three equal groups. The first three chapters read Randian texts in the context of psychoanalysis and psychology; the middle set deals with Objectivism and the arts, especially literature and film; chapters in the final group locate Rand's work in the context of wider political and economic debates.

Ian Parker opens the book proper with an investigation of Ayn Rand's reliance on frameworks held in common with psychoanalysis, a discipline she dismissed. Parker introduces the work of one of Objectivism's most vocal contemporaneous critics, Thomas Szasz, and demonstrates not only that his American ego-psychological libertarianism chimes with the Objectivism it questions, but claims also that more recent critiques from the psychoanalytic left, including most famously that by Slavoj Žižek, also fail to work through the extent to which they are caught up in the logic they seek to subvert. Parker commits to an approach that attends to the psychoanalytic implications of these texts, rather than the application of a stable set of psychoanalytic 'rules': 'The task is not to discover what is secretly psychoanalytic in [Rand's] writing, unconsciously buried in it, but to track the signifiers of a form of subjectivity to which psychoanalysis attaches itself and then explicates'. Parker argues that it is only such an open-ended and contextually aware form of analysis that can counter the limited and calcified power relations and unacknowledged repressions that characterise both Objectivism and the discourses that have traditionally been set against it.

Jan De Vos also takes as his starting point Rand's surprisingly intimate relationship with psychology and psychoanalysis. He is interested in the extent to which Objectivism calls upon what has come to be termed 'psychologisation', an 'overspill of the psychological in discourse to non-psychological areas' that is often met with consternation by right-wing commentators.[23] Psychology is regarded in such commentary as repressive and irrelevant, and this leads to the suggestion that we should go back to a time before psychology, when things were simpler and we were authentically ourselves. The rejection of psychology seemingly allows access to a pure subjectivity, and thus the move against psychologisation proves to be one of its most forceful articulations. De Vos begins by reading this move in Rand's work, where a clear boundary between the psychological and the pure logic of Objectivism is quickly dissolved, as the latter claims to show us who we 'truly' are. Again, Objectivism is not opposed to psychologisation, but insists instead that it grants access to a psychology so authentic that it should not really be classed as a psychology at all. It just is what is. De Vos then makes a connection to narratives produced and repeated within Silicon Valley, as its entrepreneurs often cite Rand as an influence, with praise for individuality, and a hatred of the state, seen as the connecting threads. De Vos claims instead that one of their central ties is this mutual entanglement in the dialectic of psychologisation. Both Rand and Silicon Valley are invested in the notion of an independent and assessable reality, yet neither can acknowledge the alienating movement necessary to this seemingly natural state.

In De Vos's understanding, then, the desired pure or authentic state is not prior to its inauthentic other, but rather its surplus or supplement: purity only comes to us through the rejection of dirt and detritus. To rearticulate this in the terms that organise this book, we might say that it is revelation that brings into being what, now revealed, seems always to have been waiting for its moment in the light. From this understanding, De Vos makes a connection between the place of the 'literary' in Randian philosophy and that of the 'virtual' within contemporary techno-utopian discourse, arguing not that these two realms signal a move away from the demands of 'real life' but, instead, that 'real life' is framed as such through these phantasmatic discourses. It is such a notion that I take up in Chapter 4, which addresses Rand's novel *The Fountainhead* as well as her anti-communist testimony to the House UnAmerican Committee. My central contention is that the purity of Rand's narratives is always compromised, not least through their literary status: Rand is constantly disavowing the narrative frame that is necessary for her philosophy to be 'revealed'. I further claim that a comparable disavowal can be read in the work of her most radical of critics, specifically Slavoj Žižek, thus bringing the first section of the book to a close by returning to arguments set out by Ian Parker in its opening chapter.

Kristina West begins the book's second section with a chapter that develops a reading of the literary construction of the Randian subject, introducing the psychological theories necessary to Rand's aesthetics. To this end, West contrasts Randian individualism with that forwarded by another greater American mythologiser of the self, and self-declared 'Romantic' thinker, Ralph Waldo Emerson. West's sustained interest is in their constructions of childhood. Childhood is often understood to hold very little interest for Rand. Whittaker Chambers, in the review quoted previously, declared that 'the strenuously sterile world of *Atlas Shrugged* is scarcely a place for children' (Chambers 1957). As West argues, however, Rand's writing repeatedly returns to the child, as it presents a problem for Objectivist philosophy. Does the good Objectivist look back on herself when a child to see something entirely other, a being lacking the rationality that defines the mature individual? Or does the Objectivist self, so resistant to the influence of the outside world, remain fundamentally unchanged throughout its existence? Emerson encounters some of the same deadlocks, West contends, and argues that engaging the ways they both work through, and are defeated by, the challenge of the child, can help bring to light what is at stake in Rand's particular brand of self-reliant subjecthood.

Individualism is also the subject of Lisa Downing's analysis of two very different films: King Vidor's 1949 cinematic version of *The Fountainhead* and Chris Menaul's 1999 made-for-television biopic *The Passion of Ayn Rand*. Downing disrupts and extends Randian notions of heroism through returning to them the question of gender that they more usually repress. The Objectivist hero is more usually abstracted from such concerns, seemingly unmarked by existing societal divisions that see agency and action equated with men, and connectiveness and cooperation with women. Downing is interested in the extent to which Rand's work can realise the possibility and enable a representation of the female hero. In this, she is also concerned with the degree to which the purity of Rand's authorial vision in this regard is challenged by the seemingly supplementary processes and negotiations necessary to film production.

Returning to the strange retrospective logic introduced by Jan De Vos, Bonnie McGill ends the second section of the book with a further meditation on the difficulties that attend narratives of realisation, whether these concern a work of art or a political project. For McGill, one of the challenges involved in such accounts is that of 'pre-history', that is: how are we to identify the conditions necessary for a given process outside of and prior to that process? This might appear a somewhat abstract concern, but, as McGill demonstrates, for Rand the issue is urgent. Objectivism is, after all, invested in the notion that each individual is tasked with fulfilling his or her potential. From the point of completion, however, how can such potential by known *as potential*, that is, known as itself, as the A that is nothing other than A? McGill's first audacious move is to contrast Rand's difficulty in this area with that of Karl Marx, the figure who, for Objectivists, encapsulates all that is wrong with the world. Might these two seemingly opposed philosophers share an uncanny bond through their writing on pre-history? In a second move, equally audacious, the neat opposition between Rand and Marx is further troubled by the introduction of a third figure: Steve Ditko. As you may know, the Spiderman author was an Objectivist, and, through a close reading of his classic origin story of Spiderman's foe The Lizard, McGill draws out the strange logic both of the prehistoric and of 'life' in order to return these as disruptive forces to both Marxist and Objectivist accounts of history.

Jerome Cox-Strong begins the final section of the book by turning to Objectivist accounts of education to point to constitutive inconsistencies within the Randian political project. Cox-Strong engages the medical metaphors upon which these discourses depend, arguing that their ambivalence relates to the idea that pedagogy can be figured as a cure to a societal disease. When forwarded by progressive educationalists, this is taken to be indicative of state control, but such an understanding both of the virulence of competing discourses and the certainty with which these can be countered are also forwarded within Objectivist accounts. Cox-Strong concludes by relating his reading to contemporary higher education debates, suggesting that the legacy of Objectivist pedagogy can be encountered even within radical or progressive discourse.

In the penultimate chapter, Stephen Thomson articulates the political urgency of an attentive reading of Objectivism through contrasting it with the philosophy of Hannah Arendt, a writer who, unlike Rand, has been widely and positively engaged within recent academic work. The focus for the chapter is on issues of de-segregation in American schools, especially the 1957 'Little Rock incident'. Both Arendt and Rand came out against moves to promote integration in classrooms, and through contrasting what might seem their aligned positions, Thomson draws out the wider stakes involved in a comparative reading of the two authors. Central to this reading, and central also to recent 'alt-right' contributions to debates on 'liberalism', are questions of topography. What, Thomson asks, are the demarcations that must be called upon when separating a celebrated theorist such as Arendt from a seemingly peripheral and problematic thinker such as Rand? And how might the difficulties involved in corralling these two impact on the kind of physical and social separations that are evoked and evaded within their racist discourse, and, indeed, in any reading of such discourse?

In the concluding chapter of the book, I make further connections between the analysis offered in the preceding chapters and Randian economic ideas through engaging Objectivism's continued commitment to the gold standard. I argue that gold in *Atlas Shrugged* is asked to fulfil a range of incompatible demands: a discrete substance, yet positioned within a substitutive structure of relation; an intrinsic value, but one that is also supplemental; supremely present, yet consistently lacking. My interest is not simply in questioning Randian surety through the return of difference, but in emphasising also the necessity of such difference to the efficacy of the political project of Objectivism.

Notes

1. Business leaders who have praised Rand include Jimmy Wales, Peter Thiel, Travis Kalanick, Steve Jobs and Jeff Bezos. Political admirers include Rex Tillerson, Mike Pompeo, Paul Ryan, Rand Paul, and in the UK, Sajid Javid. A 1991 survey of American readers funded by the Library of Congress, found *Atlas Shrugged* came second only to *The Bible* when they were asked to name the book that had most influenced them (Heller 2009, xii). Rand's published work remains extraordinarily successful, with *Atlas Shrugged* having sold 9 Million copies, *The Fountainhead* 6.5 million. See Ayn Rand Org. https://aynrand.org/novels. For more on the political influence of Rand, see Byrd (2015), Duggan (2019), Burns (2009).
2. Chapter 9 of this present book addresses this speech in more detail.
3. Diana Trilling reviewing the novel in the *Nation*, as discussed by Berliner (2017).
4. Mae Tinne for the *Chicago Tribune* and Eileen Creelman for the *New York Sun*, quoted in Berliner (2017, 83). For an extended reading of Rand on film, see Chapter 6.
5. Rand was, however, working on a new novel when she died. See Leonard Piekoff's introduction to Harriman (1999, xiii).
6. Burns is referring to Rand in relation to the Barry Goldwater campaign. For a criticism of this position on Rand and race, however, see Myka Tucker-Abramson (2018).
7. Sciabarra and Cox remain as editors, now joined by psychologist Robert L. Campbell, who shares Sciabarra's views on the dialectic (see note below, and Chapter 7), and 'left Libertarian' Roderick Long, a senior fellow of the Mises Institute.
8. See also Harrison (1999).
9. Duggan (2019, 11). The most celebrated queer reading of Rand is Hardie (1999). For a particularly nuanced feminist reading of Rand, see Wilt (1999).
10. Gladstein wrote a study of *Atlas Shrugged* that, although appealing to traditions of gynocriticism, also comes from a clear Objectivist position (Gladstein 2000). To give an idea of the kind of work included in Sciabarra and Gladstein (1999), see this from Robert Sheaffer: 'While it has been common for many decades for male doctors to marry female nurses, there is absolutely no hint of any trend suggesting that female doctors and male nurses, both non-traditional and presumably non-sexist, are linking up. Women, feminists included, try to marry men above them on the socioeconomic ladder, holding out as long as necessary (indeed, sometimes forever) to find such men', 312.

11. Duggan's book is preceded by Byrd (2015), who focuses on a critical assessment of Rand and Theology. There have been other critical books, for example Weiss (2012). This journalistic text offers a compassionate, broadly liberal, yet pointed assessment of Objectivism at the beginning of the twenty-first century, charting the connections between Rand's work and The Tea Party movement.
12. Duggan (2019, 81).
13. See also Slobodian (2018), Klein (2007). Quotation from Duggan (2019, 82). For the rise of neoliberalism, see, of course, Mirowski and Plehwe (2009). For a critique, see Higgins and Larner (2017). For more on Rand and disaster capitalism, see the final chapter of this book.
14. For a further critique of Rand's appeal to rationalism in terms of the history of free-market economics, see Comyn (2018).
15. See, for example, Rand (1975, 31).
16. Rand's aesthetic and literary theory is set out in this text. Despite its declared rationalist, system-building approach, this offers, I would argue, a convoluted and contradictory argument, which I do not have space here to work through in detail. For a critique of some of its claims, however, see Chapters 5, 9, and 10.
17. Rand's claim, for example, is that a 'basic premise is an absolute that permits no co-operation with its antithesis and tolerates no tolerance' (Rand 1957, 741). For an example of this kind of Manichean thinking in a contemporary advocate of Rand, see Barrowman (2018).
18. Counter to this, and as indicated briefly above, Objectivist philosopher Chris Matthew Sciabarra argues that Rand's philosophy *is* dialectical in nature. His argument is dependent on the dialectic being thought of in terms of the total connections necessary to the functioning of a given dynamic system: dialectics 'compels scholars towards a comprehensive grasp of the many factors at work in a given context'. See the Introduction to Sciabarra (2001). I take this to be a problematically positivist account, one resistant to the repetition, retrospection, and downright strangeness of the dialectic as I read it. See Chapter 7 of this present book for a further critique of Sciabarra on this issue.
19. See Tucker-Abramson (2018) for a recommended alternative reading of the uncanny in *Atlas Shrugged*.
20. Here I am quoting my own quotation of Sigmund Freud (1919). See Cocks (2016, 363).
21. See Derrida, (1967).
22. For what I take to be a good example of the first, see Brühwiler (2016), and for the second, Champagne (2006). The first approach is also to be read in the work of historians of the right such as Burns and Heller introduced above. The ethics of the 'non-partisan' approach to Rand are discussed at length by Jan De Vos in Chapter 3.
23. See De Vos (2013).

Bibliography

Ayn Rand Org. https://aynrand.org/novels. Accessed 3 December 2019.

Barrowman, Kyle. 2018. Signs and meanings: Film studies and the legacy of post-structuralism. *Off Screen* 22 (7). https://offscreen.com/view/signs-and-mea ning-film-studies-and-the-legacy-of-poststructuralism. Accessed 18 February 2020.

Berliner, Michael. 2017. The fountainhead reviews. In *Essays on Ayn Rand's the fountainhead*, ed. Robert Mayhew, 77–85. Lanham: Lexington Books.

Brownmiller, Susan. 1999. Ayn Rand: A traitor to her own sex. In *Feminist interpretations of Ayn Rand*, ed. Mimi Gladstein and Chris Matthew Sciabarra, 63–68. University Park: Pennsylvania State University Press.

Brühwiler, Claudia Franziska. 2016. Pitiless adolescents and young crusaders: Reimagining Ayn Rand's readers. *Canadian Review of American Studies* 46 (1): 42–46.

Burns, Jennifer. 2017. Ayn Rand. https://www.jenniferburns.org/ayn-rand-god dess-of-the-market/. Accessed 13 May 2019.

———. 2009. *Goddess of the market: Ayn Rand and the American right*. Oxford: Oxford University Press.

Byrd, Dustin. 2015. *A critique of Ayn Rand's philosophy of religion: The gospel according to John Galt*. Lanham, Boulder, New York: Lexington Books.

Chambers, Whittaker. 1957. Big Sister is watching you. *National Review*, 28 December.

Champagne, Marc. 2006. Some convergences and divergences in the realism of Charles Peirce and Ayn Rand. *The Journal of Ayn Rand Studies* 8 (1): 19–39.

Cocks, Neil. 2016. Uncanny repetitions in Lillian Hellman's *Children's Hour*. *Modern Drama* 59 (3): 363–379.

Comyn, Sarah. 2018. *Political economy and the novel: A literary history of 'homo economicus' (Palgrave studies in literature, culture and economics)*. Basingstoke: Palgrave.

Derrida, Jacques. 1997 [1967]. *Of grammatology*, trans. Gayatri Chakravorty Spivak. Baltimore and London: Johns Hopkins University Press.

De Vos, Jan. 2013. *Psychologization and the subject of late modernity*. Basingstoke: Palgrave.

Duggan, Lisa. 2019. *Mean girl: Ayn Rand and the culture of greed*. Oakland: University of California Press.

Freud, Sigmund. 1955 [1919]. The uncanny. In *The complete psychological works of Sigmund Freud*, vol. XVII, trans. J. Strachey, 217–252. London: Hogarth.

Gladstein, Mimi Reisel. 2000. *Atlas shrugged: Manifesto of the mind*. New York: Twayne.

Glenn, David. 2007. Advocates of objectivism make new inroads. *Higher Education Chronicle*, 13 July.

Hardie, Melissa Jane. 1999. Fluff and granite: Rereading Rand's camp feminist aesthetics. In *Feminist interpretations of Ayn Rand*, ed. Mimi Gladstein and Chris Matthew Sciabarra, 363–390. University Park: Pennsylvania State University Press.

Harrison, Barbara Grizzuti. 1999. Psyching out Ayn Rand. In *Feminist interpretations of Ayn Rand*, ed. Mimi Gladstein and Chris Matthew Sciabarra, 67–76. University Park: Pennsylvania State University Press.

Heller, Anne C. 2009. *Ayn Rand and the world she made*. New York: Doubleday.

Higgins, Vaughan, and Wendy Larner (eds.). 2017. *Assembling neoliberalism: Expertise, practices, subjects*. New York: Palgrave Macmillan.

Hoberek, Andrew. 2006. *The twilight of the middle class: Post World War II America and white collar work*. Princeton: Princeton University Press.

Long, Roderick. 2001. Review. *The Independent Review* 15 (4): 615–619.

Klein, Naomi. 2007. *The shock doctrine*. London: Penguin.

Mayhew, Robert. 2009. Review: *The goddess of the market*. *The objective standard*. https://www.theobjectivestandard.com/issues/2009-winter/ayn-rand-jennifer-burns/. Assessed 13.5.2019.

Mirowski, Philip. 2013. *Never let a serious crisis go to waste: How neoliberalism survived the financial meltdown*. London and New York: Verso.

Mirowski, Philip, and Dieter Plehwe. 2009. *The road to Mont Pelerin: The making of a neoliberal thought collective*. Cambridge: Harvard University Press.

Murnane, Ben. 2018. *Ayn Rand and the posthuman: The mind-made future*. Basingstoke: Palgrave.

Norton, Ben. 2015. Libertarian superstar Ayn Rand defended Native American genocide: 'Racism didn't exist in this country until the liberals brought it up'. https://www.salon.com/2015/10/14/libertarian_superstar_ayn_rand_d efended_genocide_of_savage_native_americans/. Accessed 3 December 2019.

Peikoff, Leonard. 1999. Introduction. In *The journals of Ayn Rand*, ed. David Harriman. New York: Plume.

Rand, Ayn. 2007 [1943]. *The fountainhead*. London: Penguin.

———. 1957. *Atlas shrugged*. New York: Random House.

———. 1974. Graduation address, West Point. https://www.salon.com/2015/10/14/libertarian_superstar_ayn_rand_defended_genocide_of_savage_native_americans/. Accessed 17 March 2020.

———. 1975. *The romantic manifesto*. New York: Signet.

———. 1988. Introducing objectivism. In *The Ayn Rand lexicon: Objectivism from A–Z*, ed. Harry Binswanger. New York: New American Library.

———. 2000. *The art of fiction*, ed. Tore Boeckmann. New York: Plume.

Rose, Jacqueline. 2016. Donald Trump's victory is a disaster for modern masculinity. *The Guardian*, 15 September.

Sheaffer, Robert. 1999. Rereading Rand on gender in the light of Paglia. In *Feminist interpretations of Ayn Rand*, ed. Mimi Gladstein and Chris Matthew Sciabarra, 299–317. University Park: Pennsylvania State University Press.

Sciabarra, Chris Matthew. 2001. *Total freedom: Toward a dialectical libertarianism*. Philadelphia: University of Pennsylvania Press.

Slobodian, Quinn. 2018. *Globalists: The end of empire and the birth of neoliberalism*. Cambridge: Harvard University Press.

Tucker-Abramson, Myka. 2018. *Novel shocks: Urban renewal and the origins of neoliberalism*. New York: Fordham University Press.

Weiss, Gary. 2012. *Ayn Rand nation: The hidden struggle for America's soul*. New York: St. Martin's Griffin.

Wilt, Judith. 1999. The romances of Ayn Rand. In *Feminist interpretations of Ayn Rand*, ed. Mimi Gladstein and Chris Matthew Sciabarra, 173–198. University Park: Pennsylvania State University Press.

Žižek, Slavoj. 2002. The actuality of Ayn Rand. *Journal of Ayn Rand Studies* 3 (2): 215–227.

———. 2011. *Did somebody say totalitarianism?* London: Verso.

PART I

Psychoanalysis and Psychologisation

CHAPTER 2

Reading Ayn Rand Psychoanalytically: Ethics, Libertarian and Otherwise

Ian Parker

1 Introduction

Ayn Rand, who was born in Russia in 1905 and moved to the United States in 1926, developed an avowedly anti-communist philosophical system of thought which she propagated in the novel *The Fountainhead* and, in the Bible of the Objectivist movement she founded, *Atlas Shrugged*, which was published in 1957. A film version of *The Fountainhead* starring Gary Cooper as uncompromising architect hero Howard Roark was released in 1949, boosting a group of admirers called 'The Collective' who gathered around Rand in New York. The main protagonist of *Atlas Shrugged*, 'John Galt' became a fiction figurehead for supporters of free-enterprise capitalism, leading a strike of the 'wealth-makers' in the novel.

For Rand, it was not the working class who created wealth through their labour from which surplus value was extracted, but talented individuals. In the book, then, it was individuals who refused to 'work', refused to subordinate themselves to the dependent masses who looked to the

I. Parker (✉)
Manchester, UK

© The Author(s) 2020
N. Cocks (ed.), *Questioning Ayn Rand*,
Palgrave Studies in Literature, Culture and Economics,
https://doi.org/10.1007/978-3-030-53073-0_2

welfare-state for support, those characterised by Rand in the book and in other writings as conformist 'second-handers'; 'This', says John Galt, 'is the mind on strike' (Rand 1957, 677). Ayn Rand died in 1982, after breaking with her acolyte Nathaniel Branden who carried on working on 'self-esteem' as the psychological correlate of Objectivism, and after alienating most of her other supporters. She continues, however, to attract extraordinarily passionate abuse and continues to inspire alt-right activists and mainstream career politicians.

Her own fraught émigré biographical narrative is ripe for pop-psychoanalytic 'interpretation', for a reframing of her political project as the expression of pathological resentment of the kind of regime at home in Russia that would deprive her and her family of its bourgeois comforts. One could easily home in on pathological resentment that would launch Rand into a search for robust independent individuals who would refuse to compromise with the state and would propel her into the milieu of right-libertarian celebrity culture in post-war US America. Such a reductive pathobiographical approach to Rand, which would include attention, perhaps, to her disavowal of an assigned Jewish identity as 'Alisa Zinovyevna Rosenbaum' and the construction of a new identity with her new chosen name, would also need to account for the replication of this process of disavowal and self-nomination in the group she led. We might then note the uncannily close identification of followers in the group with her, signalled in the incorporation of the signifier 'rand' into the assumed identity of Nathaniel Branden, formerly Nathan Blumenthal (Levine 2011). Her near-future didactic novels wipe away the existence of Jews and black people in a white world populated only by adults driven by power, power which is intimately linked, for the protagonists, the ones who matter to her, to sex; coercive sadomasochistic scenarios bind the characters together just as they seem to have underpinned Rand's own desperate manipulative sexual relationship with Branden (Heller 2009).

Rather than search for private personal hidden sources for the vaunted 'ethics' of Ayn Rand, an approach that would treat Howard Roark and John Galt as fantasy screens of the desire that structured Objectivism, we should instead ask how it is that psychoanalytic discourse as such comes to operate in a philosophical system that is designed to shut out, 'repress' we might say, anything Freudian. Psychoanalysis which is operative in the text of Rand's novels and the post-war transformations of psychoanalysis in the US as it adapts itself to and resists adaptation to the peculiar moral-political universe of free-market capitalism is also to be found in her life-work.

Rather than 'apply' psychoanalysis to Ayn Rand, however, we need to read the fate of psychoanalytic ethical discourse with her work in order to trace the trajectory of libertarianism as a lure and trap. The following sections of this chapter address the question, first, as to how we should read Rand before turning, second, to psychoanalytic discourse in her work and then, third, to the explicitly ethical discourse of two psychoanalytic fellow-travellers, Szasz and Žižek, allies and opponents of Objectivism.

2   Reading Ayn Rand

To read Ayn Rand today is to be sucked into a weird parallel universe, one all the more uncanny because its coordinates resonate so closely with those of present-day neoliberal capitalism. Her depictions of near-future alternate worlds in her fiction blockbusters were designed to make a moral point, to ram home the moral system elaborated in her political-philosophical writings. Her Objectivism is one of the ideological forms of free-market capitalism, telling us that there is no alternative to it and that therefore we should respond objectively while also subscribing to a form of subjectivity in which we freely will ourselves, each of us, to strive to compete and succeed. Her fictional characters operate as crude obvious ciphers for good and evil, easy to grasp objects of identification, and that, perhaps, is why the writing is so compelling, both for those on the right delighted to be interpellated by the text and for those on the Left by turns bewitched and repelled by it. For those of us on the Left it is as if we are faced with the worst of Lenin, the claim that consciousness is or should be a direct reflection of reality, combined with the most despairing diagnosis of capitalist realism a century later in the work of Mark Fisher, that it is easier to imagine the end of the world than the end of this wretched political-economic system (Fisher 2009; Lenin 1909).

For readers on the right there are glaring ideological contradictions that make it tempting but risky to declare adherence to Ayn Rand as part of the apparatus of career realpolitik, the most obvious being the tension between her atheism and the requirement that one link one's personal religious faith to civic responsibility, a requirement that is usually played out in US-American politics in relation to Christian fundamentalism of some kind or another. We see this tension expressed in the early career moves of many American politicians who say they admire Ayn Rand, before they have actually read her it would seem, and are then alerted to her hostility to Christianity, and so quickly backtrack.

One of the pulls is precisely the intimate link between Ayn Rand's fiction, her explicitly programmatic writing and her own biography. This link expresses and reinforces the just-as intimate link between rhetoric, public policy and personal life that is demanded of politicians as good subjects of the neoliberal psy-complex; that is the psy-complex as dense meshwork of theories and practices concerning subjectivity that is relayed through the competing and complementary apparatuses of the psy professions, of psychology, psychiatry, psychotherapy and psychoanalysis in the universities, schools, clinics and prisons (Ingleby 2011; Rose 1985). That is, it is not good enough to preach a political line; you have to show that you really believe it, that you live it, inhabit and confess infractions of moral rules.[1]

Neoliberalism is a return to classical liberal political economy of the nineteenth century analysed and unravelled by Marx in *Capital*, but with a twist (Marx 1867). Neoliberalism, characterised as such by Michel Foucault consists of the stripping back of welfare service functions of the capitalist state and an intensification of its police functions in order to enforce a mode of individuality in which each one of us is responsible for accumulating and managing our own resources (Foucault 2010; Zamora and Behrent 2016). This triple-shock neoliberal capitalism also calls upon the psy-complex, requires it in order that what is objectively perceived is also subjectively experienced.

Descriptions of the psy-complex as an apparatus of discipline and confession owe something to the descriptions of repressive and ideological state apparatuses in the writings of Louis Althusser, and are elaborated in the work of followers of Michel Foucault, one of Althusser's students (Cotoi 2011; Althusser 1971). The psy-complex is one of the key apparatuses of neoliberalism, underpinning the kind of world Ayn Rand describes, instantiating it, fleshing out the conditions of possibility for it to operate. This is why she lives on, providing both an image of archaic commitment to anti-communism of the 1950s, as we have seen, and inspiration to those interpellated as neoliberal subjects searching for some moral core to the hollow life which capitalism produces.

One way of opening up the contradictions in Ayn Rand is to read her moral system in relation to psychoanalysis. This is clearly a perilous task, bringing into the frame of critical reading a theoretical framework that is complicit in the psy-complex, one that routinely reduces political-economic processes to the level of individual subjectivity, inciting personal disclosure and inviting personal responsibility for hidden as yet undisclosed desires, as Foucault pointed out (Foucault 2010). One should avoid, therefore, simply applying psychoanalysis to Ayn Rand's fiction, philosophy or biography, but one can and should interrogate how psychoanalytic discourse functions both in what we read by Ayn Rand and of her. She is herself a moral example, configures herself as exemplar of Objectivism, and just as her followers were usually drawn to her through her fiction, so they repeated the moral forms they found there in the formation of the Ayn Rand 'Collective'. This was a tight-knit obedient group often symptomatically characterised by detractors using psy discourse to label and dismiss it as a kind of 'cult' (Rothbard 2017). This use of the term 'cult' would be an instance of what Rand called 'psychologizing' (Rand 1971).[2]

Her fiction also faithfully follows two of the three rules of creative writing programmes, writing programmes that aim to express and transmit the authentic life project of the author and which set supposedly objective standards by which good writing should be assessed.[3] These creative writing programmes effectively operate as adjunct soft apparatuses of the psy-complex. Intending authors who want to break into the market-place and sell the products of their labour against competitors, and who are willing to invest in creative writing programmes in order to do that, configure themselves in the process as subjects true to themselves, neoliberal subjects.[4] These are subjects ripe for induction into Objectivism. Hence, the intimate link between Ayn Rand's biography, political commitment and novels. She explicitly follows and evangelises for the rule that the author should write what they know, first rule, and find their own voice, rule two, while systematically breaking and reversing the third rule that one should show not tell. She tells it straight in *Atlas Shrugged*, that, as she puts it there, 'The code of competence is the only system of morality that's on a gold standard' (Rand 1957, 76).[5]

Rand's claim about morality that is at the heart of Objectivism raises a question about how psychoanalytic discourse finds its way into her writing, and how she takes up and reworks forms of discourse to which she was ostensibly so opposed. Objectivism today is forthright in its rejection of Freud who, we are told by her followers, peddled an image of man as 'a loathsomely small, ordure-strewn pervert', a 'smutty pawn shaped by sexual aberrations and toilet training' (Peikoff 1982). This caricature of Freud neatly expresses what Rand's noble self-sufficient man of reason must pit himself against; he must also then pit himself against a Platonic and Kantian image of subjectivity that debases and misleads him about his own nature. Neoliberal subjectivity configured by our repeated and unavoidable encounters with the psy-complex, however, is actually today, for readers and followers of Ayn Rand, a good deal more flexible in its quasi-psychoanalytic accounts of ethics. Different competing representations of Freud in psychoanalytic discourse, inside and outside the clinic, have been tamed and adapted in such a way as to render its ethics into something more canny and compatible with Objectivism.

Let us look at how psychoanalysis operates as a discursive resource in Ayn Rand's writing, at why we need to take psychoanalysis seriously while reading her, before turning to the ways in which misreading of psychoanalysis and distortions of psychoanalytic ethics, their transformation into moral systems, enable particular accounts of neoliberal subjectivity in the psy-complex to underwrite Rand's own moral-political project.

3   Rand's Psychoanalytic Writing

The methodological route I want to take in this reading is focussed not on particular kinds of imagery that can be reframed and so 'interpreted' in psychoanalytic terms, re-transcribed into a psychoanalytic vocabulary, but on the traces of psychoanalytic subjectivity in Rand's work. So, I am not, for example, so interested in a semiotic analysis of *The Fountainhead* that would highlight the links between the title as such as phallic image and the sharp clear lines of the upward-thrusting architecture that Howard Roark favours and that Rand clearly admires.[6] The task is not to discover what is secretly psychoanalytic in her writing, unconsciously buried in it, but to track the signifiers of a form of subjectivity to which psychoanalysis attaches itself and then explicates. It is precisely that psychoanalysis attaches itself to and explicates such a kind of text that leads Rand and her followers to take pains to distance themselves from Freud.

My claim is not simply that Rand's writing is saturated in psychoanalysis, for there are clearly stretches of the text when she is able to circumnavigate it, and clearly a whole terrain of textual representation of the self in US-American culture in the mid-twentieth century that draws on a range of other conceptual resources. I do claim, though, that Rand does absorb and regurgitate psychoanalytic discourse. She does this in *The Fountainhead* and, more so, in *Atlas Shrugged*, a book produced when Freud's ideas were even more deeply implanted in US literary and popular culture. And, not incidentally, she does this in the way she configures personal relationships in and around 'The Collective', a domain in which therapeutic notions are explicitly mobilised in order to ensure obedience to the group and buttress Objectivism as an ideological project. Here in this domain of the reproduction of Objectivism as a life project, the imperative to distance the therapeutic ambitions of the psychologist Nathaniel Branden from Freudianism is most apparent. Let us turn to Branden for a moment.

Branden's classic text *The Psychology of Self-Esteem* which was cobbled together from articles published in *The Objectivist*, and which Rand attempted to block publication of following her fall-out with Branden in 1968, sets out a programme for self-improvement which is predicated on the idea that a sense of self-worth is key to success. It combines elements of humanistic therapy which was already indebted to quasi-Freudian notions of 'self-actualisation' and which carried with it residues of the Hegelian notion that we should proceed from dependence on others, and dependence on the recognition that others give us, to independence.[7] This independence is clarified by Branden as being an index of psychological maturity. This is not the place to evaluate this self-enclosed self-sufficient notion of self-esteem, but it should be noted that critiques of it claim that this libertarian vision of autonomous psychological functioning is of a piece with increased self-esteem not so much as a prerequisite for mental health but of authoritarian if not paranoiac modes of relating to others.[8]

Members of the Collective were encouraged to undergo therapy, and required to do so at times of conflict in the group in order to bring them back into line and atone for their infractions of group rules.[9] Ayn Rand was herself in therapy for many years with Branden before he became her rather reluctant lover in a contractual arrangement brokered by her. In practice, Objectivist forms of therapy seem to have been closer to cognitive-behavioural approaches; these were approaches, it should be noted, that themselves were developed by psychoanalysts in the tradition of US-American ego psychology who were looking for quicker cheaper ways of curing their patients, arriving at a cure that was, moreover, assumed to entail the adaptation of the individual to society.[10]

The paradox in the Branden approach endorsed by Ayn Rand was that while recognition from others was conceptually bypassed, treated as a problem rather than as a foundation for later independent mental functioning—Freud and Hegel were both viewed as antithetical to Objectivism—the treatment did rely on a series of signs of identification with other members of the group, of taking up smoking because Ayn Rand smoked for example; in this, the approach effectively concurred with the worst claims of quasi-Freudian ego psychology at the time, that the end of analysis entailed identification of the ego of the patient with the ego of the analyst.[11]

There are no particular claims for the primacy of sex as instinct or drive in Branden's self-esteem therapy, but there are for sure such claims about the centrality of sex to the relationships between the key protagonists in the two key Rand novels; between Dominique Francon and Howard Roark in *The Fountainhead*, and between Dagny Taggart and John Galt in *Atlas Shrugged*. The fourteen years between the two novels, from the early 1940s to the late 1950s, mark a period in which the ambivalent nature of sexual desire, the entanglement between love and hate, affection and destruction, life and death described in pop-psychoanalytic writing becomes a reflexively worked topic of emotion-talk in relationships, and so it does for Ayn Rand.

The Fountainhead does not shy from describing Dominique Francon's first sexual encounter with Roark as rape, Dominique names it herself; 'the act of a master taking shameful, contemptuous possession of her', Rand tells us, 'was the kind of rapture she had wanted' (Rand 1943, 231). One might already see here something of the predicament of a divided subject in which 'she felt the blood beating in her throat, in her eyes, the hatred, the helpless terror in her blood. She felt the hatred' and, Rand reminds us, 'One gesture of tenderness from him - and she would have remained cold, untouched by the thing done to her body' (ibid.).[12] This is not so much psychoanalytic as the worst representation of what reactionary pop-psychoanalysis warrants for women's sexuality; it is as if it were the recipe for Freudian sex written jointly by Kate Millett and Susan Brownmiller (Millett 1977; Brownmiller 1975).

Atlas Shrugged, on the other hand, plays in more subtle but no less pernicious way with the mingled attraction of the woman for her man Galt, represents it as a power-play in which subordination and domination are tied together, and tied together all the more so for Dagny as the woman, as the one who positions herself as object while voicing the contradictions of subjectivity that this entails. In this, Rand tells us exactly what Dagny thinks and feels in line with her tell-not-show style of writing, and in the process lays bare the internal life of a subject torn between something rational, which Rand obviously values, and something of the unconscious which she refuses to name as such. Rand tells us right out that 'a man's sexual choice is the result and the sum of his fundamental convictions' (Rand 1957, 489). And so the stakes are high in the long-awaited encounter between Dagny and John Galt; we are to discover something of the tension between 'fundamental convictions' between human subjects and also, crucially, inside them.

For the man, Rand tells us, 'only the possession of a heroine will give him the sense of an achievement, not the possession of a brainless slut' (490). The woman knows her place, knows, when she turns up at Hank Rearden's party that she should display 'the most feminine of all aspects: the look of being chained' (136). Dagny half-knows what she wants from Galt, is prepared for it from the slap she receives from another lover Francisco d'Anconia and enjoys it; she grasps something of the nature of pleasure in pain, and she reflects upon 'pleasure in what she suddenly grasped about him, about herself and about his motive' (99).

There is a deep paradox here in the way that Ayn Rand renders the subject visible as divided in her fiction on the one hand and then sutures that division in her pronouncements about the nature of moral action. We are told in *Atlas Shrugged*, for example, that 'man is an indivisible entity, an integrated unit of two attributes: of matter and consciousness, and that he may permit no breach between body and mind, between action and thought, between his life and his convictions', but then we witness the protagonists living with the impossibility of overcoming this breach (122). Those around her in the Collective also lived that impossibility, resorting to therapy, rather improbably to enable them to take 'moral responsibility'.

4   Psychoanalysis as a Moral Project

This paradox also riddles psychoanalysis itself. There are traditions of work in psychoanalysis that see the ego-psychological revision of Freudian practice that gave rise to cognitive-behavioural therapy focused on self-efficacy and 'self-esteem' as a betrayal of psychoanalytic ethics, but we also see attempts to stitch ethics back into psychoanalysis in the US that is deliberately geared to the kind of libertarian right agenda that Rand advocated. I want to turn now to one of these attempts, for it spells out one version of ethics that is simultaneously almost Objectivist and almost psychoanalytic, showing that it is possible to work through the contradictions at the level of subjectivity that are a necessary correlate of the kind of apparently rational unitary subject that Rand herself promoted.

Thomas Szasz would seem at first glance to be an unlikely bedfellow of the Objectivists, but his own particular approach to moral responsibility traces an uncanny parallel trajectory to that of Rand. He will be known to undergraduate psychology and social science students as author of *The Myth of Mental Illness*, a full-blown attack on the conceptual confusions and abuses of authority that enable psychiatrists to present themselves as experts on other peoples' lives (Szasz 1961). He is often represented in secondary literature as an anti-psychiatric campaigner, even as a man of the Left, the US-American equivalent of the British anti-psychiatry movement around R. D. Laing. This is a mistake.

Szasz was an anti-communist Jewish-Hungarian émigré, who actually criticised psychiatry from the right, a right-libertarian who was concerned with the power of the state to exonerate the individual for failing to take responsibility for their own actions as well as the power of the state to incarcerate people. He was, he said, 'equally opposed to psychiatric coercions and to psychiatric excuses' (Szasz 1997, 43). This is what made possible some alliances between Rand and Szasz; Szasz was willing to ally with anyone who would challenge psychiatry, and was with Rand in challenging, as an unapologetic atheist, anti-scientific quasi-religious systems of thought (Szasz 2002, 40).

What is not so well-known, and not often fully acknowledged among critics of psychiatry keen to enrol Szasz into a broader critique of the psy-complex, is that Szasz not only trained as a psychoanalyst as well as a psychiatrist before he wrote *The Myth of Mental Illness*, but carried on practicing as a psychoanalyst for the rest of his life. This was a form of psychoanalysis that was in tune with the transformations in ego psychology in the US that turned it into part of the machinery of adaptation, transformations that also required that the theory adapt itself to the ideological apparatus of free-market capitalism.[13] He spells out this approach in a 1965 book *The Ethics of Psychoanalysis* in which he characterises psychoanalysis as a '*moral exercise*' which would be based on a '*fully* contractual' approach (Szasz 1988 [1965], 113, 202). This adherence to a version of psychoanalysis is at the root of dissension between Szasz and Objectivists, even though Szasz was departing from some key tenets of psychoanalysis in order to shore up the ego as a master in the house while the Objectivists were utilising some kind of therapeutic approach that required acknowledgement of non-rational processes in order to keep their house in order.

The two libertarian approaches cross paths at the point where the individual subject takes responsibility, and it is here that Ayn Rand's therapeutic relationship with Nathaniel Branden comes under fire from Szasz. Rand's essay 'The psychology of psychologizing' is not enough to throw Szasz off the scent. She writes that what she calls 'psychologizing' consists of condemning or excusing specific individuals on the grounds of their psychological problems, real or invented, in the absence of or contrary to factual evidence (Rand 1971). One might read this statement, written three years after the break with Branden, as special pleading. Szasz goes for the jugular in his 2004 book on different libertarian critiques of psychiatry, pointing out that Branden himself was always proud to call himself a psychologist and, Szasz argues, 'he ignores the coercions and excuses intrinsic to the legal and psychiatric use of the term "mental illness"' (Szasz 2004, 135). A review in the *The Journal of Ayn Rand Studies* focused on the criticisms of Branden and played up the compatibility between Rand and Szasz (Richman 2006).

This encounter between one of the most prominent psychoanalysts in the US, Thomas Szasz, and Ayn Rand, draws attention to two crisscrossing paths in a global culture that is increasingly undergoing processes of psychologisation.[14] Jan De Vos will explore this connection further in the following chapter, but for now it is worth establishing the fundamental tension at work. On the one hand, psychoanalytic notions of subjectivity were becoming embedded in popular culture, with Rand an unwitting, unwilling carrier of this discourse. On the other hand, psychoanalysis was steadily being evacuated from mainstream clinical practice, with Szasz as an exemplar of this shift away from a concern with desire to calculative rational discourse. This is the basis of the repeated attempts by followers of each to speak with each other, and of the failure of those attempts. Szasz was abandoning psychoanalysis while Rand was embracing it.

5   Psychoanalysis as an Ethical Project

There is another psychoanalytic take on these questions, one diametrically opposed to the ego-psychological tradition that Szasz represents, by the author of a book with exactly the same title, *The Ethics of Psychoanalysis* by Jacques Lacan. One can hardly accuse Lacan of being an 'antipsychiatrist', though Szasz did include him in a list of enemies clustered under that rubric that Szasz himself always refused, but Lacan was an angrier critic of free-market capitalism in the US, a political-economic system Szasz always endorsed, as Ayn Rand did, of course (Szasz 2009; Lacan 2006). The stakes for Lacan were precisely that psychoanalysis was incorporated into a system of rule in which ethics was transformed into morality; the ethical responsibility of the subject was made subordinate to a moral order which defined what the 'good' was for them.

It is pertinent to pit Lacan against Szasz here as a quite different way into the ethics that is assumed to be operative in Ayn Rand's Objectivism, not only because Lacan refuses each of the dominant systems of moral coordinates that Szasz borrows from in his own particular version of 'ethics' compatible with the psy-complex, but also because Lacanian 'ethics' is itself also subject to pop-psychoanalytic discourse that risks turning it from being a critique of neoliberal society into its helpmeet.[15] That is, the ostensibly most radical alternative approach to ethics from within psychoanalysis could also be read in line with the right-libertarianism of Ayn Rand. Her own albeit reluctant subscription to some kind of psychoanalytic subjectivity in her novels provides the hinge-point for a misreading of Lacan, a recruitment of Lacan to Objectivist ethics.

One might, for example, pin our hopes on the idea that Rand unwittingly brings us up against welfare-state capitalism, the capitalism of the 'second-handers', and does this in the name of a 'pure capitalism', an impossibly pure capitalism that functions as such, as impossible, opening the way to the overthrow of capitalism.[16] This would be, as a rhetorical move, a way of tactically giving voice to the 'prime movers', those who believe they are the wealth-makers, and so giving voice to those who pretend they are masters. The identification of Dominique Francon with her rapist Howard Roark in *The Fountainhead* and of Dagny Taggart with John Galt in *Atlas Shrugged* would thus be accomplished by way of a hysterical revolt, psychoanalytically conceived; this is the kind of hysterical revolt which aims at deposing the master.

Such would be the impact of subversive overidentification with the enemy, according to Slavoj Žižek. Indeed, it is Žižek's contention that such overidentification would deconstruct the presumptions of capitalism in the process. One wonders why *The Journal of Ayn Rand Studies*, who published this work, would have allowed such an enemy inside the gates if they did not believe they could tame him, but maybe they were wrong. In this Žižekian reading 'Rand gives us capitalism in its pure, unmediated, basic form' which is difficult to argue with, indeed she does, but one then needs a motor force to power that deconstruction, something a good deal more than the quasi-Hegelian and Lacanian-psychoanalytic master-slave dialectics of relationships voiced by Dominique Francon when she asserts that 'I want to be owned, not by a lover, but by an adversary who will destroy my victory over him' (Barnard-Naude 2012; Rand 1943, 290).

This might at least be one way of working through Lacan's formulations of the ethics of psychoanalysis in Seminar VII where it would seem, at first glance, as if there were a 'pure desire' at work in the subject, against which they should not give ground (Lacan 1992 [1986]). However, there are a number of problems with this use of Lacan. Lacan's Seminar VII is not at all an account of psychoanalytic ethics, but of the ethics of psychoanalysis as a clinical practice; such formulations and consequences that there are in that seminar about the assumption of subjectivity outside the domain of the clinic need to be handled very carefully.[17] One then needs to take care not only not to extrapolate from an idealised image of what happens in the clinical space to the social realm but also not to read back that romanticised vision of political action as 'act' back into Lacan's own text. This is what Žižek does.

The kind of 'act' that changes the symbolic coordinates of the subject, and which is the crux of much of Žižek's politics, for example, is not only often reduced to the level of the individual—this is where the clinic becomes the anchor-point and model for political action—but presupposes that such an act in the clinic would necessarily need to be recognised by others in order to be effective. Many acts in the clinic are not even noticed by the analyst; the assumption that they should be is one that we would find located in the discourse of the hysteric.[18]

For Žižek, hysterical revolt, hysterical revolt as part of intense overidentification, is what makes Rand radical, what gives us a 'radically atheist, life-assertive, "selfish" ethics', he claims, and so the act, the 'act of assuming existential indifference is perhaps the very gesture of absolute negativity which gives birth to the subject' (Žižek 2012).[19] Žižek is no fool, and so while most of his examples of political acts are of resolute individuals, those who have remained true to Lacan's oft-cited injunction from Seminar VII 'don't give ground relative to your desire', he is enough of a Hegelian to know that what is at stake is not what goes on between individuals but within them: 'The true conflict', as he puts it, 'runs within the prime movers themselves: it resides in the (sexualised) tension between the prime mover, the being of pure drive, and his hysterical partner' (ibid.). It is this reflexive replication of inter-subjective process into the interiority of the subject that makes Hegel a quasi-psychoanalytic writer and which, on a cultural-historical level, makes psychoanalysis as such possible.

Whether or not Žižek wills it, this moral imperative 'don't give ground relative to your desire' is at the heart of Ayn Rand's own Objectivist argument against welfare-state capitalism and she would be quite happy, as was her journal, to hear that she was an advocate of 'pure capitalism'. However, there is a further problem here in this reading, in this apparent immediate compatibility between Rand and Lacan, a problem which is rather fortunate for us Lacanians, for it actually distances us from Rand. While Lacan's formulations in Seminar VII are indeed sometimes framed as if they are obeying a Freudian 'categorical imperative', the import of them for Lacan is actually very different. What Lacan actually says in the Seminar is that 'from an analytical point of view, the only thing of which one can be guilty is of having given ground relative to one's desire' (Lacan 1986, 319).[20]

Nowhere does Lacan formulate this as an injunction. As Marc De Kesel remarks, 'This reference is valid solely in the specific situation of an analytic cure whose goal it is to direct the analyst's and analysand's attention to desire' (De Kesel 2009, 262). We have to be clear, if we are to avoid idealised readings of individual action, the kind of idealised readings that both Žižek and Rand would license, that the intention of Lacan's formulation 'is not to require that the analysand realize this desire in her personal life' (ibid.). Even within the reduced frame of the clinical setting, the 'marks' of an analysis are intimately bound up with the social bonds which tie the subject to others and to the symbolic (Izcovich 2017). This is, perhaps, why Žižek sometimes cites Lacan's Seminar VII but still views it as 'conservative'; it does not go all the way with desire and drive (Žižek et al. 2010).

6 CONCLUSIONS

There is a temptation for those taken with psychoanalytic discourse to wield it as a weapon, and to repeat the claim, much-beloved of psychoanalysts who are over-keen to defend their territory and employ the armature of psychoanalysis as a meta-narrative, that the truth of psychoanalysis is revealed in every attempt by detractors and opponents to combat it.

Their opposition to psychoanalysis speaks of a deeper resistance to the truths that Freud and his followers discovered; they resist psychoanalysis, so the story goes, because they repress and defend themselves against the presence of the dirty secret that sex is central to their lives, the deep core around which their lives revolve. An attack on Freud can then be easily interpreted as a sign that they are actually more obsessed by sex than Freudians are, and enraged when this is commented on. Ayn Rand's disclaimers about unconscious drives and assertion of the sovereignty of the ego could be read as a case in point.

Rand and her followers evidently recognised the nature of the threat that psychoanalysis poses to Objectivism, and railed against it accordingly. This was the case in the 1950s when psychoanalytic discourse was a rival popular resource for understanding the nature of the self in the US and when Rand was explicitly allied with the McCarthyite purges which were purges not only of the Left but also of left-Freudians. This is still the case when psychoanalysis as a theoretical framework is almost as fractured as the neoliberal subjects it sets itself to work upon, and when Objectivism has also mutated, flourished and adapted itself to post-Trump politics.

If we step back, and step up a level to attend to psychoanalytic discourse, we find the temptation of appealing to this discourse in order to frame those who inveigh against it almost as strong, but the reflexive loop which binds friends and enemies of Freud together is structured differently at this level. The question now is not whether psychoanalysis is right or wrong, or in which particular version of psychoanalysis an ethical position should be grounded, but how subjects are positioned within a discourse that frames and inhabits contemporary subjectivity.[21] It is in this sense that psychoanalysis is unavoidable. It is difficult to avoid Freud today, and difficult to avoid Rand.

We read Ayn Rand because we must. We encounter her ideas as ideological condensations of commonsense under capitalism whether or not we directly read her books, but reading her books brings us face to face with underlying assumptions made about capitalist realism and neoliberal subjectivity. This gives us an opportunity to clarify not only where we stand ethically and politically in relation to capitalism as economic scaffolding of the symbolic order today, and so of what is configured as Other to us. It gives us an opportunity also to clarify where we stand in relation to psychoanalysis as an historically constituted theory and practice of subjectivity that both locks us into this order and promises us a way out of it. It just locks us in according to Thomas Szasz, and a good thing too.[22]

Perhaps it does offer us a way out, but we have to make it so, we have to work at it, opening up the contradictions in it, and looking not to the fantasy of a pure desire that could erupt against the capitalist order and sweep it away. That reduction of the psychoanalytic 'act' to the level of individual desire and drive recurs in Žižek's writing. [23] That would be but a bizarre mirror-image of what Ayn Rand presented as pure unfettered capitalism. Our psychoanalytic readings of Freud and Rand, and Szasz and Lacan, need to ground ethics in social bonds, discourse, in links with emancipatory politics, and so with the communist vision of collective action and solidarity that Ayn Rand tried so hard to bury.[24]

NOTES

1. For more on this, see Duggan (2019).
2. For more on this, see De Vos (2012). See also Chapter 3 of this present book.
3. See, for example, McGurl (2012).
4. See Jameson (2012).
5. See the final chapter of this book for an extended discussion of this quotation.
6. See Kunkle (2007).
7. See Branden (1999).
8. See Emler (2001).
9. For more on this, see Heller (2009).
10. See Jacoby (1983).
11. See Hartmann (1958 [1939]).
12. See Chapter 4 for an extended discussion of this issue.
13. See Parker (2019).
14. See again De Vos (2012), and see also the following chapter of this present book.
15. See Parker (2019).
16. For more on this, see Chapter 9 of this book.
17. See Neill (2011).
18. See Pluth (2008). For more on this, see Chapter 3 of this book.
19. This is a version of the essay discussed by Cocks and De Vos below. Žižek (2002).
20. See Critchley (1999).
21. See Parker (1997).
22. See Parker (2019).
23. See Parker (1994). See Chapters 3 and 4 for further discussions of Žižek and Rand.
24. See Parker (2011).

Bibliography

Althusser, Louis. 1971. Ideology and ideological state apparatuses (notes towards an investigation). In *Lenin and philosophy, and other essays*. London: New Left Books.

Barnard-Naude, Jaco. 2012. The spectrality of Ayn Rand. *Mail & Guardian*, March 26. http://thoughtleader.co.za/jacobarnardnaude/2012/03/26/the-spectrality-of-ayn-rand/. Accessed 3 July 2018.

Branden, Nathanial. 1999. *The psychology of self-esteem: A new concept of man's psychological nature*. Los Angeles, CA: Nash Publishing.

Brownmiller, Susan. 1975. *Against our will: Men, women and rape*. New York: Simon & Schuster.

Cotoi, Călin. 2011. Neoliberalism: A Foucauldian perspective. *International Review of Social Research* 1 (2): 109–124.

Critchley, Simon. 1999. *Ethics, politics, subjectivity*. London: Verso.

De Kesel, Marc. 2009. *Eros and ethics: Reading Jacques Lacan's seminar VII*. New York: State University of New York Press.

De Vos, Jan. 2012. *Psychologization in times of globalisation*. London: Routledge.

Duggan, Lisa. 2019. *Mean girl: Ayn Rand and the culture of greed*. Oakland: University of California Press.

Emler, Nicholas. 2001. *Self-esteem: The costs and causes of low self-worth*. York: Joseph Rowntree Foundation.

Fisher, Mark. 2009. *Capitalist realism: Is there no alternative?* Winchester and Washington: Zero Books.

Foucault, Michel. 2010. *The birth of biopolitics: Lectures at the Collège de France, 1978–1979*. Basingstoke: Palgrave Macmillan.

Freedland, Jonathan. 2017. The new age of Ayn Rand: How she won over Trump and Silicon Valley. https://www.theguardian.com/books/2017/apr/10/new-age-ayn-rand-conquered-trump-white-house-silicon-valley. Accessed 3 July 2018.

Hartmann, Heinz. 1958 [1939]. *Ego psychology and the problem of adaptation*. New York: International Universities Press.

Hegel, G.W.F. 1997 [1807]. *Philosophy of spirit*. Oxford: Oxford University Press.

Heller, Anne C. 2009. *Ayn Rand and the world she made*. New York: Doubleday.

Ingleby, David. 2011. Professionals as socializers: The 'psy complex'. In *Critical psychology: Critical concepts in psychology, volume 1, dominant models of psychology and their limits*, ed. Ian Parker, 279–307. London and New York: Routledge.

Izcovich, Luis. 2017. *The marks of a psychoanalysis*. London and New York: Routledge.

Jacoby, Russell. 1983. *The repression of psychoanalysis.* New York: Basic Books.

Jameson, Frederic. 2012. Dirty little secret. *London Review of Books* 34 (22): 39–42.

Kunkle, Sheila. 2007. Žižek's choice. *International Journal of Žižek Studies* 1 (3). http://zizekstudies.org/index.php/IJZS/article/view/50/47. Accessed 3 July 2018.

Lacan, Jacques. 1992 [1986]. *The ethics of psychoanalysis 1959–1960: The seminar of Jacques Lacan book VII*, trans. Dennis Porter. London: Routledge.

———. 2006. *Écrits: The first complete edition in* English, trans. Bruce Fink. New York: Norton.

Lenin, V. I. 1909. *Materialism and empirio-criticism: Critical comments on a reactionary philosophy.* https://www.marxists.org/archive/lenin/works/1908/mec/index.htm. Accessed 9 July 2018.

Levine, Bruce. 2011. How Ayn Rand seduced young men and helped make the U.S. into an uncaring nation. http://brucelevine.net/how-ayn-rand-seduced-young-men-and-helped-make-the-u-s-into-an-uncaring-nation/. Accessed 29 June 2018.

Marx, Karl. 1867. *Capital: A critique of political economy.* https://www.marxists.org/archive/marx/works/1867-c1/. Accessed 10 July 2018.

McGurl, Mark. 2012. *The program era: Postwar fiction and the rise of creative writing.* Boston, MA: Harvard University Press.

McKeever, Paul. 2017. Top Ayn Rand ad hominems: A guide for the misogynistic, anti-Semitic, and otherwise ignorant. http://blog.paulmckeever.ca/uncategorized/top-ayn-rand-ad-hominems-a-guide-for-the-misogynistic-anti-semitic-and-otherwise-ignorant/. Accessed 3 July 2018.

Millett, Kate. 1977. *Sexual politics.* London: Virago.

Neill, Callum. 2011. *Lacanian ethics and the assumption of subjectivity.* London: Palgrave.

Parker, Ian. 1994. *Slavoj Žižek: A critical introduction.* London: Pluto Press.

———. 1997. *Psychoanalytic culture: Psychoanalytic discourse in Western* society. London and Thousand Oaks, CA: Sage.

———. 2011. *Lacanian psychoanalysis: Revolutions in subjectivity.* London and New York: Routledge.

———. 2019. Psychology, psychiatry and the ethics of psychoanalysis. In *Routledge handbook of psychoanalytic political theory*, ed. Y. Stavrakakis. London and New York: Routledge.

Peikoff, Leonard. 1982. *The ominous parallels.* New York, NY: Stein and Day.

Pluth, Ed. 2008. *Signifiers and acts: Freedom in Lacan's theory of the subject.* New York: State University of New York Press.

Rand, Ayn. 1943. *The fountainhead.* New York: Bobbs Merrill.

———. 1957. *Atlas shrugged.* New York: Random House.

————. 1971. The psychology of psychologizing. https://campus.aynrand.org/works/1971/01/01/the-psychology-of-psychologizing/page1. Accessed 9 July 2018.

Richman, Sheldon. 2006. Szasz and Rand. *The Journal of Ayn Rand Studies* 7 (2): 429–444.

Rose, Nikolas. 1985. *The psychological complex: Psychology, politics and society in England 1869–1939*. London: Routledge and Kegan Paul.

Rothbard, Murray N. 2017. The sociology of the Ayn Rand cult. http://rothbard.altervista.org/essays/the-sociology-of-the-ayn-rand-cult.pdf. Accessed 29 June 2018.

Szasz, Thomas. 1961. *The myth of mental illness*. New York: Harper & Row.

————. 1988 [1965]. *The ethics of psychoanalysis: The theory and method of autonomous psychotherapy*. Syracuse, NY: Syracuse University Press.

————. 1997. In conversation with Thomas Kerr. *Psychiatric Bulletin* 21: 39–44.

————. 2002. Rothbard on Szasz. *Liberty* 16: 33–34.

————. 2004. *Faith in freedom: Libertarian principles and psychiatric practices*. New Brunswick, NJ: Transaction Publishers.

————. 2009. *Antipsychiatry: Quackery squared*. Syracuse, NY: Syracuse University Press.

Walker, J. 1999. *The Ayn Rand cult*. Chicago, IL: Open Court.

Zamora, Daniel, and Michael C. Behrent (eds.). 2016. *Foucault and neoliberalism*. Cambridge: Polity Press.

Žižek, Slavoj. 2002. The actuality of Ayn Rand. *The Journal of Ayn Rand Studies* 3 (2): 215–227.

————. 2012. The lesbian session. *The Symptom*, 13. http://www.lacan.com/symptom13/the-lesbian.html. Accessed 3 July 2018.

Žižek, Slavoj, Maria Aristodemou, Stephen Frosh, and Derek Hook. 2010. Unbehagen and the subject: An interview with Slavoj Žižek. *Psychoanalysis, Culture & Society* 15: 418–428.

CHAPTER 3

Psychologisation, What It Is and What It Is Not: Objectivism, Psychology, and Silicon Valley

Jan De Vos

1 THE OVERSPILL OF PSYCHOLOGY

In the previous chapter Ian Parker introduced Ayn Rand's 'The Psychology of Psychologizing', and the often unacknowledged connections between her philosophy and psychological and psychoanalytic narratives.[1] When I began researching Rand for this book, I certainly found it surprising to learn that she wrote specifically on 'psychologization', that is, she criticised psychologising discourses. But should this really come as a surprise? For, as we can observe, we critics of psychology often find ourselves in the rather uncomfortable company of conservative neoliberals attacking, for example, 'therapeutic culture' and the political correctness embedded in psycho-programmes implied in education and other spheres.[2] It is a familiar discomfort: think of those well known, left-situated critics like Christopher Lasch and Slavoj Žižek who verge/or are accused of verging (I leave this in the middle) toward a conservative

J. De Vos (✉)
Cardiff University, Cardiff, UK

© The Author(s) 2020
N. Cocks (ed.), *Questioning Ayn Rand*,
Palgrave Studies in Literature, Culture and Economics,
https://doi.org/10.1007/978-3-030-53073-0_3

right-wing position.[3] From here, we might need to reinterpret Žižek's argument on Ayn Rand, also introduced in the preceding chapter, that she is one who, as a useful fool, takes the right-wing ideology at its most serious and thus shows the consequences, the very logic, the embarrassing kernel of capitalism. We might have to twist this a bit: is Ayn Rand not above all one of those right-wingers who might reveal to us the embarrassing kernel of our leftist position? In other words, might Ayn Rand be one of our own demons that we should confront? And might Ayn Rand's critique on psychologisation help us to confront also the limits of our—or, my—well-meant critique on psychology?

Let me start by explaining the title of my chapter: 'Psychologisation, What It Is and What It Is Not'. The trivial issue here is that I have been misunderstood and even misquoted concerning what I have written previously on psychologisation. Hence, I sometimes think I should engage not with 'my critics', but 'those who misunderstood me', but this might be the perfect way to make things even worse.

In my book *Psychologization and the Subject of Late Modernity*, I stated that one might consider psychologisation as the overspill of psychological discourse to non-psychological areas. I then proceeded to question and critique this conception from the argument that this definition opens up the claim that we should return to pre-psychologisation times and non-psychologising conceptions of the human. This is a claim which, of course, repeats the simplistic, essentialist position I rejected.

But here the possible link to a conservative/right-wing discourse is immediately clear. That is, defining psychologisation as the unwarranted overspill of psychological discourse to all sort of life-domains (education, parenting, culture economy...) opens up the claim that we should stick to what the human being *really is* beyond all this soft leftist psycho-blah-blah. I contend that this is actually the pinnacle of psychologisation: to claim that it is as such possible to define what the human being really is. Put simply, the critique of psychologisation runs the risk of stranding in psychologisation itself.

This is what I precisely contend in *Psychologization and the Subject of Late Modernity*, in the pages following upon my first provisory description of psychologisation as the overspill. But as you can guess, I am more than often quoted in this way: 'De Vos defines psychologisation as the overspill of psychology to society'.[4]

What, then of Ayn Rand's discussion of psychologisation? If, as said, many critiques denounce psychologisation as obscuring 'the real human being'—what I call a fantasy—Ayn Rand immediately testifies to this phantasmatic level as she starts her critique on psychologisaton with a *fictitious example*, of course, as you might guess, from her own novel *Atlas Shrugged*. Her claim is that psychologisation obscures what the human being *objectively* is, and this is followed by: let my give an example of my novel. Hence a phantasmatic example.

Rand refers to Hank Reardon from *Atlas Shrugged* who psychologises his wife: he wonders if, behind her sarcasm and her contemptuous way of treating him, the truth of a disavowed love is hidden. Rand rejects this and claims that the sarcasm and contempt of the wife might be what is at stake. In a way Rand could be said to profess: there is a truth in the symptom itself! Which would sound very psychoanalytic.

As you might know, psychoanalysis is not about searching for a hidden truth behind a reality, such as what a symptom would mean or signify, but, rather, it concerns the *lack of, or within, meaning* leading to, for example, symptomatic manifestations. Remember the Jewish joke mentioned by Sigmund Freud:

> Two Jews met in a train at a Galician railway station. 'Where are you travelling?' asked one. 'To Cracow,' was the reply. 'Now see here, what a liar you are!' said the first one, bristling. 'When you say that you are travelling to Cracow, you really wish me to believe that you are travelling to Lemberg. Well, but I am sure that you are really travelling to Cracow, so why lie about it?' (Freud 1981, 63)

Of course this refers to some kind of surplus, a Real embedded in the symptomatic. Think, for example, of telling the truth in order to conceal something (a well-known strategy within propaganda), which is far removed from the dimension of the objective which forms the backbone of Ayn Rand's philosophy.

Ayn Rand rejects psychologisation as it would obscure the objective state of things. And here, and this is central, she does not reject the psychological or the science of psychology as such. Her argument is the following: philosophy is the realm of reason, cognition, objectivity; the realm of psychology is the 'subconscious', concerning wishes, feelings, beliefs; the subconscious, can, when some pathological conditions are in play, hamper reason, cognition and morality (the field of objectivist philosophy); in 'normal' circumstances the psychological level does not play a role (Rand 1971, 23–31). According to Rand, this is what psychologisers miss as they start to psychologise the as such non-psychological fields of reason and cognition. Hence, Rand is a prime example of those who see psychologisation as the inappropriate overspill of psychology. It is here that Rand does not reject the potential validity of the science of psychology (above all as a 'future science'), and acknowledges that there are 'conscientious psychotherapist[s]' (24). This is what I always have contested: the phenomena of psychologisation, in my opinion, are closely connected with the basic antagonisms within psychology itself. This, of course, is in line with the psychoanalytic, and above all Lacanian, tradition that sees psychology as a per definition problematic and impossible science, trying to objectify subjectivity.

Counter to such an understanding, Rand writes:

> The task of evaluating the processes of man's subconscious is the province of psychology. Psychology does not regard its subject morally, but medically — i.e., from the aspect of health or malfunction (with cognitive competence as the proper standard of health). (27)

She thus concedes a positive place to psychology: in the medical realm. Or, the (neuro)biological, as the most common buyout for a psychology drowning in its own paradoxes and fallacies. And this move for Rand, I argue, has its particular reasons. Rand needs psychology as 'the other science' filling the hole in her Objectivist philosophy itself.

2   RAND NEEDS PSYCHOLOGY

Let me make this argument starting with the claim that the division, required by Rand, between a psychological field (the jurisdiction of psychology) and the non-psychological field (for Rand the field of Objectivist philosophy) is as such problematic. While it would allow a firm 'Stop you psychologisers, don't cross this line', Ayn Rand testifies how the defence of non-psychological grounds is rapidly achieved in psychologising ways. Rand writes: 'The basic motive of most psychologisers is *hostility*. Caused by a profound self-doubt, self-condemnation, and fear, hostility is a type of projection that directs toward other people the hatred which the hostile person feels toward himself' (25). What is this else than: *vade retro*, you psychologisers, *vade retro*, in the name of psychology? Here is a further quotation: 'It is not man's subconscious, but his *conscious* mind that is subject to his direct control — and to moral judgment. It is a specific individual's *conscious* mind that one judges (on the basis of objective evidence) in order to judge his moral character' (29). The 'conscious mind' and 'his moral character' are the jurisdiction of Objectivist philosophy, or should we not say *the Objectivist psychology*? Ayn Rand shows that those who believe that psychologisation is the unlucky, inappropriate overspill of psychological science cannot but defend the supposedly non-psychological fields in psychological terms.

Of course, this is quite obvious. Objectivist authors such as Robert Campbell and Nathaniel Branden already have pointed out that despite Rand's critique on psychologisation this is exactly what she is relapsing into. But, clearly, Ayn Rand is more or less aware of this: the title of her essay is 'The Psychology of Psychologizing'. But nonetheless, I claim, neither Rand nor her critics like Campbell and Branden understand the true character of the paradox Rand problematically acknowledges (Branden 1969; Campbell 2015).

Consider for example the following formulation, where Rand rejects Immanuel Kant's basic proposition that we cannot know the Thing (Das Ding) as such: for Kant there is a 'noumenal' reality which escapes our phenomenological knowledge. Rand writes: '[Kant's] metaphysical inferiority of this world (as a "phenomenal" world of mere "appearances"), is a rationalization for the hatred of reality. The notion that reason is unable to perceive reality and deals only with "appearances" is a rationalization for the hatred of reason [...]' (Rand 1984a, 19). One cannot miss the paradox here: according to Rand, Kant rationalises for the hatred of the ratio.

It is a contention that may well ring a bell: I once argued, based on my reading of Christopher Lasch, that one psychologises *for the hatred of the psyche* (De Vos 2013). One takes recourse to the psychological ego in order to escape the split subject, the zero-level of subjectivity, or perhaps more understandable: one psychologises to escape the horror of the unconsciousness.

With Rand we have a particular form of this logic, as she puts rationality, cognition and morality at the centre of her Objectivist philosophy, the first thing she claims is that these are as such unproblematic issues. If there is something wrong on the level of rationality, cognition and morality, then there is a psychological/medical problem in play. Psychology, hence, as the keystone of Ayn Rand's philosophy: psychology as the Other Science serving to provide the closure of Objectivism. Simply put, Rand needs psychology in order to ward off the possibility that the fields of rationality, cognition and morality might themselves be flawed, might be themselves ridden by antagonisms. And the unacknowledged paradox here is that, once again, this requires her relapse into psychologisation. That is, sketching out an agent capable of rationality, cognition and morality, she depicts a strong Ego, and this is where she shies away from the Split Subject, the subject of the unconscious.

Of course, with this psychoanalytic *unconscious* I do not mean the psychologising *subconscious* that Ayn Rand tries to fence in. The *unconscious* is not the story which would fill up or explain medically the gaps of the conscious story, it is the fundamental failure of closure, that what makes the conscious story unable to fully coincide with itself. If one would agree that this is in a way a depiction of what the Lacanian Real is about, then perhaps one could argue, building on Rand's argument on the rationalisation for the hatred of reason, that Rand takes recourse to reality and objectivity *for the hatred of the Real*.

At the very most, Rand's depiction of the human being needs to be one of wholeness and of fullness. This is why Rand loathes so much B.F. Skinner's contention: 'To be for oneself is to be almost nothing. The great individualists so often cited to show the value of personal freedom have owed their successes to earlier social environments' (cited in: Rand 1984a, 145). Rand takes issue with this: she wants to save the ego, the individual set apart from society. Just consider how in her essay 'The Property of the Airwaves' she writes: '[…] there is no such thing as the "public interest" (other than the sum of the individual interests of individual citizens)' (Rand 1986, 136). This is, perhaps, where Margaret Thatcher's famous line comes from. Of course, for us psychoanalysts, there is a point here: *there is no Other*. But for Lacanians the issue is: *there is no Other of the Other*. Society is not a whole, it is ridden by a fundamental antagonism. Missing this part, Rand and Thatcher believe that there is such a thing as the individual. This is where Ayn Rand's 'philosophy' is necessarily psychologistic, as it attempts to depict the ego as a firm and objective issue.

3   THE DIGITAL RAND

If one of the reasons for my interest in Ayn Rand is that she wrote on psychologisation, another is the idea that Silicon Valley loves Ayn Rand. For after having written on psychologisation and neurologisation I would like here to expand my 'field of fire', with yet another 'isation', that is the digitalisation of subjectivity.

Let me start out with a passage in Rand's text on 'The Psychology of Psychologizing' which struck me. As Rand criticises psychologisation she writes:

> The result is the stupor and lethargy of those who are neither infants nor adults, but miserable sleepwalkers unwilling to wake up. Anything can enter the spongy mess inside their skulls, nothing can come out of it. The signals it emits are chance regurgitations of any chance splatter. (...) They have abdicated the responsibility for their own mental processes, yet they continue to act, to speak, to deal with people — and to expect some sort of response. (Rand 1990, 31)

Now, these wordings are almost the same that the philosopher Bernard Stiegler uses as he describes the perils of digitalisation: it leads to infantilisation and the decline of responsibility (Stiegler 2016). Let us leave this aside for the moment, however, and first turn to the issue that it is bon ton to connect Ayn Rand to Silicon Valley. And yes, the Silicon Valley boys do refer to Ayn Rand: they of course centre their technology on the self. That is their business model.[5] One might think here also of Adam Curtis's documentary *All Watched Over by Machines of Loving Grace* in which he introduces the claim that: '[computers] could turn everyone into heroic individuals' (Curtis 2011).

Nevertheless, could one not argue that Rand would be horrified by digitalisation? Consider for example again her critique on B.F. Skinner: according to Rand, Skinner advocates 'a single culture for all mankind', and is keen to set up a totalitarian world state, which would 'rul[e] every cell of every man's brain and every moment of his life'. Rand writes:

> Who will be the 'designers' of his proposed global culture and the rulers of mankind? He answers unequivocally: the 'technologists of behaviour.' What qualifies them for such a job? They are 'scientists.' What is science? In the whole of the book, no definition is given, as if the term were a self-evident, mystically hallowed primary. (Rand 1984b, 149)

But, if there is a truth in the idea that the Silicon Valley pundits are inspired by Ayn Rand, is it not also the case that it is the Objectivist philosophy/psychology that provides the 'science' for today, and I repeat Rand's words, 'technologists of behaviour'? And is it not precisely the fact that Ayn Rand's 'science' passes over fiction and novels that make her so apt to be used in today's digitalisation of reality? That is, if the Silicon Valley pundits claim a Randian inspiration, they testify to how they give form to the virtual (to the avatar, to the smart environment, the placeholders of subjectivity and intersubjectivity) starting from fiction.

Digitalisation, one could argue, is not about modelling science, it is about giving fiction a larger-than-life form. Digitalisation is always a second order virtualisation, relying on a prior virtualisation or fictionalisation. This is why Rand's 'Objectivist philosophy' is so usable. In Rand's essay on Skinner that I just mentioned, criticising yet another author she writes: 'If you have read *The Fountainhead*, you will understand the relationship: he is the Gus Webb to Mr. Skinner's Ellsworth Toohey' (Rand 1984b, 159). Is this then the ultimate Objectivist stance: to understand how things really are, read my novels! This is the same structure as: to understand how the world is, go to the World Wide Web. Hence, it is within the digital that Ayn Rand's *fictions* will be realised and made objective. Because if you are into naturals, the objective, the way things are in themselves, you are in the realm of the phantasmatic and the mythical (that is why Ayn Rand had to write fiction). Today the realm to turn fantasies into reality is the digital and the virtual.

Think in this respect of Fred Turner contending in a recent television documentary that for the Silicon Valley moguls the Internet is about, I quote: 'The hope that we can build technologies of consciousness that will transform the social world without government' (Turner quoted in Meerman 2018).[6] This is, of course, Rand's political world view, realised via technology. This is the guiding idea: put people in the network, use the right/good algorithms and people will most naturally start to steer themselves. It may seem neutral, that is, it might seem beyond ideology, but of course, it is precisely there, at the level of the algorithms, that the psychological theories and models come in. It is the latter that provide the fictional scripts to organise, to give form to, and consequently to exploit subjectivity and sociality.

Whilst driving around the campuses of Google and Apple in the television documentary mentioned above, Fred Turner comments on the bland and unobtrusive architecture: 'they don't want to show power

...'; '...they don't want to become public' ...; '...they don't believe that there is a genuine public space that they should be serving'; 'Google, Apple, they want to build their world [...] we want to help people brand themselves [...] to engage in complex, collaborative consumption. Great. The public, what's that? People will take care of themselves [...]'[7] For the companies mentioned by Turner, the social does not exist; society, the public do not exist. The world and the people then? Well, we just fabricate these along the lines of our fantasies. Hence, this is not about touching the right buttons, of having a technology aligned with science, aligned with human neuropsychology whether unintentionally or by design. This is, instead, about making fiction work, just as Ayn Rand made her Objectivist philosophy work within her novels.

All this might offer a different way to think about the problems we face today with digitalisation. According to the current mainstream argument, the web offers a new kind of public sphere, and for some it resembles the local pub, where people easily become rude, offend others, shout indecent things...A bit human all too human, no? So, the typical argument is that more and better algorithms are needed to steer human nature, or (for the moment?) we need more human eyes/ears to do what algorithms cannot themselves (yet) do. Or a similar mainstream argument: people will have to adapt, as we are atavistic, we are testing the boundaries of the new social spheres, we will have to learn and we will have to educate. This, however, leads me to question the excesses that we see in the first place: is this truly (natural) human psychology and sociology set free or aggrandised? Perhaps we should think this differently: the excess is at the side of the digital itself. It is digital/virtuality running itself amok, the derailing of digital reality as such. That is, the aberrances and the problems of the digital should not be linked to our true human psychology or sociology, but to the ideological fantasies we have put in the digital, the psychological/sociological models and theories.

Turning to Rand once more, we read that, in her estimation, psychologisation is bad fiction:

> The old lady who talks about her operation is a well-known bore; she is nothing compared to the youngish lady who talks on and on and on about her psychological problems, with a lameness of imagination that prevents them from being good fiction. (Rand 1990, 29–30)

Of course, for me, Rand's objectivist fiction suffers from and amounts to the same, lame ego-psychology, celebrating the strong ego, in the figure of the white, smart, handsome, successful, bright heroic man, that she—am I allowed to psychologise here?—loved to fantasise about.

This bad fiction has now gone digital.

4   The Good Mother Argument

How should we oppose bad fiction? Should we ourselves write novels and explain the world with it? Or do we already have a leftist *Atlas Shrugged*? And should we then give this leftist *Atlas Shrugged* to the Silicon Valley heroes, or those from Zhong Guan Cun, the technology hub in the Haidian District of Beijing in China? But, of course, this could not simply be us, leftists, for are we not the ones doing the critique, doing the explanations of why people are caught in ideology? Should we then, concerning Rand's *Atlas Shrugged*, explain to the public and especially her aficionados that they are trapped in fiction? Should we do a literary analysis and explain the luring mechanisms in order to counter them? Of course, this would only redouble Ayn Rand's own stance: you are lured, let me show how so that you can escape it. Should we then be inspired by Lacanian leftists such as Yannis Stavrakakis and acknowledge there is 'jouissance' involved in all this. In order to what, to lay it bare, or perhaps, to use these mechanisms ourselves? (Stavrakakis 1999). Or should we follow William Connolly, the Deleuzian political theorist, who argues that the right uses neuropsychological techniques to influence the people: his argument, then, let us from the left do the same but explain the people in the meantime what we are doing and why (Connolly 2002).

I've written against Connolly elsewhere, arguing that he mistakes neuropsychology for the real thing, for an uncontested and unproblematic science, whereas I claim that in order to do neuroscience, you need psychology. The question is, therefore: which psychological theories and models do you choose to use when you do neuroscience? And I made this point: psychoanalysis is not an alternative in this instance. That is, I claimed, in the end issues such as the death drive, the object *a* and transference are not *scanable*. Or put differently, psychoanalysis is not a psychology, and thus cannot offer natural categories, or those of a simple and plain psychological kind, to be laid under the scanner: it can only deconstruct them, showing their paradoxes and show their lack of any final ground.

Now the question today could be, are we to use psychoanalysis for the virtual and the digital: that is, is psychoanalysis *algorithmisable*? Again, I claim not. In the same way that the revolution will not be televised, the object *a* will not be digitalised. The singular is not algorithmisable, the singular is the deadlock in the algorithm. I've tried to make this argument elsewhere. But for now, let me approach this from another angle. For, maybe more important than 'what to do with psychoanalytic conceptions in the virtual' is perhaps the question 'what to do with the psychologising issues that are now structuring digitalisation?' That is, from a political, leftist point of view, if we would want to nationalise Facebook and the others, how then would a 'Nationalised Book' be organised? Should it ask its users how they feel and prompt them to share their feelings? Should it use any or none of these psychologising features? And what about a nationalised Tinder or other dating apps? Would swiping be still allowed in the nationalised versions? Or should we as such have to get Tinder and Grindr from the net, as they, as the Hungarian philosopher Srećko Horvat argues, turn our 'emotional life' into a commodity and trap teenagers in digital narcissistic culture?[8]

Perhaps here we can look to an older discussion, of how to control or censor the Airwaves in the old radio and television times: Ayn Rand wrote a few essays on this matter, including 'The Property Status of Airwaves'. In this article she writes : 'What was needed was *legality*, not *controls*' (Rand 1986, 135). Or as she wrote in 'Have Gun, Will Nudge': 'in a free society there is no place for regulation' (Rand 1966). Rand's argument against her opponents who plead for regulation in the best of public interest centres on the difficulty of government defending something as 'public interest' (which for Rand does not exist) without getting bogged down in censorship: 'If a commissioner has to judge which applicant for a broadcasting license will best serve the "public interest," how can he judge it without judging the content, nature and Value of the programs the applicants have offered or will offer?' (Rand 1986, 137–138) Ayn Rand's argument here is that this control and regulation would have no place in a neutral and minimal government which would only ensure legality. Is this Ayn Rand's dream: picturing a good enough neutral Mother?

Consider in this respect how she criticises the academic grant system in academia channelling public money to a clique of established scholars and their protégés: this is what she wrote in the context of the already mentioned essay criticising B.F. Skinner: 'This is the way an "establish-ment" is formed and placed beyond the reach of dissent. What chance would a beginner, a nonconformist, an opponent of behaviourism, have against the entrenched power of a clique supported by government funds?'[9] Rand's main point here is while being against the state, she does not plead for anarchy, she takes this legalist position: a state would only provide a minimal law to protect basic issues such as private property.[10]

I must say, reading Rand's various pleas on these and different matters, that I recognised some of my own (former) ideas and their deadlocks. Ayn Rand, for example, questions the idea of the fairness doctrine in the USA, which demands that equal opportunity be given to all sides of a controversial issue in radio and television channels. Rand of course rejects this, as for her a true capitalist market would not need this control. But outside such reasoning, does she not have a point here when she claims the unworkability of the fairness doctrine?

For example, when in my writings and my comments I critiqued the government-induced and facilitated psychologisation of education, did I also not dream of an education sticking to its mere formal assignment, to be a non-psychological education? Does this not in the end celebrate an education *before* psychologisation? In the same vein I critiqued the Flemish government's promotion of evidence-based methods and of CBT in psychotherapy and social care institutions, did I also not proclaim: *vade retro state, stay neutral.* But in what should such neutrality consist? Should the state defend the spectrum: secure for example that in each philos-ophy department there would be one phenomenologist, one Kantian, one Zizekian, one Randian... Or, concerning our psychotherapeutic and care institutions, should each service have one psychoanalyst, one Rogerian, one behaviourist? I don't know, one could imagine a dear one going to a centre, and the team deciding, well let's give this case to Burrhus our behaviourist... There is an argument for some radicalness here: one behaviourist is already too much.

That is, a partisan censorship might be needed: silencing all those theories and their subsequent practices which are, at least to me, clearly problematic. So in the end perhaps we should say, against Ayn Rand, no, the government should not be neutral, politics are not neutral, they should be partisan. Thus, if I were in control I would simply close down the psychology departments nationwide. I would make psychoanalysis the state theory. However, knowing that amongst psychoanalysts there are 'very bad people' too, I would have to instal a thought police too, and foresee 'truth trials'...

But as, most probably, the opportunity to be in control will not present itself to me (nor to any reader of this book, I would guess), perhaps the question is, for those of us from the left, for whom do we write? For those intelligent or open-minded right-wingers, or for the social democrats still sympathetic to the Real Left, so that they would pick something up, and soften or amend their policies? Or that they would make sure there is in each department/social care centre at least one critical person. Or do we write for the future drop outs, that is the future drop outs of the totalitarian digital society that is awaiting us? Do we write for them, the future *homo sacer*? But then the question could be, would they still be able to read us, would we not better write our critiques in the format of fiction? Better still, perhaps, fiction that is orally transmittable?

If this is what we would need to do, write novels for the future, let us turn for a penultimate time to Ayn Rand, and ask ourselves, why is it that her novels are so enthusiastically read and especially by younger people? Can we learn something here?

5   Conclusion: The Appeal to Rand by the Youth[11]

Ayn Rand addresses her reader as an apprentice in her Objectivist philosophy, she writes:

> If you keep an active mind, you will discover (…) that every challenge you examine will strengthen your convictions, that the conscious, reasoned rejection of false theories will help you to clarify and amplify the true ones, that your ideological enemies will make you invulnerable by providing countless demonstrations of their own impotence […]. (Rand 1984a, 21)

Note the strong interpellative 'you' here. Is this not why Ayn Rand is appealing? She promises enlightenment to the initiated. And are we not trapped in the same ambition when we would argue: *do you think Ayn Rand's writings tell you the truth and show you the way out? Well, let me tell you this: you were blinded and these are the psychological mechanisms and rhetoric tricks she uses to promise you salvation.* And from here, we might think we are entitled to claim: at least we, the leftists, are not promising you any bright road to salvation…

But maybe this is too simple as it misses the double layer with Ayn Rand. Perhaps, she is actually not promising her aficionados the road to heroism. She writes: 'If you reach the day when these essentials become your absolutes, you will have entered Atlantis—at least psychologically; which is a precondition of the possibility ever to enter it existentially' (Rand 1986, 22). What does this mean, psychologically? You must and can first become a hero in your mind (psychologically), that is for us psychoanalysts, in your fantasy? In order to do what? The answer is of course: in order to remain there, stuck in your fantasy.

To properly read this, let us introduce Myka Tucker-Abramson's analysis of the fate of the characters such as Eddie Willers and Cheryl Taggart in *Atlas Shrugged*. According to Tucker-Abramson, in the novel no characters actually transcend their class positions and this failure is always coded as a personal failing. Tucker-Abramson writes: 'so the reader must identify with capital if they are to identify with the novel's developmental arc' (Tucker-Abramson 2017, 90). Readers must identify with Dagny and Galt while they remain Eddies and Cheryls. Tucker-Abramson continues: 'Yet the novel's ending is a happy one because the reader no longer identifies with the victimized middle class but rather with the forces of capital' (ibid.). Hence, the reader is above all led to an 'identification' with the winners, while remaining stuck in his/her own current position. If we are to follow this critique, our task would be to explain to the Rand reader and adept: you are lured in this story about how things really are, but in the end you are locked up in that position, as you are told 'stay where you are, just look up to the real heroes'.

Perhaps this chimes with my critique on neurologisation: you are lured into the neurodiscourse ('you are you brain') in order to identify, not with your brain as such, but, rather, with the perspective of the expert. *Look this is what you are*, interpellates you to identify with the gaze of the expert and not with the thing that you are said to be. But this expert position itself you will never attain, you are just invited to look up to the expert. So in the end the message is: resign and let go any resistance to those who tell you what the fate of the human being is.

The Randian identification follows the same path: identify with the forces of capital and remain within your subdued position. And perhaps this is precisely what digitalisation is about. To readjust Rand's words: become a hero in the digital and the virtual, in this way you will have entered Atlantis—at least psychologically; which is a precondition of the possibility *never* to enter it existentially. Hence, Rand might not lead to overidentification as Slavoj Žižek has it, undermining contemporary capitalism Rather, she leads to identification properly. Reread in a twisted

Althusserian way, Rand interpellates you to identify with the hero so that you are locked up in the position of the aficionado.

So in conclusion, to overcome all this, to write a leftist Great Novel for the future drop outs, one should read Ayn Rand very well, and discern her deadlocks.

Here, then, is my final recourse to Ayn Rand. In 'The Psychology of Psychologizing' she writes: 'The mind is a processing organ; so is the stomach. If a stomach fails in its function, it throws up; its unprocessed material is vomit' (Rand 1990, 31). The stomach failing in its functions is what happens when a psychopathological process hampers the processing, or the entrance of psychologisers has the same effect. So for Rand and Objectivist philosophy it is essential to keep psychology and the psychologisers at bay so ensure a proper processing, so that, instead of vomit, we will have shit properly evacuated.

Which might be yet a different way of approaching the future drop outs.[12]

Notes

1. This chapter is based on the transcript of a lecture I gave at the 'Ayn Rand From the Left' conference at The University of Reading, UK, November 2018.
2. See, for example, Furedi (2004).
3. See, for example, Rankin (1996); Browne (2016).
4. For one of my job applications, I had to mention the number of citations I attracted, and was asked to subtract the self-quotations. Which made me think: what if they asked me to subtract all those quotations in which I was misquoted?
5. Here it is worth extending a note in Neil Cocks's introduction to this book. When the CEO of Uber, Travis Kalanick, had to choose an avatar for his Twitter account in 2015, he opted for the cover of *The Fountain-head*. Peter Thiel, Facebook's first major investor and a rare example of a man who straddles both Silicon Valley and Trumpworld, is a Randian. Meanwhile, Steve Jobs is said by his Apple co-founder, Steve Wozniak, to have regarded *Atlas Shrugged* as one of his 'guides in life'. See Freedland (2017). Reading Rand against and with the Valley presents problems that are not recognised within such accounts.
6. See also Turner (2019).
7. Fred Turner: 'they don't want to become public [...] they don't believe that there is a genuine public space that they should be serving [...] Google, Apple, they want to build their world [...] The idea of promoting

a public good… is not there. We want to provide complex consumer services, we want people to connect to one another, on a one to one basis […] we want to help people brand themselves so that they can find each other, we want people to collaborate in complex elaborate consumption. The public, what's that, people can take care of themselves…'. See Meerman (2018).

8. See, for example, Van Valkengoed (2019).

9. How could I, at the moment of writing this out of academia proper, working under temporarily and precarious conditions, not be sympathetic to this, knowing all too well how cliques protect their interests and exert power, keeping different views and opposing scholars out?

10. See also Nathaniel Branden in 'Alienation', also from Rand (1986): 'in a free society there is no place for regulation', 318.

11. For the serving of narcissistic grandiosity (Yes, it's about you, you can be the hero!), see Cummins (2016).

12. Hence my argument: we are all turned into little entrepreneurs, looking up to the big entrepreneurs, or to capital as such, and thus letting them to have their way. And this obfuscates our seeing of the drop outs, the waste products, those not able to be in one way or another an entrepreneur. As Tucker-Abramson writes: 'The result of this reconceptualization is that if the subject's life is entirely of her own making, they have two choices when economic or personal disaster occurs: they can either identify with the winners, those who profit from the shocks, or they can identify with the losers, those who fail to profit from the shocks. As the novel's conclusion shows, the choice is clear' (Tucker-Abramson 2017, 90).

BIBLIOGRAPHY

Branden, Nathaniel. 1969. *The psychology of self-esteem*. Los Angeles: Nash Publishing.

Browne, Marcus. 2016. Slavoj Žižek: 'Trump is really a centrist liberal'. *The Guardian*, April 28.

Campbell, Robert L. 2015. The prohibition against *psychologizing*. *The Journal of Ayn Rand Studies* 15 (1): 53–66.

Connolly, William. 2002. *Neuropolitics: Thinking, culture, speed*. Minneapolis: University of Minnesota Press.

Cummins, Denise. 2016. What happens when you take Ayn Rand seriously? https://www.psychologytoday.com/intl/blog/good-thinking/201602/what-happens-when-you-take-ayn-rand-seriously?amp. Accessed 19 May 2019.

Curtis, Adam, dir.. 2011. *All watched over by machines of loving grace*. BBC.

De Vos, Jan. 2013. *Psychologization and the subject of late modernity*. Basingstoke: Palgrave.

————. *Psychologisation in times of globalisation*. London: Routledge.

Freedland, Jonathan. 2017. The new age of Ayn Rand: How she won over trump and silicon valley. *The Guardian*, April 10.

Freud, Sigmund. 1981 [1905]. *Complete works of sigmund freud, vol VIII*, trans. James Strachey. London: Vintage.

Furedi, Frank. 2004. *Therapy culture: Cultivating vulnerability in an uncertain age*. London: Routledge.

Meerman, Marije, dir.. 2018. *Cybertopia: Dreams of Silicon Valley*. Indigenous.

Murnane, Ben. 2018. *Ayn Rand and the posthuman: The mind made future*. Basingstoke: Palgrave.

Rand, Ayn. 1962. Have gun, will nudge. *The Objectivist Newsletter*, March 9.

————. 1984a. Philosophical detection. In *Philosophy: WHo needs it?* 12–22. New York: Signet.

————. 1984b. The stimulus and the response. In *Philosophy: Who needs it?* 127–161. New York: Signet.

————. 1986 [1966]. The property of the airwaves. In *Capitalism: The unknown ideal*, 131–140. New York: Signet.

————. 1990 [1971]. The psychology of psychologizing. In *The voice of reason: Essays in Objectivist thought*, ed. Leonard Peikoff, 23–31. New York: Meridian.

Rankin, Aidan. 1996. Christopher Lasch and the moral agony of the left. *New Left Review*. https://newleftreview.org/issues/I215/articles/aidan-rankin-christopher-lasch-and-the-moral-agony-of-the-left. Accessed 21 Feb 2020.

Stiegler, Bernard. 2016. The digital, education, and cosmopolitanism. *Representations* 131 (4): 157–164.

Stavrakakis, Yannis. 1999. *Lacan and the political*. Abingdon: Routledge.

Tucker-Abramson, Myka. 2017. *Atlas Shrugged*'s shock doctrine. *Modern Fiction Studies* 63 (1): 73–94.

————. 2018. *Novel shocks: urban renewal and the origins of neoliberalism*. New York: Fordham University Press.

Turner, Fred. 2019. Machine politics: The rise of the internet and a new age of authoritarianism. *Harpers*. https://harpers.org/archive/2019/01/machine-politics-facebook-political-polarization/. Accessed 20 Apr 2019.

Van Valkengoed, Ellyn. 2019. Protesting in the age of social media. https://magazine.areweeurope.com/stories/silentrevolutions/ellyn-valkengoed-protesting-in-the-age-of-social-media. Accessed 20 Apr 2019.

CHAPTER 4

Narrated Rand: HUAC, Engraved Invitations and the Real of Sexual Difference

Neil Cocks

1 RAND WITH HUAC

I will begin with an extraordinary exchange between Ayn Rand and John Stephens Wood, Democratic Congressman for Georgia, during the former's 1947 testimony before the House Un-American Activities Committee [HUAC]. Rand was called as a friendly witness for the prosecution of this standing committee, tasked with identifying extremist activists working in and against America, and asked for her opinion on *Song of Russia*, an American film understood by her to be pro-communist propaganda. Although Wood does not doubt that the film is propaganda, he suggests the possibility that its aim was not to overthrow the state, but to convince American citizens of the power and nobility of a newly acquired ally against Germany:

N. Cocks (✉)
Department of English Literature, University of Reading, Reading, UK

© The Author(s) 2020
N. Cocks (ed.), *Questioning Ayn Rand*,
Palgrave Studies in Literature, Culture and Economics,
https://doi.org/10.1007/978-3-030-53073-0_4

> *Mr. Wood*: Do you think, then, that it was to our advantage or to our disadvantage to keep Russia in this war, at the time this picture was made?
> *Miss Rand*: That has nothing to do with what we are discussing.
> *Mr. Wood*: Well—
> *Miss Rand*: But if you want me to answer, I can answer, but it will take me a long time to say what I think, as to whether we should or should not have had Russia on our side in the war. I can, but how much time will you give me?
> *Mr. Wood*: Well, do you say that it would have prolonged the war, so far as we were concerned, if they had been knocked out of it at that time?
> *Miss Rand*: I can't answer that yes or no, unless you give me time for a long speech on it.
> *Mr. Wood*: Well, there is a pretty strong possibility that we wouldn't have won at all, isn't there?
> *Miss Rand*: I don't know, because on the other hand I think we could have used the lend-lease supplies that we sent there to much better advantage ourselves.
> *Mr. Wood*: Well, at that time—
> *Miss Rand*: I don't know. It is a question. (Rand 1999 [1947a], 378–379)[1]

Why extraordinary? Because despite Rand's testimony before HUAC constructing a divided world of us and them, her formulations above repeat the very moves the Committee is set up to condemn. In replying to Wood, Rand questions the questions asked of her, and refuses to give a yes or no answer. Within the committee hearings, such questions and refusals elsewhere are met with severe censure. Indeed, it can be argued that evasions of this kind are what HUAC was, in part, designed to elicit from those brought before it: such a response is usually met with a charge of contempt, and it is this that lands those accused of Communist Party or Screen Writers Guild membership in jail. In Rand's case, however, there is no call for court security to remove her. She is free to continue her account of the film, her words flowing so freely that the stenographers struggle to keep up: 'Am I speaking too fast?' asks Rand at one point. Compare this to chief prosecutor Robert E. Stripling's reaction to the testimony of screenwriter Herbert Biberman:

Mr. Stripling: Mr. Biberman, are you a member of the Screen Writers' Guild or have you ever been a member of the Screen Writers' Guild?

Mr. Biberman: Mr. Stripling, I would like to reply to this very quietly — Mr. Chairman, also. If I will not be interrupted, I will attempt to give you a full answer to this question. It has become very clear to me that the real purpose of this investigation

The Chairman: (pounding gavel) That is not an answer to the question.

Mr. Biberman: is to drive a wedge

The Chairman: (pounding gavel) That is not the question (pounding gavel).

Mr. Biberman: into the component parts

The Chairman: (pounding gavel) Not the question.

Mr. Biberman: of the motion-picture industry.

The Chairman: (pounding gavel) Ask him the next question.

Mr. Biberman: And by defending my constitutional rights here I am defending

The Chairman: (pounding gavel) Go ahead and ask him the next question.

Mr. Biberman: the right not only of ourselves

Mr. Stripling: Are you a member

Mr. Biberman: but of the producers and of the American people

Mr. Stripling: of the Communist Party?

The Chairman: Are you a member of the Communist Party or have you ever been?

Mr. Stripling: Are you a member...

Mr. Biberman: What is the question now?

Mr. Stripling: Are you now or have you ever been a member of the Communist Party? [...][2]

This continues for another minute before the Chairman, J. Parnell Thomas, declares 'All right, you are excused. Take him away', and Biberman is escorted from his seat. Biberman here is later understood by Rand to 'howl' in protest, yet, it would seem, there are instances where the yes or no formula that he rejects can only be engaged if one is given time and allowed a 'long speech on it' (Rand 1999 [1947b], 383). In such a case, fidelity to the binary is possible only through supplementation, not compliance with the demand to limit oneself to one of two options.[3]

Rand's testimony can be further contrasted to her subsequent commentary upon it. Rand is concerned that it might be argued that HUAC has infringed the free speech and personal liberty of those it has accused, an argument taken to be invalid because:

> The Thomas Committee was inquiring, not into a question of opinion, but into a question of fact, the fact being membership of the Communist Party. The Thomas Committee did not ask anyone whether he believed in Communism, but asked only whether he had joined the Communist Party. (Rand 1999 [1947b], 382)

HUAC cannot be seen to engage ideas or beliefs, as this would not only counter Rand's claim that 'a citizen has a right to hold and advocate his own ideas, even when they are unpopular, and that no legal penalty (no restraint by force) will be imposed on him for it', but also because HUAC must limit itself to 'fact' (384). Focusing on membership is understood to ensure certainty, bypassing the challenge of interpretation as much as the realm of individual belief that must be free from institutional intrusion. Membership allows the committee to limit its inquiry to a seemingly stable space. In this, however, a double move can be read. In one sense, the self is externalised, with any questions pertaining to its responsibility resolved only through the 'fact' of its action. With this notion of a performative self, however, comes the idea of an inner, sacred self that is being protected from the reach of the law. This can result in a condemnation of those to be judged, in so far as the move to keep the individual self untouched opens up also the possibility of that self's disappearance, the notion of an identity that exists only at the level of display. A comparable move can be read in Rand's novels, where the enemies of Randian individualism are figured as 'masses', with individuality available only to those whose actions and thoughts qualify them for it. The enemies are those who preach collectivity, and their fate, within the philosophy of individuality, is to be understood as a collective. In Rand's understanding of HUAC, in other words, the subject judged by his external actions is one who, through signing a membership card, has left himself open to judgement through such actions, and can be condemned as an externalised subject, rather than praised as one whose actions speak to something other than them: a private self, unavailable to the world.

At this point a further difficulty arises, as Rand does not sustain her construction of the communist as a purely performative subject, nor does she limit the role of HUAC to investigating externalised matters:

> It is not the right of Congress to inquire into anyone's ideas – but neither is it the duty of Congress to protect deceit by withholding from the public any information which may involve someone's ideas. If, in the course of an inquiry into criminal and treasonable activities, Congress reveals the nature of the political beliefs of certain men – their freedom of speech has not been infringed in any matter. (384–385)[4]

This is, of course, how HUAC operated: by placing material obtained through dubious means on the record, the committee could open up fresh lines of inquiry. There can be no investigation into individual beliefs, only the fact of party membership, but if asking a question about membership 'reveals' the nature of beliefs, then that is perfectly acceptable, and is even to be encouraged.[5] Within this formulation, the individual subject has not been asked about beliefs, and she has not necessarily spoken about them. How is it then that they have been 'revealed'? The answer, I would suggest, is that belief is not bound to articulation in Rand's formulation. The conclusion to be drawn is that the nature of certain political beliefs are not changed in being 'revealed'. What is revealed is the general 'nature' of the beliefs in question, not any specific formulation. My belief can be abstracted from my utterance and still be my belief, it would seem. Here we might return to the resistance on the part of HUAC to Biberman's 'attempt to give [...] a full answer to the question'. Such an attempt is not taken to aid an understanding of the accused's beliefs.

Rand's testimony before HUAC might be understood in terms of hypocrisy, as she does not afford her enemies the rights she enjoys: practicing what the committee she praises rails against; failing to maintain a commitment to individuality; defending the institutional exposure of that which should remain wholly private. This, I think, will not quite do, as hypocrisy requires an original belief that is betrayed. My suggestion instead is that Rand's testimony, like her philosophy, is inevitably touched by the other it moves to expel, and in a crucial sense very much opposes. As I discussed in the Introduction to this book, Objectivism, the philosophical movement that Rand founded, is based on the notion of non-contradiction, that 'A = A'.[6] Rand's testimony works against such an understanding, caught up as it is in an uncanny repetition of that which it is set against.[7]

2   THE ALIENATED INDIVIDUAL

I would like to begin to question what I take to be this always compromised Randian purity of identity through engaging Rand's constructions of individuality, externalisation and privacy in a little more detail. As such, I will turn now to one of Rand's own accounts of ideal individuality. Here is a description of Howard Roark, the single-minded hero of Rand's novel *The Fountainhead*:

> Nothing can really touch him. He is concerned only with what he does. Not how he feels. How he feels is entirely a matter of his own, which cannot be influenced by anything and anyone on the outside. His feeling is a steady, unruffled flame, deep and hidden, a profound joy of living and of knowing his power, a joy that is not even conscious of being joy, because it is so steady, natural and unchangeable. If outside life brings him disappointment – well, it is merely a detail of the battle. He will have to struggle harder – that's all. The world becomes merely a place to act in. But not to feel in. The feeling – the whole [realm] of emotions – is in his [power] alone. He is a reason unto himself. He cannot feel differently. He was born that way. (Rand 1936, 94)

At this point, a warning: to really work through what I take to be at stake in this quotation, I'm afraid I am going to have to slow things right down, and read in detail. It is, I will argue, through such detailed reading that I can best dislodge the certainties of Rand's philosophy. To begin this process, let us think about the claim that it is Roark's limited concern with 'what he does' that makes him untouchable, with 'what he does' understood as pure externality. As Roark's 'concern' is necessarily something other than 'what he does', such action is, in one sense, left scrupulously clean of any mark of privacy or reflection. There is a difficulty here, however: 'what he does' is not simply held within itself, as it calls upon a concerned subject, a 'he' that exceeds the untouchability of pure, externalised action, and this, it might be assumed, is the same 'he' who engages in externalised action. One might conclude either that 'he' is strangely doubled, thus troubling Rand's law of non-contradiction, or that there is but one 'he', with this opening up the possibility of a 'he' who transcends 'what he does'. In this last, in other words, it is the doing that is out there, not the 'he'.

Against what I take to be the compromised externality of act, Rand sets up 'feeling'. Feeling is understood not to occur in the world, being 'entirely a matter of his own'. It is further argued that to be 'his own', a thing must escape 'his' concern: complete ownership is of no concern to the subject. This situation becomes more problematic still, as 'his feeling' is also 'his knowledge' and a joy 'that is not even conscious of being a joy'. This is a joy that is private because it is hidden, but such is the extent of this privacy that the subject is prevented from accessing the truth of his joy. Instead, the hidden nature of the owned feeling is wholly framed by another: it is the narrator who knows 'his' feeling to be a joy, and this to be knowledge of 'his' power, and knows that 'he' does not know the truth of what this joy is. As I read it, there is an advantage to Roark's own lack of awareness of his knowledge of his own qualities: the Randian hero can be understood to be free from division, liberated from a divided consciousness. Just as the 'feeling' is unchangeable, so Roark has an all-of a-pieceness, and this can be understood to inform both his external existence as pure action, and the internal unawareness that keeps him free from destabilising difference.

As Kristina West argues in her Chapter on Rand and Emerson that opens the following section of this book, it is such a 'natural', unchanging identity that results in a problematic account of childhood in Rand's writing. The singularity of the ideal individual, and its resistance to influence, means that education is always going to be a difficulty for Rand's philosophy of Objectivism, with accounts of learning that are sympathetic to this philosophy consistently seeing a return of the very divisions they seek to expel. And it is precisely such divisions that are addressed above by Ian Parker, when working through what he takes to be those 'contradictions at the level of subjectivity that are a necessary correlate of the kind of apparently rational unitary subject that Rand herself promoted'. One difficulty with Rand's account of Roark above, then, is simply that it is through self-division that he is liberated from division. Roark must, in the words of Judith Wilt, be 'streamline[d] [...] to irreducible essence, pure line/movement always embodied, never fractured, manifested as immoveable object', yet through this he is caught between concern, feeling and knowledge, defined by a joy from which he is always separate (Wilt 1999, 178). Such contradictions are necessary for the unitary subject to be known. Even the minimal recognition of a subject that resists being known, either through its availability as pure action, or in being an occult mystery to itself, requires the return of what was repressed, hence both the 'contradictions at the level of subjectivity' and the problem of a radically independent essence that is narrated by a third.

The unchanging quality of feelings might, however, suggest a reason for the external narration of the self not being taken to impinge upon its radical individuality. For Rand, the true individual is above all rational, and rationality is 'truth to the facts of the outside world' (Rand, 1999 [1943], 251). Although the individual's feelings are 'in his power alone', and this because he is 'reason to himself', this is so in strict fidelity to the truth of the external world, despite the world not being the site of such feelings. In other words, the hero's feelings are his own because they remain unaffected by the demands and delusions of society, being faithful instead to unalterable, rational truth, yet this means that such feelings inevitably coincide with any rational understanding. One implication of this is that there is nothing particularly individual about an individual point of view. And this means that those accused by HUAC are not alone in being deprived of their testimony in Rand's philosophy. The feelings and beliefs of the pure Randian subject, too, can be constituted from a position other than his own, this is the condition of their being genuinely 'his'.

3   'Rape by Engraved Invitation'

What I take to be the urgency of the problem of Randian purity can perhaps be best read through an engagement with the most debated episode in any of Rand's fictions, the rape of Dominique Francon by Howard Roark in *The Fountainhead*. Rand's erstwhile friend and colleague Nathaniel Branden famously recounted how the scene was described to him by its author as 'rape by engraved invitation' (Branden 1999, 230).[8] This has led certain critics of an Objectivist persuasion to claim that what occurs between Roark and Francon is not rape.[9] I would suggest the fact of there being an 'engraved invitation' *to a rape* confirms rather than alters the status of the event. If one were to argue that that 'invitation' modifies the rape, however, there remains a further 'modifier' to be addressed: the 'engraved' status of the invitation. If there is deliberation and purpose to be read in this, it is constructed through an appeal to physicality. It is the material condition of the invitation, rather than its wording, that is significant. This understanding is confirmed if we turn to what I suppose to be the description of this invitation in *The Fountainhead*: 'The delivery truck had not left the grounds, when she [Francon] was at her desk, writing a note on a piece of exquisite stationery. She wrote: "The marble is here. I want it set tonight"' (Rand 2007 [1943], 217). Francon has used the marble as an excuse to engineer a meeting with Roark, yet, in my reading, the physical quality of the invitation, as it is described to Branden, suggests a permanence and certainty that Francon's words do not have. 'The marble is here. I want it set tonight' does not, after all, simply and certainly mean 'could you rape me?' The invitation, as it is narrated by Rand to Branden, is free from linguistic content, and it can be understood to bypass the need to engage the uncertainty of meaning. In one sense, the engraving can be taken to repeat the 'fact' of Communist Party membership, as both resolve issues of belief or consent through exteriorisation and materiality. Both can also be understood to set such exteriorisation against a more genuine or sacred truth. Here I am thinking about the 'exquisite' quality of the invitation: Francon's house is understood to share in this quality, but it fails to have the desired effect on Roark when he visits, as he does not register such external markers of success, and recognises instead something far more intimate and true in his female counterpart.[10] Oddly enough, then, the invitation does not simply deliver certainty, the exteriorisation it offers having both the stability of non-linguist materiality and a kind of borrowed, inauthentic sophistication.

In its opposition to the more authentic self that Roark perceives in Francon, the invitation differs from Rand's reading of externality in HUAC, as there the fact of membership promises, at one stage, to be a defence against those who would trespass on the purity of the self. In *The Fountainhead*, I would contend, the self radically fails to escape the intrusion of others:

> He [Howard Roark] stopped.
> They said nothing. They looked at each other. She [Dominique Francon] thought that every silent instant passing was a betrayal; this wordless encounter was too eloquent, this recognition that no greeting was necessary.
> She asked, her voice flat:
> 'Why didn't you come to set the marble?'

> 'I didn't think it would make any difference to you who came. Or did it, Miss Francon?'
> She felt the words not as sounds, but as a blow flat against her mouth. The branch she held went up and slashed across his face. (218)[11]

Wordlessness is eloquence, but it is so from a point of view that is other to, yet constitute of, Francon's own. There is recognition, this remains unsaid, and what is recognised is the fact that no greeting is necessary, yet all this is understood not simply by Francon, but a textual perspective that knows that she knows what is and is not necessary for both Roark and herself. In *The Fountainhead* the exteriorisation of consent is thus established in at least two ways. It is secured through the external materiality of the engraving, this echoing Roark's feelings as read in the section above, remaining certain and unchanging because seemingly unreadable, while also promising the material certainty that defines Roark's active engagement in the world. Consent is, however, also established through a constitutive perspective on the self and its other that stands outside both, and, as we have read, the understanding this guarantees is taken to oppose and invalidate the 'exquisite' quality of the invitation.

Here we might turn to the narration of the rape scene itself: '[t]hen she [Francon] felt him shaking with the agony of a pleasure unbearable even to him, she knew that she had given that to him, that it came from her, from her body, and she bit his lips and she knew what he had wanted her to know' (220). Although Francon will later think to herself 'I have been raped by some redheaded hoodlum from a stone quarry', this is an event that is initially framed by a narration that can guarantee the truth of what she knows about what Roark wanted her to know (223). There have been numerous exacting and politically astute readings of the rape scene, and the critical debate that surrounds it, yet, as we shall read, the question of narration is never understood to problematise the terms of discussion. In my understanding, however, it is this external authority that compromises whatever edgy sexual politics Rand might be understood to be offering. The rape occurs in a world of seemingly sacred privacy, but it is also one in which there is an unproblematic access to the truth of the other, a truth constituted as such by a perspective on that other. For a faithful Objectivist such as Wendy McElroy, the discursive frame simply is not a problem: in her account of 'hidden consent' in *The Fountainhead* she claims that '[i]n every one of Rand's sex scenes, a clear indication of consent is present either in the revealed thoughts of their characters or in their behaviour' (McElroy 1999, 161). Revelation is taken only to confirm the truth of the independent self. For Objectivists, the fundamental truth of their philosophy is indeed 'A = A', with any mechanics of revelation understood to fall outside this self-confirming equation: purity wants no supplement. Counter to this, my suggestion is that the supplement stages a disruptive return, with the necessary and constitutive frame of revelation invalidating the non-contradiction it is tasked with upholding.

4 Žižek with Rand

As I noted in the Introduction to this book, the chapters within it cannot claim to be the first to counter Randian purity. There have been a number of significant critics who have managed to see her work not as a Dickensian 'horrible wonder apart', but as strangely and disturbingly familiar (Dickens 2009 [1870], 176).[12] This approach is certainly an advance on those critiques that simply oppose Rand, and thus feed into her narrative of purity. I am interested, however, in questioning the most celebrated of these more nuanced readings, Slavoj Žižek's 'The Actuality of Ayn Rand'. As Ian Parker and Jan De Vos have argued, this work is more bound up with Objectivist discourse than it acknowledges. Indeed, it seems to me there is something altogether uncanny about its own uncanny approach: in this most disarming disruption of Randian purity, purity stages a disruptive return.

For Žižek, Howard Roark should not be understood simply as a figure of liberal individuality, one at odds with more left-leaning and questioning accounts of the subject. Instead, in her 'excessive identification' with the 'ruling ideological edifice' of capitalism, Rand is understood to have created a hero who is 'properly subversive' (Žižek 2002, 215). In this, Žižek's argument rests on a distinction between the psychoanalytic terms 'drive' and 'desire'. The former is taken up by a subject who has a 'perfect indifference to the Other', the latter defining one captured within 'the desire of the Other'.[13] Whilst the subject of desire finds itself 'always already gazed at by the Other', that is, by the empty position of authority that vouchsafes identity and possessions in the normal run of things, the subject of drive is 'no longer bothered by the Other's gaze' (218, 219). To be free in this way is to be 'desubjectivised', liberated from the various social fantasies and 'entanglements' that are understood to alienate us from the fundamental 'kernel' of our being (225). Put simply, the 'desubjectivised' subject is one who has ceased wasting its time obsessing over what is wanted of it, and has instead kept to its own path. In doing so, it has become unrecognisable, as it works outside of the network of societal differences that structure—and defer—identity. For Žižek it follows that:

> far from signalling the 'end of subjectivity,' [the] act of assuming existential indifference is, perhaps, the very gesture of absolute negativity that gives birth to the subject. What Lacan calls 'subjective destitution' is thus, paradoxically, another name for the subject itself, i.e., for the void beyond the theatre of hysterical substitutions. This subject beyond subjectivisation is free in the most radical sense of the word. (222)

The Randian subject and the kind of 'Lacanian saint' promoted by Žižek are thus 'uncannily close': 'only an invisible line of separation distinguishes them' (217). And this means that a character such as Howard Roark should not be thought of as simply reactionary. Untouched by the demands of the world, and seeking no validation from it, he is not tied to the replication of existing social structures. Instead, Roark can be regarded as potentially revolutionary:

> The pure being of drive that emerges after the subject undergoes 'subjective destitution,' is not a kind of subjectless loop of the repetitive movement of drive, but, on the contrary, the subject at its purest, one is almost tempted to say: the subject 'as such'. Saying 'Yes!' to the drive, i.e., precisely to that which can never be subjectivized, freely assuming the inevitable, i.e., the drive's radical closure, is the highest gesture of subjectivity. (226)

Here, a difficulty in Žižek's account of the birth of the subject can be read. It is claimed that subjectivity at its purest is non-hysterical: it does not sit within any symbolic structure, and opposes subjectivisation. At some stage, however, '"Yes!"' has been said to the drive, and this is taken to be a gesture of subjectivity. Certainly, there is a sense in which this gesture might be understood as that of the subject undergoing 'subjective destitution', rather than the 'pure being of drive' that emerges from this. It is also the case, however, that the pure being is also the subject '"as such"', and thus 'the highest gesture of subjectivity' must be its own. This gesture, I would contend, cannot keep within the 'drive's radical closure', in so far as saying '"Yes!"' to the drive' is a linguistic and externalised 'gesture'. The subject is known through a gesture, yet it is unclear to me how this can be safely secured as other to the hysteria of 'the theatre'. The subject is known, moreover, from a seemingly authoritative position in language. How is the boundary between language or theatre and their beyond to be policed, if the one is framed by the other?[14]

To think through the problem of the 'being of pure drive' a little further, we might turn to the passage from *The Fountainhead* with which Žižek introduces Howard Roark as its exemplar. At this stage in the novel, Roark has been arrested after blowing up a building he designed, this because he feels it has been compromised by the inept intervention of another architect. Roark decides to conduct his own defence:

> It is [the] ethical stance of inner freedom that accounts for the authenticity clearly discernible in Rand's description of the momentary impact Howard Roark makes on the members of the audience in the courtroom where he stands trial:

> 'Roark stood before them as each man stands in the innocence of his own mind. But Roark stood like that before a hostile crowd – and they knew suddenly that no hatred was possible for him. For the flash of an instant, they grasped the manner of his consciousness. Each asked himself: do I need anyone's approval? – does it matter? – am I tied? And for that instant, each man was free – free enough to feel benevolence for every other man in the room. It was only a moment; the moment of silence when Roark was about to speak.' (Žižek quoting Rand 2002, 224–225)[15]

For Žižek, this is indicative of a subject who has 'suspend[ed] the inter-subjective game of mutual (mis)recognition', yet rather than constructing Roark as a subjectless subject, delivered from substitution, I read instead a subject constructed by otherness. Roark stands as all men stand, after all. There is a difference, to be sure, as wherever he finds himself, Roark can stand as all men stand in the innocence of their own minds, but this means that his standing is nonetheless defined by the standing of others: he stands precisely *as* others stand. Furthermore, the claim is that all men, at certain points in their life, stand in the same way. In this, these men are not simply constituted against symbolic structures of deferral and opposition, as they are also understood to be other to their minds. There is a division in the subject, and that which is pure within it is not a phantasmatic core liberated from hysteric structures, but instead a quality of the property it dwells within: while Žižek begins his essay by stating that it is 'the prime mover' Roark who is himself 'innocent', 'innocence' is for *The Fountainhead* that of an 'own mind'.

In keeping with the readings introduced thus far, all of this is, of course, known from a perspective other than that of the parties involved. It is the narrating third that constructs a collective 'they', a 'hostile crowd'. It is this perspective that knows that 'they' 'knew suddenly'; 'grasping' 'the manner of his consciousness' in 'the flash of an instant'. There is an added difficulty with the Randian interiority of the self, however, in that consciousness is understood to have a 'manner', grasp-able for the audience because Roark has stood before them. In so far as this 'manner' is concerned with outward bearing, I read a disturbance of the tight distinction between an external world of act and an inner being crucial to Rand's previous description of Roark. We have moved on from this description in another sense, as here consciousness is not opposed to the most private aspect of the self, but is instead a necessary part of it. And this outward yet private consciousness is available to all who witness Roark taking the stand, a fact that is guaranteed by the external authority of the narration, and though this is, for Žižek, more generally 'discernible'.

5   'The Real of Sexual Difference'

My argument, then, is that the 'shift' from desire to drive in the court-house scene is necessarily narrated, and cannot wholly circumvent the symbolic. Against this, as I read it, Žižek offers precisely a philosophy of the 'discernible'. It is his claim, after all, that 'Roark displays the perfect indifference towards the Other characteristic of drive' (Žižek 2002, 217). 'Display' carries much the same weight in Žižek's analysis as 'revelation' in that offered by Wendy McElroy. Display and revelation are not under-stood to impact upon their objects. They are supplements of the safest variety. In this final section, I would like to think through the political implications of the rejection of perspective, in a way that will allow me to return to the question of rape as introduced above.[16]

Part of what makes Žižek understand his engagement with Rand as 'properly subversive' is the contention that there is a feminist angle to his celebration of the Randian hero and the 'Lacanian saint'. He argues that '[t]he true conflict in the universe of Rand's two novels [is between] the prime mover, the being of pure drive, and his hysterical partner, the potential prime mover who remains caught in the deadly self-destructive dialectic' (Žižek 2002, 221). In *The Fountainhead*, for example, Roark goes his own way with no interest in anyone else, whilst Francon attempts to follow her own path, but is still caught up in the world of others. This is why she spends so much of the time attempting to destroy what she loves, Roark included. At one stage, for example, she destroys a statue because she thinks it is beautiful, and cannot abide the thought of the ignorant gazing upon it. What she must learn is not to combat such a gaze, but to be indifferent to it. Only when she does not care in the least about the other can she accept her drive. And that means she can only be with Roark when her desire for him will no longer be bothered by the Other's gaze, that is, when her desire is, in the strictest terms, *selfish*.

Žižek argues that it would be wrong to conclude from this that the novel is about a women learning the trick of sublime indifference from a man, as this would be to understand Roark as 'phallocratic'. Counter to this, and '[p]aradoxical as it may sound, the being of pure drive who emerges once the subject "goes through the fantasy" and assumes the attitude of indifference towards the enigma of the Other's desire, is a feminine figure' (225). This is because:

> What Rand was not aware of was that the uptight, uncompromising masculine figures with a will of steel with whom she was so fascinated, are effectively figures of the feminine subject liberated from the deadlocks of hysteria [...] Rand's ridiculously exaggerated adoration of strong male figures betrays the underlying disavowed lesbian economy, i.e., the fact that Dominique and Roark, or Dagny and Galt [in *Atlas Shrugged*], are effectively lesbian couples. (ibid.)

For Žižek, the figure, in opposing the difference of the symbolic, is ironically something other than itself: the being of pure drive. A being is a figure, in other words. This figure is taken to be other than the masculine figures that fascinated Rand, a fascination that constructs such figures in terms of desire.[17] It is not stated for whom a feminine figure 'emerges', presumably because this figure now transcends such hysteric questions. What these figures are 'effectively' is what they are free from 'fascination'. The effective knows no audience. Here I think a tension can be read in the account of what I might term 'revelation'.[18] The feminine figure 'emerges' when hysteria is gone and done, yet the 'disavowed lesbian economy' is 'betray[ed]' by 'Rand's ridiculously exaggerated'—that is, hysteric—adoration of 'strong male figures'. The effective is both underlying and emergent, accessed through hysteria, and through hysteria's end. A comparable difficulty can be read in Žižek's splitting of hysteria and drive through the difference between two figures, as this requires 'figure' to transcend the divide. Figure has a consistency that problematises the necessary opposition it secures. One could say, therefore, that in its *insistence*, in its inability to be located on one side of the binary of drive and desire, 'figure' is a figure of drive, and drive thus does not keep to its proper place.

What I am reading here is a compromised theory of the a-hysteric, one in which, to recall Ian Parker's previous formulation, the commitment to a 'sublime' figure has, as its correlate, contradictions at the level of the symbolic. Such hysteric disturbance cannot be tolerated. Instead, for Žižek, the lesbian couple is the *answer* to the hysteric uncertainty of Francon and Roark. The effective truth that Roark is a lesbian is not taken to be a disturbance in and of meaning.[19] Instead, the effective seemingly does away with the excess through which it is constituted: *that* does not matter, it is only *this* that really counts. Again, and in short, the claim is that there can be an answer to hysteria's endless questioning: Roark and Francon are somehow neither themselves, nor anything else, only figures.

I realise, of course, that Žižek is arguing for 'the real of sexual difference'.[20] The idea is that the kind of textual encounter I am setting up in this chapter cannot hope to do anything other than getting caught up in the endless cycle of the symbolic. In trying to work through the complexity of identity constructed in Rand's novels, the kind of reading I am offering will betray what I would term *différance*, finding itself instead wedded to the idea of the 'sexual relation'.[21] Put simply, those that would accuse Žižek of avoiding the frame of his own debate will find themselves committed to the idea that there are already existing hard-impacted identities that have complex relations to each other. Žižek opts for what he takes to be the more radical option, of the zero-point of identity necessary to identity as such, the unthinkable difference that must be in place for any cultural difference to be debated, for the symbolic to be engaged in general. My issue with this is that Žižek's account of the effective conforms to the logic of the empiricist, according to Louis Althusser:

Knowledge: its sole function is to separate, in the object, the two parts which exist in it, the essential and the inessential – by special procedures whose aim is to *eliminate the inessential real* (*by* a whole series of sortings, sievings, scrapings and rubbings), and to leave the knowing subject only the second part of the real which is its essence, itself real. Which gives us a second result: the abstraction operation and all its scouring procedures are merely procedures to purge and eliminate *one part of the real in order to isolate the other*. (Althusser and Balibar 2009 [1986], 38–39)

The effective seemingly isolates what really matters—even if that turns out to be a void—but the process itself compromises the result, with what falls outside never truly eclipsed. The practice of isolation is not interested in this unforeseen effect, however, and holds out instead the hope that reading Rand is not necessary to understanding her work, just as messy discourse is not required when accessing the effective truth of gender.

It follows from this, of course, that there can be no textual reading of the rape in *The Fountainhead*. It is Žižek's contention that 'the crucial scene' in the novel is that discussed above, in which Francon meets Roark by chance upon a road, and attacks him with a branch in response to his perceived, silent insolence. For Žižek, although she is a '[m]aster confronting a slave', 'her whipping is an act of despair, an awareness of his hold over her, of her inability to resist him—as such, it's already an invitation to a brutal rape' (Žižek 2002, 220).[22] My argument is not that Rand's text at this stage has a secure meaning that Žižek is betraying, but rather that any engagement with the beyond of meaning cannot simply bypass the text to fix instead on the meaning that is 'effective'.[23] We should be aware of the difficulty of maintaining a sure divide, however 'thin' or 'invisible' this might be, between such an analytic approach and the appeals to the unreadable that allow Objectivist hot-takes on sexual assault the preposterous security of 'hidden consent', or those crucial to, yet compromised within, Rand's own account of the good of the House Un-American Activities Committee (Žižek 2002, 225).

NOTES

1. One should not take from this the idea that Wood is trying to subvert the will of the Committee. A member of the Klu Klux Klan, he was instrumental in directing HUAC towards New Deal and communist subjects, and away from 'UnAmerican' activity on the right. See O'Reilly (1983). For an account of why it is crucial here to resist any easy and total separation of the Republican and the Democrat, the laissez-faire and the Keynesian, see Cooper (2017). I return to this text in the conclusion of this book.

2. I am relying on the HUAC transcripts for this quotation, but be aware that rather than the neat sequence of one speaker following the other, the video record shows Stripling and Chairman J. Parnell Thomas speaking over Biberman, and Parnell, in fact shouting 'That is not the question! That is not the question! Not the question! Not the question! Not the question!' as he continually pounds the gavel, rendering Biberman's speech almost incomprehensible.

3. It is important to note here, however, that if Rand was allowed her uninterrupted time upon the stand, she was not asked back. Lisa Duggan convincingly argues that this was because Rand misunderstood the way in which HUAC was approached by powerful Hollywood players: redirect anti-Semitism towards a few perceived troublemakers, and shore up anti-Union power, but other than that, keep the investigation contained. In accordance with Žižek's reading below, Ayn Rand over-identified with American capitalism, and in so doing threatened to upset this scheme. She attacked popular films, and threatened to draw anti-union executives into HUAC's line of fire. See Duggan (2019, 40–41). For an Objectivist defense of Rand before HUAC, see Mayhew (2004).

4. Rand (1999, 384–385).

5. As Kenneth O'Reilly summarises: 'the purpose of the committee and its constituency, chiefly conservative journalists and other publicists, was not to investigate subversive activities but to disseminate information already known to the FBI.' O'Reilly (1983, 7).

6. This is a repeated formulation, but see, for example, Rand (1975, 31).

7. At one level, the failure of Randian purity before HUAC can be understood simply in terms of the inability of her Manichaean worldview to engage the history of HUAC. The committee resists the secure binaries that a philosophy of purity requires. HUAC utilised FBI powers, and built on practices that infringed civil liberties, that were introduced and developed in the New Deal, yet it arose out of a propaganda machine designed to subvert New Deal policies, and was antagonistic to the FBI. HUAC

occasionally fulfilled its obligation to disrupt fascist and far right organ-isations, yet was run by racists. See Douglas (2007), Gladchuk (2009), O'Reilly (1983).

8. See also Branden (1986, 134).

9. A number of such essays are collected in Gladstein and Sciabarra, eds., (1999). As I indicate above, Judith Wilt rigorously reads such claims in her crucial overview of the controversy, anthologised in the same volume.

10. I am thinking, for example, about the following: 'He's [Roark is] only a common worker, she [Francon] thought, a hired man doing a convict's labor. She thought of that, sitting before the glass shelf of her dressing table. She looked at the crystal objects spread before her; they were like sculptures in ice- they proclaimed her own cold, luxurious fragility; and she thought of his strained body, of his clothes drenched in dust and sweat, of his hands. She stressed the contrast, because it degraded her. She leaned back, closing her eyes. She thought of the many distinguished men whom she had refused. She thought of the quarry worker. She thought of being broken—not by a man she admired, but by a man she loathed. She let her head fall down on her arm; the thought left her weak with pleasure', Rand (2007 [1943], 208–209); 'She [Francon] asked her old caretaker and his wife to remain in the house that evening. Their diffident presence completed the picture of a feudal mansion. She heard the bell of the servants' entrance at seven o'clock. The old woman escorted him to the great front hall where Dominique stood on the landing of a broad stairway [...] He wore his work clothes and he carried a bag of tools. His movements had a swift, relaxed kind of energy that did not belong here, in her house, on the polished steps, between the delicate, rigid banisters. She had expected him to seem incongruous in her house; but it was the house that seemed incongruous around him' Rand (2007 [1943], 214).

11. Rand (2007, 218).

12. For more on this, see Chapter4 of Cocks (2014).

13. Žižek (2002), 217–218.

14. To be clear, my issue here is not with drive as such: I have no wish to claim there is no 'beyond' to the pleasure principle. My reading instead is that in Žižek's reading of Rand such a principle returns to and as its own beyond, with the resistant 'beyond' constituted in the impossible antagonism between the symbolic and its beyond.

15. Žižek quoting Rand (2002, 224–225).

16. It is worth noting here just how complex and contradictory the rela-tionship is between the court house scene and Rand's take on HUAC. Certainly, there is irony in the fact that Roark, unlike those accused of communist membership, is allowed the space to make a long, didactic speech at his trial, wholly uninterrupted, and praised by all who witness it, despite this testimony calling into question the authority of the court. At

the same time, however, the necessity of an individual perspective is undermined, the guarantee of the third person narration securing the truth of the individual subject from a perspective that is not their own. My concern here is not with setting up such a perspective as a site of truth or point of pure origin, but rather questioning any account that engages the subject, however compromised, without it.

17. For an alternative view of Roark as fascistic, patriarchal rapist, see Stockton (2006).

18. I acknowledge the difficulty of the term here.

19. I am thinking here about Judith Butler's celebrated working through of the demands of coming out, especially Butler (1983, 309): 'To claim this is what I *am* is to suggest a provisional totalization of this 'I'. But if the "I" can so determine itself, than that which it excludes in order to make that determination remains constitutive of the determination itself. In other words, such a statement presupposes that the "I" exceeds its determination, and even produces that very excess in and by the act which seeks to exhaust the semantic field of that "I"'.

20. See, for example, Žižek's reading of the work of Judith Butler in Žižek (2009). See also Copjec (2005 [1994]). For a critique, see Ziarek (1997).

21. See Lacan [1969]. See also, for example, Žižek (1992), Žižek (1996).

22. Žižek (2002, 220).

23. For an overview of this kind of 'effective' reading see Copjec (2005, 138).

BIBLIOGRAPHY

Althusser, Louis, and Balibar, Étienne. 2009 [1986]. *Reading capital*, trans. Ben Brewer. London & New York, NY: Verso.

Branden, Barbara. 1986. *The passion of Ayn Rand*. New York, NY: Doubleday.

Branden, Nathaniel. 1999. Was Ayn Rand a feminist? In *Feminist interpretations of Ayn Rand*, ed. Mimi Reisel Gladstein, and Chris Matthew Sciabarra, 223–230. Pennsylvania, PA: Pennsylvania University Press.

Butler, Judith. 1983. Imitation and gender insubordination. In *The gay and lesbian studies reader*, ed. Henry Abelove, Michele Aina Barale, and David M. Halperin, 307–320. London: Routledge.

Cocks, Neil. 2014. *The peripheral child in nineteenth century literature and its criticism*. Basingstoke: Palgrave Macmillan.

Cooper, Melinda. 2017. *Family values: Between neoliberalism and social conservatism*. New York, NY: Zone Books.

Copjec, Joan. 2005 [1994]. *Read my desire: Lacan against the historicists*. Cambridge, MA: MIT Press.

Dickens, Charles. 2009 [1870]. *The mystery of Edwin Drood*. Oxford: Oxford University Press.

Douglas, M. Charles, M. Douglas 2007. *J. Edgar Hoover and the anti-interventionists: FBI political surveillance and the rise of the domestic security state, 1939–1945*. Columbus, OH: Ohio State University Press.

Duggan, Lisa. 2019. *Mean girl: Ayn Rand and the culture of greed*. Oakland, CA: University of California Press.

Gladchuk, John J. 2009. *Hollywood and anticommunism: HUAC and the evolution of the red menace, 1935–1950*. London and New York, NY: Routledge.

Lacan, Jacques. 2006 [1969]. *The seminar of Jacques Lacan: The other side of psychoanalysis*, trans. Russell Grigg. New York, NY: W. W. Norton.

Mayhew, Robert. 2004. *Ayn Rand and song of Russia: Communism and anti-communism in 1940s hollywood*. Lanham, MD: Scarecrow Press.

McElroy, Wendy. 1999. Looking through a paradigm darkly. In *Feminist interpretations of Ayn Rand*, ed. Mimi Reisel Gladstein and Chris Matthew Sciabarra, 157–171. Philadelphia, PA: Pennsylvania University Press.

O'Reilly, Kenneth. 1983. *Hoover and the un-Americans: The FBI, HUAC, and the red menace*. Philadelphia, PA: Temple University Press.

Rand, Ayn. 1975. *The romantic manifesto*. New York, NY: Signet.

———.1999 [1936]. Notes. In *Journals of Ayn Rand*, ed. David Harriman, 77–116. New York, NY: Plume.

———. 1999 [1943]. The moral basis of individualism. In *Journals of Ayn Rand*, ed. David Harriman, 243–310. New York, NY: Plume.

———. 1999 [1947a]. Testimony before the house un-American activity. In *Journals of Ayn Rand*, ed. David Harriman, 371–381. New York, NY: Plume.

———. 1999 [1947b]. Suggestions regarding the congressional investigation of communism. In *Journals of Ayn Rand*, ed. David Harriman, 381–386. New York, NY: Plume.

———. 2007 [1943]. *The fountainhead*. London: Penguin.

Stockton, Sharon. 2006. *The economics of fantasy: Rape in the twentieth century*. Columbus, OH: Ohio State University Press.

Wilt, Judith. 1999. The romances of Ayn Rand. In *Feminist interpretations of Ayn Rand*, ed. Mimi Reisel Gladstein and Chris Matthew Sciabarra, 173–198. Philadelphia, PA: Pennsylvania University Press.

Ziarek, Ewa Plonowska. 1997. From euthanasia to the other of reason: Perfomativity and the deconstruction of sexual difference. In *Derrida and feminism: Recasting the question of woman*, ed. Ellen Feder and Mary C. Rawlinson, 115–140. Abingdon: Routledge.

Žižek, Slavoj. 1992. *Looking awry: An introduction to Jacques Lacan through popular culture*. Cambridge: MIT.

———. 1996. There is no sexual relationship: Wagner as a Lacanian. *New German Critique* 69: 7–35.

———. 2002. The actuality of Ayn Rand. *The Journal of Ayn Rand Studies* 3/2: 215–227.

———. 2009. *The ticklish subject: The absent centre of political ontology*. London and New York, NY: Verso.

PART II

The Arts

The American Mythology of Individualism: Emerson, Ayn Rand, and the Romantic Child

Kristina West

1 Negotiating the Boundaries

Ralph Waldo Emerson and Ayn Rand might seem like a politically odd coupling, with tensions between Rand's right-wing capitalist manifesto and Emerson's socialist support of issues including education, anti-slavery, and women's rights that developed throughout his lifetime and writings; yet parallels have been drawn between their philosophies of American individualism since Rand's time. Academics and popular readers claim a connection between and inspiration from the two writers, particularly through linking Rand's philosophies of Objectivism and Individualism with Emerson's works on self-reliance. Yet there are frequently contradictions embedded in the 'proof' provided to support such claims: for example, a CUNY blog aims to be 'bridging the gap between Emerson and Rand', thereby establishing them as separate in the very attempt to bring them together (Anon 2018).

K. West (✉)
London, UK

© The Author(s) 2020
N. Cocks (ed.), *Questioning Ayn Rand*,
Palgrave Studies in Literature, Culture and Economics,
https://doi.org/10.1007/978-3-030-53073-0_5

This claim to congruity between the two writers can cause problems for those readers invested in left-wing political views.[1] Roxanne J. Fand, discussing her college teaching of Rand, comments: 'I could not dismiss Ayn Rand out of hand, as many of my literary and leftist friends did, because Rand's novels resonated with Emerson's "Self-Reliance", which had inspired my youth' (Fand 2005, 487). While Fand does not fully situate herself as 'leftist' (or even 'literary'), with a division between her and her friends, her claim to 'could not' establishes a troubled desire to dismiss Rand and an assumption that being 'leftist' should, and does, result in that very dismissal, while also claiming that taking inspiration from Emerson might trouble both desire and dismissal through her reading of a resonance between the two writers. As such, Fand brings the two writers together—particularly through the concept of self-reliance—in her own reading and her subsequent teaching, despite her attempt to keep a 'leftist' boundary between them.

That such a congruence was read even during Rand's lifetime is apparent as she denies, and therefore establishes, a link between Emerson's works and philosophy and her own. In 'Philosophy: Who Needs It? ', Rand discusses hypothetical people who claim never to have been influenced by philosophy, arguing: 'They might say: "Consistency is the hobgoblin of little minds". They got it from a very little mind, Emerson' (Rand 1982, 4–5). Despite the critical debate about whether Rand misquotes or misrepresents Emerson here through the partial quotation of his sentence, this is interesting primarily because Rand presents Emerson's views as antithetical to her own; however, in her need for denial and repudiation through the imaginary people who 'might' make such a claim, she also both creates and acknowledges a link between Emerson's philosophy and hers.[2]

Neither of these writers are widely recognised for their work on childhood, yet both engage with Emerson's question in his 1836 work, *Nature*, of 'What is a child?' repeatedly across the body of their work (Emerson 1892 [1836], 78). In much of Emerson's writing, the child is constructed in its relation to an ideal manhood—not as an exploration of childhood, but as an illustration of what man could, or should, be—while Rand constructs a relation between childhood and her philosophies of Individualism and Objectivism. Both writers also construct childhood within a claim to Romanticism: Emerson through his debt to English and German Romanticism via writers such as Goethe, and through inspiring critical readings of the Romantic child in works such as 'Domestic Life'; and Rand through her exploration of childhood in works including *The Romantic Manifesto*.

This chapter will therefore consider Rand's and Emerson's constructions of individualism, as read through their portrayals of childhood, to chart key political differences between these two great mythologisers of the American self, as well as drawing out repetitions across their work that disrupt any wholly secure separation between them. I also engage with the question of the child's relationship to capitalism. After all, as Christopher Parks argues, the Romantic child was never entirely divorced from capitalism: 'Victorian and Edwardian authors [...] were fundamentally concerned with redefining the relationship of the child to the marketplace in order to accommodate the child within capitalist society' (Parks 2012, 1). Far from the unassailable innocence of the desired and ideal child in Rousseau's *Emile*, for example, this reading disturbs such an assumption of the child's separation from the world of commerce as one that, inevitably, leads to its return and production as a capitalist subject.

2   TROUBLING SELF-RELIANCE

Despite differences in form and genre, those Rand and Emerson works related to childhood that I intend to discuss each claim to contain something other than writing and an intent other than reading; in particular, each either positions itself, or is critically read to include or endorse, what Rand terms a 'manifesto', a term which may be used simply as a synonym for 'definition', but with its political overtones can also carry the related assumption of a desired application in the reader's life beyond any reading of the text. Critics such as Lawrence Buell use the term 'manifesto' to define some Emersonian texts; while Rand uses the term herself for *The Romantic Manifesto* (Buell 2006, v). Emerson's 1841 essay, 'Self-Reliance', is read as such a 'manifesto' of American Transcendentalism via its constructions of the self-reliant adult individual; yet it does so via an assumed relation between man and child. Emerson writes:

> Trust thyself: every heart vibrates to that iron string. Accept the place the divine providence has found for you, the society of your contemporaries, the connection of events. Great men have always confided themselves childlike to the genius of their age, betraying their perception that the absolutely trustworthy was seated at their heart, working through their

hands, predominating in all their being. And we are now men, and must accept in the highest mind the same transcendent destiny; and not minors and invalids in a protected corner, not cowards fleeing before a revolution, but guides, redeemers and benefactors, obeying the Almighty effort and advancing on Chaos and the Dark. (Emerson 1841a, 45–46)

Despite his exhortation for man to 'trust thyself'—one of the key tenets of his code of self-reliance—Emerson constructs a process of deferral to those positioned as other to the self: to the child; to the father via his appeals to an unnamed and unformed deity; and to Emerson as writer in his commanding imperatives. As such, this passage appears to trouble any claim to individualism as Emerson's self-reliance rests on a diffuse web of influence beyond man. While Emerson may reject the 'sepulchres of the fathers' in *Nature*, stating that 'Our age is retrospective; it builds the sepulchres of the fathers. […] Why should not we also enjoy an original relation to the universe?', his self-reliance here is built upon acceptance of the plans of the patriarchal divine (Emerson 1892 [1836]). Further, Emerson invokes 'the genius of our age' and 'the same transcendent destiny' as indicators of what he elsewhere calls 'the oversoul': man's guiding destiny and the divine spirit that resides within each soul (Emerson 1841a).[3]

Likewise, he claims that 'great men have always confided themselves childlike to the genius of their age': adult and child are divided in that the man can only ever be 'childlike'—like the child but not the child—and yet the child provides the model for the man to follow as 'divine providence' has previously. In allying childhood with these transcendent guides—in that the example of the child should be followed, even if that example is in following others or the divine other—and in constructing childhood in contrast to man as that which does not need to be told/taught, Emerson privileges the child above even the 'great' man, whose self-reliance is troubled still further by his need to be told, by Emerson, what he should do and how he should live.

Yet even this vision of the child as only ever relational through its inspiration to man seeking his ideal state—thereby positioning the child, too, in a problematic relationship to self-reliance—comes under attack later in the paragraph when Emerson claims: 'we are now men […] and not minors and invalids in a protected corner' (ibid.). Far from the child that is to be emulated in the 'great' man's acceptance of his destiny, Emerson

constructs the status of 'minors' as contrary to that of the ideal, independent man and as undesirable, linked to 'invalids' in their need for
protection and in their positioning in 'a corner', and even to 'cowards'.
This child, then, militates against the previous status of child in that it is
not followed by man; it is not even follower, but is rather unable to be
either. Yet it remains in relation to man both in its need for adult (male)
protection and in its symbolic status as a weakness that must be cast off in
order for the status of man to be attained. However, if we read this claim
against Emerson's previous deferrals to a power behind and beyond men,
'obeying the Almighty effort', this might also place 'man' in the 'corner'
with the protected 'minors', with the need for such deferrals positioning
man within the protection and guidance of a patriarchal divine providence. Here, then, the man returns to the rejected status of 'minor' in
the very act of its rejection.

This ambivalence towards the status of the child—and therefore
the desired status of the man under this 'manifesto' of self-reliance—
continues throughout the essay. Emerson writes further:

> What pretty oracles nature yields us on this text in the face and behaviour
> of children, babes, and even brutes! That divided and rebel mind, that
> distrust of a sentiment because our arithmetic has computed the strength
> and means opposed to our purpose, these have not. Their mind being
> whole, their eye is as yet unconquered, and when we look in their faces we
> are disconcerted. Infancy conforms to nobody; all conform to it; so that
> one babe commonly makes four or five out of the adults who prattle and
> play to it. (ibid.)

The 'us and them' division between man and child continues in this
passage, although again, the positioning of the child as 'other' results in
the return of the relation between the two. Here, children—also 'babes'
and 'brutes'—are available and sought after as teaching materials for man,
positioned as 'manifesto' in the claim to 'oracles'; yet they are subject to
further deferral with their status conferred by 'nature', acting solely therefore as mediums. However, while what is to be read in the 'face' and
'behaviour' of the child can both be seen and understood by Emerson
from his status as part of the inclusive 'we' of man, it needs Emerson's
mediation to be correctly understood by others. And the message received
by Emerson is of the singularity of childhood in contrast to the 'divided
and rebel mind' of man. Despite an impending change when the child

begins grows towards manhood, inherent in the claim that 'their eye is *yet* unconquered [my emphasis]', the youngest children of 'infancy' might appear to represent Emerson's strongest claim to self-reliance: 'Infancy conforms to nobody; all conform to it'. However, the division of infancy from the 'all' who must conform continues to alienate the Emersonian child from the man who ostensibly desires its qualities, while the infant has no choice but to enter into this child—adult relationship as 'all conform to it' despite its rejection of conformity to others.

Yet in the claim that 'one babe commonly makes four or five out of the adults who prattle and play to it' lies a possibility for man to return to the status of child, one that is predicated again on following the unconforming child. While Emerson's children are always divided from their adult counterparts, neither will each stay in what Emerson constructs as their own or rightful place: both child and man are forever crossing the divide, even as that divide remains and is reinforced by that very crossing. As such, any claim to self-reliance is troubled as each depends on the other, despite their status as separate.

3   Individualism and 'the Sepulchres of the Fathers'

Children are conspicuous by their absence from the adult world of Rand's *Atlas Shrugged*; yet, like Emerson, Rand draws on childhood to illustrate her philosophy of an ideal adulthood from the outset. Eddie Willers, Dagny Taggart, and Francisco d'Anconia are each introduced through recollections of their childhood; James Taggart's childhood is also recalled by his friends and sister, though he rarely indulges in such mawkishness himself; and even Hank Rearden is not immune from his mother's less flattering recollections of his boyhood, as she claims: 'That's the way he's been since he was five years old—the most conceited brat you ever saw—and I knew he'd grow up to be the most selfish creature on God's earth' (Rand 1957, 42). Rearden's mother clearly subscribes to Wordsworth's Romantic philosophy that 'the child is father to the man' (Wordsworth 1994 [1802, 91]). As part of this childhood recollection, each muses on their position within the family, their ancestry, and their relation to Emerson's key claim to reject 'the sepulchres of the fathers'.

These recollections begin with Eddie Willers, Dagny Taggart's right-hand man on the Taggart Transcontinental railroad:

He did not know why he suddenly thought of the oak tree. Nothing had recalled it. But he thought of it – and of his childhood summers on the Taggart estate. He had spent most of his childhood with the Taggart children, and now he worked for them, and his father and grandfather had worked for their father and grandfather. [...] [T]he one precious companion of his childhood told him what they would do when they grew up. (Rand 1957, 12–13)

Willers' recollections of his childhood appear rooted in nature via the trigger of the oak tree, and in that they are suffused by 'a still, brilliant sunlight' from which 'a few rays reached into his present'; yet (as we will also see with the child in Emerson's essay, 'Domestic Life') nature precipitates or accompanies a new beginning (13). In this memory, Willers' child self is always relative to someone or something other in that he spent his summers 'on the Taggart estate' and 'with the Taggart children', although this apparent challenge to his individualism appears at least part of the very happiness of his childhood. Indeed, the summers have expanded in his memory to such a degree that '[h]e had spent most of his childhood with the Taggart children'.

This relative status is, however, less about a relationship with the children—James and Dagny—than a connection with their surname and their ancestry via 'the Taggart estate' and the 'Taggart children'. Both estate and children are constituted in terms of an ownership, as possessions or property, with a family name that precedes both ownership and owned. Such claims to children as property are also made by Emerson in works such as his 1844 essay, 'Experience', frequently read to be about the death of his young son, Waldo, and attracting considerable critical vilification about the link he makes between property and childhood. Emerson writes: 'In the death of my son, now more than two years ago, I seem to have lost a beautiful estate,—no more' (Emerson 1844). Critical responses include Sharon Cameron, who claims that 'the [...] comparison of Waldo's death with the loss of an estate—is shocking' and describes 'the vulgarity of alluding to these losses as if they were comparable', while Max Cavitch writes: 'This is no mere matter of tact or sincerity. The question of what Emerson has lost in his son resonates chillingly with American slavery's collapsing of distinctions between offspring and property' (Cameron 1991, 208; Cavitch 2007, 154). That such complaints are made about Emerson's conflation of child and property and not Rand's marks Emerson's take as a digression in the critical mind; with Rand, perhaps, such a claim is less 'shocking'. However, in reading the two together, what remains is that neither writer feels that childhood is incompatible with capitalism via a claim to ownership and its associated value or, in Emerson's case, its lack. After all, despite the outraged howls from his critics, Emerson is not claiming the link between child and property as a desirable one. In both cases, however, a present or ideal relationship between childhood and individualism is troubled, with the child existing necessarily within a relationship to its ancestors, and one in which the power belongs solely to the adult.[4]

Beyond the claims to the child as property, Willers' recollections are also tied to the ancestry of both the Taggart family and his own: 'his father and grandfather had worked for their father and grandfather'. As such, Rand places her children within a social hierarchy predicated on that of their ancestors, one that is—and will be—unchanging, at least in Willers' eyes; after all, he accepts his own relative and subordinate place when Dagny, 'the one precious companion of his childhood told him what they would do when they grew up'. That her command is realised can be attributed both to the strength of her will and the social hierarchy of adults, reflected and repeated in childhood, that secures its status within their adult future: if Rand's socially superior children make decisions, they must be carried out to ensure the dynastic hierarchy remains unchallenged. In a seeming reversal of Emerson's adult–child relationship, the assumption here is that the child will follow the adult and embrace the very 'sepulchres of the fathers' that Emerson attempts to reject.

By this point, both Rand and Emerson problematise their own constructions of self-reliance as individualism: Rand prizes a capitalist economy built up through multiple generations of the same families in which each knows its place, with self-reliance a family affair rather than a claim to a personal individualism; while Emerson explicitly rejects 'the sepulchres of the fathers' in his desire for each generation to remake the world anew, yet struggles with his own premise as he claims that 'Our age is retrospective' and asks 'Why should not we also enjoy an original relation to the universe?' After all, in the claim to the multiples of 'our' and 'we', Emerson is desiring the individualism not of a man but of a generation; despite the fissures in many aspects and practices of American Transcendentalism, there is still a desire for unity, one that also undermines Emerson's claims to independence of the self.

In *Atlas Shrugged*, Dagny Taggart considers both her childhood and her place within the family business as Rand establishes her character and philosophies, again through the filter of an adult's memory of her own childhood:

> [Dagny Taggart] felt a bored indifference toward the immediate world around her, toward other children and adults alike. [...] She had caught a glimpse of another world and she knew that it existed somewhere, the world that had created trains, bridges, telegraph wires and signal lights winking in the night. She had to wait, she thought, and grow up to that world. She was twelve years old when she told Eddie Willers that she would run the railroad when they grew up. She was fifteen when it occurred to her for the first time that women didn't run railroads and that people might object. To hell with that, she thought – and never worried about it again. (Rand 1957, 54)

Dagny's status as 'other' is secured through her otherness to both children and adults but with her assumed affiliation to childhood at this stage remaining intact. The world that she desires, the one that 'had created trains, bridges', etc., is therefore apart from the 'immediate world' of children and adults, yet—like her link to childhood—retains its connections to adulthood in that she must 'grow up to that world', one which therefore both precedes her and waits for her to join it. Likewise, while her assumption of power over Willers stems from their childhood, and from the patriarchal imperative of family lauded by Rand, they still must wait until they become adults to put her directions into practice. Like Emerson's constructions of childhood as both apart from and intrinsically linked to adulthood, Rand attempts to separate the two groups but the tie between them returns with that very attempt and need for separation. Yet in Rand's claim that Dagny 'never thought about it again', she constructs a circularity between adulthood and childhood in that Dagny, like Willers before her, must revisit her child past to establish her subsequent claim to adulthood. As with Emerson's claims in 'Self-Reliance', Rand's characters can move between adulthood and childhood without ever fully disrupting the individual status of each.

Rand considers the issues of individualism related to one's family status further in Dagny's meditation on the statue of her ancestor, Nathaniel Taggart, which stands on the station concourse:

> Dominating the concourse, but ignored by the travellers as a habitual sight, stood a statue of Nathaniel Taggart, the founder of the railroad. Dagny was the only one who remained aware of it and had never been able to take it for granted. To look at that statue whenever she crossed the concourse, was the only form of prayer she knew. (ibid., 62)

While Rand's novel largely avoids the question of religious belief, in contrast to Emerson's engagement with a divine providence, Dagny's response to the statue of Nathaniel Taggart troubles what this might entail. There may be no deity of the kind established by Emerson in 'Self-Reliance', but there is assuredly worship: of a utopian capitalist society and of those who have enabled the earliest steps of its creation. Yet, in contrast to Emerson's advice for fellow men to follow his route to self-reliance via obedience to a deity—albeit one that is frequently positioned within man's own soul—Dagny suffers here from a certain lack of control: she 'had never been able to take it for granted'. There is still something above and beyond her—both figuratively and literally larger than her—that commands her obedience and 'the only form of prayer she knew'. As such, while organised religion may play no part in Rand's manifesto of individualism, Dagny's spiritual life and reliance on a patriarchal and adored figure lends itself to readings of Emerson's quasi-Christian Oversoul (Emerson 1841b).

Rand discusses this ambivalence further via a meditation on family love and loyalty:

> Dagny regretted at times that Nat Taggart was her ancestor. What she felt for him did not belong in the category of unchosen family affections. She did not want her feeling to be the thing one was supposed to owe an uncle or a grandfather. She was incapable of love for any object not of her own choice and she resented anyone's demand for it. But had it been possible to choose an ancestor, she would have chosen Nat Taggart, in voluntary homage and with all her gratitude. [...] In her childhood, his statue was Dagny's first concept of the exalted. (Rand 1957, 63)

Dagny struggles throughout this passage with the concept of personal choice, spiritual devotion, and the patriarchal system embodied by the Taggart family, caught as she is between her 'voluntary homage' and the 'unchosen family affections' she rejects. Yet despite her protestations of individualism here via Rand's narrator, that which made Nat Taggart's statue her 'first concept of the exalted' in her childhood—thereby creating other concepts of the exalted in the time since the first, either within or beyond the stage of childhood—is part of the very system she attempts to reject: the taking of her place within the confines of family tradition and inclination. In her worship of the statue via the prayer of her 'look', however, Dagny's form of religion is less the Emersonian internalisation of divinity than the worship of a Midas-like pagan idol.

Dagny and Eddie Willers shared their childhood experiences with a third child: Francisco d'Anconia, who Rand also constructs within an appeal to the Romantic tradition of the child as 'the father of the man'. Rand writes:

> Francisco [d'Anconia] found it natural that the Taggart children should be chosen as his companions: they were the crown heirs of Taggart Transcontinental, as he was of D'Anconia Copper. 'We are the only aristocracy left in the world – the aristocracy of money,' he said to Dagny once, when he was fourteen. [...] 'The reason my family has lasted for such a long time is that none of us has ever been permitted to think he is born a d'Anconia. We are expected to become one'. (ibid., 89)

This passage differs from the recollections of Dagny and Willers in a number of ways. Despite this childhood, too, appearing solely as recollection, d'Anconia is permitted direct speech and, as such, he brings childhood into the present tense of 'we are' while establishing himself as leader of the three children, even if he addresses Dagny alone here and at other points. According to these recollections, like attracts like as d'Anconia finds it 'natural' that 'the crown heirs' of each family should grow up together, although he fails to question the patriarchal imperative of 'should be chosen' and the lack of individual freedom this entails. Rather than questioning this morality or any apparent troubling of claims to individualism in the concept of inherited capital concerns, Rand revels in it as 'the aristocracy of money'. Yet the figure of d'Anconia, in particular, problematises such an easy assumption, both here in the claim that nobody is 'permitted to think that he is born a d'Anconia' but that they 'are expected to become one', and through the duration of the text. Rand zigzags between approval of the family dynasty and both the repudiation and repetition of its legacy: after all, there is no option for a family member not to become a d'Anconia, yet in doing so, they are subject to what is 'permitted' and 'expected', again ceding control to the family imperative. In reading this passage via claims to childhood,

Rand's child acts as both the difference from and the reinscription of family traits and capital structures. It may well attempt to reject Emerson's 'sepulchres of the fathers', but in doing so—as may be the case in Emerson too—it is doomed to repeat them. As such, both writers' claims to individualism/self-reliance are troubled by the very act of patriarchal rejection.

4   POWER AND THE ROMANTIC CHILD

Thus far, I have spent little time considering claims by and about these two writers on their status as Romantic thinkers; yet an exploration of childhood in particular lends itself to such an approach. Any unconnected definition of Romanticism is always going to be a problem—there is far more value in reading any such claim via critics or through an author's works—yet perhaps the most overused quote on Romanticism may be of some assistance, located as Rand's work (at least) is within a claimed Romantic tradition. In Wordsworth's Romantic child, 'trailing clouds of glory / From God, who is our home' but one that is replaced as 'shades of the prison-house begin to close / Upon the growing boy', we might consider how the Romantic child is constructed both in accordance with and against the Wordsworthian model and analyse how the very appellation of 'Romantic' problematises readings of individualism in Rand's and Emerson's works (Wordsworth 1994 [1807], 701–704; 702).

In considering these works from a Leftist perspective, I also want to consider the relationship between childhood and capitalism beyond earlier claims to the child as property; after all, the dawning of the age of the Romantic child in the early nineteenth century represented a shift in the adult understanding of childhood from what Viviana A. Zelizer has called 'the future labourer [...] security for parents in later life' to 'the economically worthless child' who was yet emotionally 'priceless' (Zelizer 1985, 5). Since the early nineteenth century, this shift in the status of the child has expanded from the affluent middle classes to most western societies, particularly with the introduction of child labour laws that severely restrict the monetised work of children. Yet in the rendering of the child as what Felix Adler described as 'a sacred thing', the child has not been divorced from capitalism at all; rather, its status has shifted from worker to 'expensive young consumer' (ibid., 4, 6).

Emerson published his essay on 'Domestic Life' in 1870, considering the child in the domestic environment and painting a picture of its development, while still evaluating that relationship between adult and child discussed in 'Self-Reliance' and other earlier works. Critical engagement with this text is limited in comparison with more celebrated Emerson essays, perhaps because of this focus on childhood. Peter S. Field designates 'Domestic Life' as 'a fine essay', but solely considers childhood in terms of Emerson's own biography: '[I]t is clear that Emerson wrote the essay with his young son Waldo gallivanting around his Concord home' in which he, Emerson, was 'deliciously distracted by his enchanting three-year-old' (Field 2003, 41). Robert D. Richardson Jr. concurs with Field's biographical reading: '[Emerson] wrote a gentle and moving piece on childhood, drawn from his times with his children and lighted also by a nostalgia for his own childhood' (Richardson 1995, 447). This language of 'deliciously' and 'enchanting', 'gentle and moving [...] lighted also by a nostalgia' lends itself to a critical view of Emerson as a Romantic writer, but with a curiously limited and limiting view of what the Romantic child might be: Peter Gregg Slater, for example, claims Emerson as one of the Romantics who 'lost sight of the humanity of the infant when they endowed him with such ineffable goodness that mere mortals [...] were not so much to love as to worship him (Slater 1977, 29). Yet such understandings of this essay—and of Emerson's vision of childhood—contrast strangely with my understanding of the text and with wider readings of the Romantic child; not just as the sentimentally valuable child discussed by Zelizer, but as under a constant threat of Wordsworth's 'prison-house' as he grows beyond infancy.

This section, from early in 'Domestic Life', again addresses constructions of the self and the child's relationship with adults, but with a more direct commentary on the American capitalist imperative than others works, such as 'Experience'. It reads:

> Carry him out of doors,—he is overpowered by the light and by the extent of natural objects, and is silent. Then presently begins his use of his fingers, and he studies power, the lesson of his race. First it appears in no great harm, in architectural tastes. Out of blocks, thread-spools, cards and checkers, he will build his pyramid with the gravity of Palladio. With an acoustic apparatus of whistle and rattle he explores the laws of sound. But chiefly, like his senior countrymen, the young American studies new and speedier modes of transportation. Mistrusting the cunning of his small legs, he wishes to ride on the necks and shoulders of all flesh. (Emerson 1904 [1859], 55–56)

The assumption here is that the male-gendered child will begin within a domestic interior, constructed in opposition to the 'out of doors' to which the child is unable to find his own way but to which he must be brought. The impact of this adult intervention is overpowering, not solely by the adult but by 'natural objects', one that removes the child's voice to leave him 'silent'. At this point, all act upon the child, including adults, nature and even the narrator who knows how the child will, and does, respond, apparently constructing the child within a Randian family hierarchy, with even the appeal to nature suggesting Willers' Romantic view of his childhood. Yet Emerson's power structure is not so simple as adult above child: rather, it exists independently of all of these forces as this child is always within a power relationship, no matter where that power may lie at any given moment: even his 'overpowering' by the natural world assumes a prior location of power within the child. However, the development of the child stems directly from the challenging of this prior power. He has been removed from the domestic environment by the adult to let nature precipitate a new beginning and to reconfigure a troubled compensatory relationship with adults that has already been established earlier in Emerson's essay. And this new beginning, occasioned by the moment of change, at first appears out of the child's control: 'Then presently begins his use of his fingers', an act constructed as outside of intent in that the child may use his fingers, but he does not take the decision to do so; it happens, rather, despite himself.

The construction of power then shifts as the child begins to exert control over his environment and himself, and regain the power lost to nature and adults. He is now the agent of his own education: 'he studies power' and 'transportation', 'he explores the laws of sound'. The power that the child studies, then, both pre-exists him and is outside of him; yet it is able to be studied and, therefore, learned with Emerson's construction of power as a learned quality, achievement, or status. In this learning of power, the child aligns himself with the adult world, but not in the sense of all adults or of Emerson's representative man; rather, in studying power he is studying 'the lesson of his race' and, crucially, in his studies, his building, and his explorations as an independent being, he becomes 'like his senior countrymen', achieving the racial status of 'young American'.

Emerson claims that the child's study of power at '[f]irst [...] appears in no great harm in architectural tastes'. The claim to 'no great harm' is, for me, where this construction of childhood splits into what Emerson observes in an American childhood and what he feels it should be; for if such studies are only 'no great harm' at 'first', then the implication is that there is, at least, some degree of harm already and that further harm will follow. Building might be an acceptable study of power at this early stage of childhood, but in the deferred building of 'his pyramid', it might be argued that the child is building his own tomb, one predicated on what Emerson deems the damaging effects of the study and learning of power.[5]

Emerson's claim to Americanism is not just in terms of geographical origin, however, but of this very study: for the American both 'senior' and 'young', the subject of study is 'new and speedier modes of transportation'. In reading *Atlas Shrugged*, of course, the claim to an American selfhood and Rand's theory of Objectivism are rooted in the fictional Taggart Transcontinental and the drive to 'speedier [...] transportation'; Emerson, rather, is reading and constructing America via the child, designating the child as symptomatic of an American desire or need to learn that supersedes youth and age, appearing to evolve from and with the country itself. Yet unlike Rand, and as with the claim to 'no great harm', this is not a model of the child-power relationship that Emerson is prepared to endorse. After all this is 'his race', not 'mine', or 'ours', in a dissociation of the narrator from the Americanism he is describing, particularly compared to inclusive claims in other essays already discussed to 'our age' and 'we are now men'.

Darker still is the chilling assertion that the child 'wishes to ride on the necks and shoulders of all flesh'. This could be read as an allusion to slavery, with the Civil War ending only five years before the essay's publication, as well as to the power of the child over the adult; yet I feel that Emerson is rather commenting on capitalism and its abuse of power in nineteenth-century America, of which slavery was, of course, a significant part. Emerson also appears to be referencing another dark period of his country's history in the assertion that the child '[m]istrust[s] the cunning of his small legs': in appropriating the language of witchcraft in his claim to 'cunning'—a language that runs throughout this essay in relation to the child—Emerson might allude to the 1692 Salem witch trials, thereby further critiquing American power and its misuse.[6] Yet it could also be read that in '[m]istrusting the cunning' of his legs, the child is conscious of the witchcraft in himself and that the 'cunning', at least as it relates to or comes from his body, is at risk of failure.

This passage speaks to some of Rand's constructions of childhood in *Atlas Shrugged* and beyond, for this Emersonian child is one whose inter- actions with adults are frequently couched in terms of a power balance. The child's 'self-reliance' appears to begin with his studies of power, at first over aspects of his own body but also over the built environment, which both precedes and is constructed by the child. The particularly American construct of transport with which this passage largely concerns itself, much as it might suggest the building of the John Galt line and Dagny Taggart's first trip in *Atlas Shrugged*, is also about the self: while the child may be mimicking or following in the footsteps of his seniors, his desire for transport is because '*he* wishes to ride' [my emphasis], but to ride on adults; to hijack them for the fulfilment of his own needs and desires. The claim to the development of self in childhood, then, is always relational for this Emersonian child; selfhood can only be gained against, or through a dominance over, the adult that is always constructed as other. Therefore, although Emerson constructs this child in terms of a growing self-reliance, a movement away from the adults who provide his early care, the adults remain necessary both as examples of how to construct an American self— which also undermines the very claim to selfhood in that it can be and is raced in this way—but also as that which must be overcome to achieve the problematic selfhood that is constructed as the aim of an American child, though this is not a model that Emerson can endorse. After all, this child can only ever grow into a model of Americanism that is exactly built on 'the sepulchres of the fathers', his apparent self-reliance a mere repetition of what has come before with the child doomed to repeat the experiences of his forefathers; and the maintenance of a capitalist imperative—despite its guarantee of 'harm'—is bitterly assured. Therefore, in this dark promise of imitation and repeti- tion, both the child's power—and the man's—are now illusory; at least as applied to Emerson's vision of capitalist America.

Reading this passage as a construction of the Romantic child is, of course, not without its problems; after all, critics Field and Richardson appear to be constructing the 'Romantic' child as Zelizer's 'emotion- ally priceless' child, one that I cannot locate anywhere in this essay. And yet, perhaps Emerson's conflation of power and childhood is more about the Romantic child than might first appear, if we return to Wordsworth's claim that 'shades of the prison-house close on the growing boy'. It is in reading the divisions within a Romantic childhood, from the innocence of its infancy to the darkening of its boyhood via an experience of the world that ultimately corrupts, that Emerson's child can be read within the Wordsworthian Romantic tradition.

In Rand's works, her claim to Romanticism is concerned with portraying the ideal man as self-defining; not with man as he is, and/or as something outside of himself has determined he is or should be, but man as he might be through what she constructs as his own agency. But even this, of course, is problematic as the Randian man, like Emerson's and Wordsworth's men, are predicated on the child as 'father'. Rand, like Emerson, considers the self-defined man via the development of the child and its relationship with adults, primarily its parents, and she positions childhood as the site of adult moral treason in the denial of its potential and pre-existing relationship with Romanticism. In this passage from her essay, 'Art and Moral Treason', introducing the child's need for Romantic art to teach him to associate morality with pleasure, Rand argues:

> In the translation of that ideal [of morality] into conscious, philosophical terms and into his actual practice, a child needs intellectual assistance, or, at least, a chance to find his own way. In today's culture, he is given neither. The battering which his precarious, unformed, barely glimpsed moral sense of life receives from parents, teachers, adult "authorities" and little second-hander goons of his own generation, is so intense and so evil that only the toughest hero can withstand it. (Rand 1971, 140)[7]

In this passage, Rand considers the relationship between child and adult as part of the child's development. Rand's child is perhaps more representative than Emerson's in that he—as with Emerson, her child is gendered male—is situated within 'today's culture' rather than the more localised domestic space; however, as Emerson's child must be brought outdoors in order to effect a shift in power roles, so Rand's must translate the ideal into a consciousness that is in and of language, and into 'his actual practice'; although an actuality and a practice that precede and do not appear to be troubled by this need for translation. Both Rand's and Emerson's children need help from adults to realise their potential and their needs, despite the difference between Emerson's and Rand's perceptions of the results in that the Emersonian child's fate is only ever undesirable: he does not suggest a positive alternative, while Rand has a vision in mind for her child, even if it is not realised in this essay. However, the 'need' of Rand's child is qualified as an either/or: 'a child needs intellectual assistance, or, at least, a chance to find his own way'. As such the adult/child relationship constructed by 'assistance' is only ever an option, and one that stands opposed to the 'chance to find his own way'. Yet the claim that 'his own way' is something that the child both needs to find—and is therefore both located outside of himself and already belongs to him, prior to any potential finding taking place—and that the finding of such is left to 'chance', but a 'chance' that must be given, also troubles the status of 'own' and therefore of selfhood in the developing Randian child.

Despite Rand's claims to the child's needs, these, she believes, are not met: 'In today's culture, he is given neither'. This lack of fulfilment in the child's need for translation is both temporal—it is 'today's' child who is so denied—and cultural. It is also specifically adult, at least in the first instance: 'The battering which his precarious, unformed, barely glimpsed moral sense of life receives from parents, teachers, adult "authorities"'. This is more than denial: Rand claims an active, 'evil', 'battering' of the child's needs and of his 'moral sense of life' from those grouped adults who stand in positions of authority over—and against—the child and therefore in a one-way power relationship; much like the children of 'Domestic Life' and *Atlas Shrugged*, whose apparent power compared to adults is only ever illusory, but unlike the shifting power status of the adult–child relationship in 'Self-Reliance'. This assault, she claims, 'is so intense and so evil that only the toughest hero can withstand it'. Both this and the comment on 'second-hander goons of his own generation' trouble the construction of the child in this passage in that this problematically representative child is now split: there are others of his generation who are, yet, not him; while only 'the toughest hero'—which may or may not be this child—can withstand the adult onslaught against his developing sense of selfhood and the 'barely glimpsed moral sense of life' that, in the claim to 'barely glimpsed', both precedes him and is separate from him.

The relationship between adult and child in this passage is both troubled and troubling: Rand's child needs the intervention of an adult in its quest for self-development, but not of *this* adult; while the adult of her claim to 'today' is invested in the child, is giving something, but not what the child needs or desires: the introduction to Romantic art. In fact, the adult is suppressing the child's 'precarious, unformed, barely glimpsed moral sense of life', one that therefore pre-exists any exposure to Romantic art and is, Rand claims, the basis of his existence as a man, 'a being of self-made soul'. The result of this is that the child 'gives up' any attempt to shape his soul, 'without knowing that what he is surrendering is morality'. Rand's child is doomed by an interaction with adults that he can neither control nor escape; as such, the next generation of adults is similarly doomed.

As in Emerson's bleak vision of childhood, Rand's child is not what it could, or ought, to be. Yet with Rand, it is an adult society standing in his way, thereby constructing a vision of an ideal development that precedes this adult interruption; while with Emerson in 'Domestic Life', it is the help and example of the adult society that shapes the 'prison-house' of the growing child: neither is permitted any attempt at self-reliance as both are locked into power relationships with the adults surrounding them, in battles they cannot ever win. And it matters that both representative children are gendered male: despite Rand's efforts to place Dagny Taggart at the centre of a male-dominated commercial world, it remains a male world, one that a girl child would not be expected to join—not even by Rand.

5   THE CAPITALIST CHILD

In reading Emerson and Rand together, I would argue that their constructions of childhood, the relationship between man and child, and their constructions of selfhood through that relationship, are quite different, despite the disturbing tenor of both passages. Each is concerned with the relationship between adult and child, particularly in terms of education and development of the child self. However, Emerson's child moves quickly from reliance upon adults to an apparent form of self-reliance and self-fulfilment, albeit one suffused with difficulties in that the selfhood he moves towards is one that is always qualified by the example of adults who he appears to mimic or follow, by the appeal to an American self, and by Emerson's disapproval of what he must become. Rand's child also needs adult intervention to self-realise—with all the difficulties that conveys—but only ever receives an education that she counts as violence and destruction, therefore splitting what might be read as a representative childhood into a childhood that is both observed and quantified by the narration that situates itself outside of childhood but also outside of the adults Rand so reviles, and one that is constructed, again beneath this problematically situated narration, as an ideal child, the child that should be but that never can be, at least 'today'; a child that is therefore simultaneously absent and present.

In both cases, the adult–child relationship is toxic. Despite the child's superficial self-reliance in 'Domestic Life', the adult retains power over the child in that the child can only repeat 'the lessons of his race'; he cannot break away from the drive to a capitalist America that also, in the claim to 'his pyramid', Emerson figures as a death drive. Similarly, Rand's child—despite the hope of Romantic art and literature as the 'major (and, today, his only) source of a *moral* sense of life' in 'the crucial, formative years' of childhood and adolescence—is in trouble, at least in her own terms. Not only do the adults holding the power in his life deny him access to Romantic thought with a violence to crush any possibility from him, in the introduction to *The Romantic Manifesto*, Rand claims: 'There is no Romantic movement today. If there is to be one in the art of the future, this book will have helped it to come into being' (Rand 1971, v). The only help for Rand's Romantic child, it seems then, is Rand herself.

Yet, in conclusion, we must consider the political stances of each in their constructions of the Romantic child, both in what 'he' is and what he should be; and in any claim to what he should be, we must ask what vision of the future each is creating. Despite the fact that both writers insist on individuality and self-reliance, each writer is also telling the child—and us, via the representative figure of the child—what their vision of society is and suggesting what we might do to achieve it: all of which opposes any claim to self-reliance in that we need to be told what we should do and who we should be, with such claims to 'manifesto' always causing problems for Individualism. Emerson's and Rand's politics may be miles apart as Emerson's denigrates the future of the capitalist child while Rand advocates it, seeing no division between this and her claims to Romanticism; but the means by which the two writers choose to promote their causes remain disturbingly similar.

NOTES

1. This chapter has been developed from my paper on Rand, Emerson and Individualism from the November 2018 conference, 'Ayn Rand from the Left', at the University of Reading.
2. See Lawrence, accessed October 2018.
3. Emerson writes, for example: 'One mode of the divine teaching is the incarnation of the spirit in a form,—in forms, like my own', 245.
4. For more on Objectivist theories of inheritance, see, for example Branden (1966). For a further, detailed reading of questions of childhood, inheritance, and capitalism, see Chapter 9 of this book.

5. Of course, Rand explores what she constructs as the privileged position of the architect in *The Fountainhead*, and architecture as the privileged form of self-expression and self-realisation. On the 70th anniversary of the novel's release, Lance Hosey wrote that '*The Fountainhead* remains the perfect representation of everything that's wrong with the profession', comparing the irresponsible individualism of Howard Roark as 'terrorism masquerading as free speech'. See Hosey (2013).

6. Emerson must have been very aware of the Salem witch trials some 110 years before his birth: his home town of Concord was just a few miles from Salem, and at least two of his neighbours—Louisa May Alcott and Nathaniel Hawthorne—were descended from witch trial judges, with much of Hawthorne's fiction predicated on his repugnance at this connection; Emerson was also descended from acused and convicted 'witch', Mary Bradbury. Charles Wentworth Upham's definitive history of the trials was published just three years before 'Domestic life', in 1867. For further discussion of this issue, see forthcoming West (2020).

7. The particular chapter is named 'Art and moral treason'.

Bibliography

Anon. 2018. Ralph Waldo Emerson and objectivism: CUNY academic commons. https://rwehdtar.commons.gc.cuny.edu/2018/05/24/ralph-waldo-emerson-and-objectivism/. Accessed 25 November 2019.

Branden, Nathaniel. 1966. Common fallacies about capitalism. In *Capitalism: The unknown ideal*, 73–100. New York, NY: Signet.

Buell, Lawrence (ed.). 2006. *The American transcendentalists: Essential writings*. New York, NY: Random House.

Cameron, Sharon. 1991. Representing grief: Emerson's 'Experience'. In *The new American studies: Essays from representations*, ed. Philip Fisher, 201–227. Berkeley, CA and Los Angeles, CA: University of California Press.

Cavitch, Max. 2007. *American elegy: The poetry of mourning from the puritans to Whitman*. Minneapolis, MN: University of Minnesota Press.

Emerson, Ralph Waldo. 1841a. Self reliance. In *Essays first series*, 41–82. New York, NY: John W. Lovell Company.

———. 1841b. The oversoul. In *Essays first series*, 235–264. New York, NY: John W. Lovell Company.

———. 1844. Experience. In *Essays second series*, 41–76. New York, NY: John W. Lovell Company.

———. 1892 [1836]. *Nature*. In *Nature, addresses and lectures*, 7–80. Boston, MA: Houghton, Mifflin, & Co.

———. 1904 [1859]. Domestic life. In *Society and solitude*, 55–72. London: George Bell and Sons.

Fand, Roxanne. 2005. Reading the fountainhead: The missing self in Ayn Rand's ethical individualism. *College English* 71/5 (May): 486–505.

Federici, Silvia. 2004. *Caliban and the witch*. New York, NY: Autonomedia.

Field, Peter S. 2003. *Ralph Waldo Emerson: The making of a democratic individual*. Lanham, MD: Rowman and Littlefield.

Hosey, Lance. 2013. The fountainhead: Everything that's wrong with architecture. ArchDaily. https://www.archdaily.com/447141/the-fountainhead-eve rything-that-s-wrong-with-architecture. Accessed 10 December 2019.

Lawrence, Richard. Did Ayn Rand misrepresent Emerson?. Objectivism reference center. Accessed October 2018; page since removed.

Parks, Christopher. 2012. *Children's literature and capitalism*. Basingstoke and New York, NY: Palgrave Macmillan.

Rand, Ayn. 1943. *The Fountainhead*. New York, NY: New American Library.

———. 1957. *Atlas shrugged*. New York, NY: New American Library.

———. 1971. *The Romantic manifesto*. New York, NY: Signet.

———. 1982. *Philosophy: Who needs it?* Indianapolis, IN: Bobbs-Merrill.

Richardson, Robert D. 1995. *Emerson: The mind on fire*. Berkeley, CA: University of California Press.

Rousseau, Jean Jacques. 2007 [1762]. *Émile, or on education*, trans. B. Foxley. Sioux Falls, SD: NuVision Publications.

Slater, Peter Gregg. 1977. *Children in the New England mind in death and in life*. Hamden, CT: Archon Books.

Stoneley, Peter. 2003. *Consumerism and American girls' literature 1860–1940*. Cambridge: Cambridge University Press.

West, Kristina. 2016. *To be boy eternal: Locating the child in the literature and criticism of Ralph Waldo Emerson*. Unpublished thesis, University of Reading.

———. 2020. *Reading the Salem witch child*. Basingstoke and London: Palgrave Macmillan.

Whicher, Stephen E. 1953. *Freedom and fate: An inner life of Ralph Waldo Emerson*. Philadelphia, PA: University of Pennsylvania Press.

Wordsworth, William. 1994 [1802 and 1807]. My heart leaps up and Ode: Intimations of immortality from recollections of early childhood. In *The collected poems of William Wordsworth*, 701–704. Ware, Hertfordshire: Wordsworth Poetry Library.

Younkins, Edward W. 2013. Economics in Ayn Rand's *Atlas shrugged*. *The Journal of Ayn Rand Studies* 13 (2): 123–139.

Zelizer, Viviana A. 1985. *Pricing the priceless child: The changing social value of children*. Princeton, NJ: Princeton University Press.

Selfish Cinema: Sex, Heroism, and Control in Adaptations of Ayn Rand for the Screen

Lisa Downing

1   INTRODUCTION

To many, the name 'Ayn Rand' stands for all that is rebarbative about today's selfish society and Global capitalism. Figures of the Right such as Rand Paul, Paul Ryan, Alan Greenspan, and Donald Trump are all professed admirers of her writings. But rather than dismissing Rand out of hand as a 'deplorable', as many in the left-leaning academic humanities have done, I would argue that it is incumbent upon us to engage with, take seriously, and try to understand on its own terms, the work of this radical and fascinating figure who is as influential as she is divisive.

Moreover, as a woman whose philosophy describes the espousal of self-interest for all, and a vision of personal heroism available to both men and women—but devoid of a feminist consciousness—Rand's concerns are timely for revisionist theoretical work in the history of women's contributions to culture, literature, and philosophy. As I argue in my recent book *Selfish Women* (Downing 2019), Rand's work has much to tell us about the difficulties of apprehending exceptional, outlier female figures who

L. Downing (✉)
University of Birmingham, Birmingham, UK

© The Author(s) 2020
N. Cocks (ed.), *Questioning Ayn Rand*,
Palgrave Studies in Literature, Culture and Economics,
https://doi.org/10.1007/978-3-030-53073-0_6

do not sit easily within familiar categories and stereotypes of what women are assumed to be: caregiving, selfless, prone to collective and cooperative action. With regard to her novel *Atlas Shrugged* (1957), Rand wrote: 'My philosophy, in essence, is the concept of man as a heroic being, with his own happiness as the moral purpose of his life' (Rand 1992, 1170). In this chapter, I will focus on a little-discussed aspect of Rand's life and work: her relationship with film.[1] In considering adaptations of Rand's work and life for the screen in this chapter, I will ask whether her old-fashioned generic use of 'man' to mean 'humankind' in the above-quoted extract can also, in any meaningful way, include women.

In what follows, I will examine two filmic adaptations of books by or about Rand. The first will be King Vidor's *The Fountainhead* (1949), based on Rand's 1943 novel, for which she was also the screenwriter. As introduced in previous chapters, *The Fountainhead*, in both its literary and filmic incarnations, was Rand's attempt to tell the story of the ideal, heroic man embodied in the figure of Howard Roark (played by Gary Cooper in Vidor's film). Roark is an individualistic architect whose single-minded desire is to design and execute his vision of what a building should be: formally, functionally, and aesthetically. Secondly, I will examine the made-for-television biopic *The Passion of Ayn Rand*, directed by Chris Menaul (1999), which is based on Barbara Branden's biography of Rand of the same name which appeared in 1986. Helen Mirren gives an intense performance as Rand in this film. Branden's book and Menaul's film focus particularly on the extramarital relationship that took place between Rand and her one-time 'intellectual heir', Barbara Branden's husband, Nathaniel. The film follows the course of the affair, which had been reluctantly consented to by Barbara and by Rand's husband, Frank O'Connor, and ends with Rand's estrangement from the Brandens, upon discovering that Nathan had taken another, younger mistress. The film seeks to examine the ways in which the politics of the Objectivist movement and Ayn Rand's relationships with the group of young students who clustered to her were intertwined, and concomitantly problematises the notion that living by the tenets of Objectivism would result in the possibility of a heroic—or a happy—life.

In comparing these two generically different films, separated by more than four decades, my aim will be to examine from a new perspective a problem that Rand had to face throughout the course of her fictional and theoretical opus, but seldom articulated explicitly: the problem of representing, or of being, the singular, heroic individual of Objectivism if one is not a powerful, white man. Rand opposed the validity of all identity politics and group-based social justice causes, most notably in the collection of essays called *The New Left* (1971), on the grounds that she dismissed class-based analysis as a product of collectivism, which she despised.[2] Her infamous essay on racism (1963), for example, blames racial prejudice on our failure to take a sufficiently individualistic view of the world. Racists are collectivists who mistakenly make identification with those of their perceived racial group, and demonise other groups, rather than apprehending individuals *qua* individuals, regardless of race.[3] This analysis completely refuses, of course, to take onboard the realities of historical and ongoing structural inequalities. On the subject of feminism, Rand is even more damning, writing: 'Every other pressure group has some semi-plausible complaint or pretense at a complaint, as an excuse for existing. [...] Women's Lib has none' (Rand 1971, 1076). However, in this regard, Rand holds somewhat contradictory views. While refusing to acknowledge the need for women's shared political cause, she understands women in a rather essentialist manner as a coherent *psychological* group. In particular, she infamously stated in a 1968 essay on women and power that: 'the essence of femininity is hero worship—the desire to look up to man' and, in a letter to Thomas Bond, a high-school history teacher correspondent, in 1964, she wrote: 'an ideal woman is a man-worshipper, and an ideal man is the highest symbol of mankind' (Rand 1988, 268; 1997, 623). Rand's views, then, betray considerable (internalised) sexism, and incredibly traditional views of the complementarity between two binary genders, leading inevitably to a concomitant homophobia.

Yet, whatever one may think of Rand's political stances, it is impossible to deny that in a number of respects she was a maverick, a thinker against the grain, devoted to overturning commonplaces. She is renowned for her claims that altruism is an evil; selfishness a virtue, in an attempt to subvert the Christian ethic. She hated the US Left and Conservatives equally, considering Objectivists to be instead 'radicals for capitalism' (Rand 1961, 1). She eschewed America's religiosity, espousing atheism and falling firmly on the side of the right of the individual woman to choose abortion in one of the most fraught and long-lived moral and political debates to dog America. It is odd, then, that the commonplace—and flawed—concept of narrow gender roles on the basis of sexual dimorphism should have gone unchallenged by her, given that she could easily have applied her (however faulty) critique of racism to sexism, affirming women as individuals, rather than asserting an innate feminine/female group nature. And what is perhaps most odd is the cognitive dissonance implied by the fact that, on one level, she so obviously saw herself as the real-life, heroic, exceptional sovereign subject reflected in her novelistic and filmic heroes, while still maintaining, with a knee-jerk sexism, that she as a woman must hero worship the ideal man whose complement she would be. It is to this dilemma—this unliveable paradox—that I will return several times through my discussion of the two films in question.

2   THE FOUNTAINHEAD

In considering the 1949 Warner Brothers production of *The Fountainhead* in light of the issues raised above concerning sex, agency, and heroism, my focus will be on two relationships imbricated in it: that between author Rand and her creation Roark, and that between screenwriter Rand and director Vidor. The film was described on its release, in a coruscating review by Bosley Crowther in *The New York Times*, as 'A long-winded, complicated preachment on the rights of the individual in society' (Crowther 1949). *The Fountainhead* is certainly an odd, awkward piece of film-making in which purely cinematic concerns are subordinated to philosophical imperatives. However, as Rand's published response to this review pointed out, 'Mr. Crowther missed the fact that Warner Brothers have given a great demonstration of courage and consistency: they have produced the most faithful adaptation of a novel ever to appear on the screen' (cited in Branden 1987, 213). It is impossible not to see a symbiotic relationship between the conditions of production of *The Fountainhead* and its narrative content and philosophical message. Roark allows nothing to stand in the way of his project to design modern architecture on which his vision is imprinted; neither the opinions of others nor the desire for fame and recognition. Indeed, he agrees to design a social housing project, Cortlandt Homes, for less talented peer Peter Keating (Kent Smith) without taking any of the credit or payment. His only demand is that the building should follow his designs to the last detail. When a committee of architects is brought into 'improve on' Roark's design, Roark responds by dynamiting the Cortlandt.

In a striking parallel with this narrative thrust, in her collaboration with Vidor, Rand demanded—and obtained—a degree of control over the screenplay that was almost unprecedented for a writer in Hollywood at the time, made all the more extraordinary by the fact that she was a woman in a very male-dominated industry. It has been pointed out (Shaw 2013) that the contractual clause Rand demanded, which gave her absolute control over the script, mirrors the conditions Roark placed on his agreement with Keating—the Cortlandt must be executed exactly according to his design. And just as Roark forewent payment for the design of that project, similarly Vidor commented of Rand: 'they didn't even have to pay her because she was so anxious to get the book on the screen' (cited in Shaw 2013). Indeed, I would argue that in *The Fountainhead*, Roark functions directly as Rand's onscreen representative: his literal, architectural edifices are meant to convey in physical form the audacity of Rand's philosophical one and his perverse resolve is an idealised projection of her own.

The ways in which Rand's and Roark's words and actions mirror each other's agendas are numerous. Artistic and formal control is an obvious starting point. The aesthetic didactic message of the film is delivered in an early scene between Roark and his mentor Henry Cameron (Henry Hull), an individualistic and brilliant, but professionally ruined, architect who drinks himself to death. Among Cameron's dying words to Roark is the exhortation: 'The form of a building must follow its function'. These words echo a principle of modern architecture, often attributed to Horatio Greenough, but probably coined by Louis Sullivan, whom Cameron represents in this *film à cle*. The principle was known simply as 'form follows function', but was later embellished by Frank Lloyd Wright as 'form follows function by way of the nature of materials'. Copious notes about this premise can be found in the journals Ayn Rand kept during her preparatory research for writing *The Fountainhead* suggesting that its meaning was particularly significant for her (Rand 1999, 144–145).

Indeed, this specifically architectural premise encapsulates also Rand's broader aesthetic claim that every element of any work of art or literature must be there for a reason, must be capable of being rationally justified, in line with her broader philosophy of Objectivism. In her lecture on the art of writing, as referenced in the Introduction to this present book, she wrote: 'I can give the reason for every word and every punctuation mark in *Atlas Shrugged* and there are 645,000 words in it by the printer's count' (Rand 2000, 4). The principal way in which Ayn Rand asserted control over form in the making of the film *The Fountainhead* lies in her insistence on the words to be spoken by her characters, brought to life by the actors on the screen. Most especially and iconoclastically, Rand demanded that, in the courtroom scene, in which Roark defends his right as Cortlandt Homes' designer to be also its destroyer, Cooper should speak the full, 6-minute-long, philosophical monologue she had written for him—the longest speech in film history at the time, according to some critics. In her journals, Rand described the function of this key speech as follows: it must convey that 'the *good* is not the *social,* but the *individual,* not the herd-instinct, but independence [...] The form of a society will be the result of this basic issue' (Rand 1999, 235).

The speech in the finished film is certainly long, and it was unusual for a Hollywood filmgoer in the 1940s to have to sit through such an extended monologue. Yet, it is not quite the case that Rand got her way and that the full speech she had written was delivered word for word by Cooper. Despite Rand's constant vigilance, turning up on set almost every day during filming to ensure fidelity to her script, she was reputedly enraged on attending the première to discover that the climactic declaration of Roark's speech—'I wished to come here and say that I am a man who does not exist for others'—had been cut from the final version of the trial scene (Vidor 2012). This was allegedly done to placate the Johnson Office, Hollywood's regulatory agency. The agency had objected more strongly to this courtroom speech, which it found immoral because it was 'materialistic', than to the forceful sex scene (some would say rape scene) between Roark and Dominique Francon (Patricia Neal), to which many subsequent feminist critics would take exception (Branden 1987, 211). This was despite the fact that it was not within the Office's technical remit to pass judgement on the philosophical content of a film.

It is clear that, to Ayn Rand, both her novels and the film were *vehicles* for a philosophical message; the message being more important than the vehicle, and the vehicle merely serving the message. Form is, in fact, *dictated* by function for Rand. Thus, where one could argue that a six-minute monologue would not serve the specificities or market demands of the cinematic medium well, Rand would surely have objected that the cinematic medium was there to serve her philosophy. Musing on this issue, Rand wrote:

> The movies have produced no great work of art, no immortal masterpiece to compare with the masterpieces of other arts. Why? [...] Because those in charge do not create what they think is good, but what they think others will think is good. [...] The movies are the perfect example of collective ideology and of 'living for others'. (Rand 1999, 87)

That films are a collectively produced art form, if not necessarily an 'example of collective ideology', is beyond dispute. One might point out, then, the inherent impossibility of Rand's project of what I am calling 'selfish cinema': the attempt to achieve a direct translation of her philosophy of individualistic creativity into a medium that she recognised as being almost structurally opposed to its tenets. That is, in her work on *The Fountainhead*, she sought to subvert the rules and codes of film adaptation and achieve instead merely a literal visual transliteration.

In parallel with these assertions, and not coincidentally, Rand has Roark voice a version of her obsessive personal and political view when he states in his courtroom defence speech:

> Everything we have, every great achievement, has come from the independent work of some independent mind. Every horror and destruction came from attempts to force man into a herd of brainless, soulless robots without personal rights, without personal ambition, without will, hope, or dignity. It is an ancient conflict. It has another name: the individual against the collective.

This idea stands in stark and literal opposition to the words of the arch-villain of *The Fountainhead*, architectural critic Ellsworth Toohey (Robert Douglas), when he states 'artistic value is achieved collectively by each man subordinating himself to the standards of the majority'. Thus, the status of the battle between individualism and collectivism for Rand is revealed—it is nothing less than a form of secular Manicheanism.

Her machinations with the script aside, Rand also appears to have had strong input into several of the film's visual and design elements. Most notably, perhaps, she identified the architectural aesthetic that would best characterise Howard Roark's work. In the journals she kept while writing the novel *The Fountainhead* and preparing the screenplay, Rand made copious notes from a comprehensive reading list of architectural textbooks and academic journals, especially those focusing on modernist theory and on the design of skyscrapers. In these notes, it becomes clear that Frank Lloyd Wright is her inspiration for Roark, and Wright's innovative modernist style the embodiment of her architectural ideal. In preliminary notes for the adaptation she wrote: 'Among present-day architects it is the style of Frank Lloyd Wright—and *only* of Frank Lloyd Wright—that must be taken as a model for Roark's buildings. [...] This is extremely important to us, since we must make the audience admire Roark's build-ings' (Branden 1987, 208–209). Accordingly, Vidor approached Wright about executing Roark's designs for the film, to which Wright agreed in exchange for 10% of the film's entire budget and full approval of the sets—a price considered too high to pay. Yet Wright's style is undoubt-edly still visible in many of the architectural designs produced by artistic director and set designer Edward Carrere for *The Fountainhead*.

However, critics have pointed out that some of Carrere's designs were simply architecturally unfeasible. For example, a drawing of a residence featured in the film includes three cantilevered overhangs and no evidence of structural support for its balcony (Schleier 2009, 126). This led Rand to reflect that the buildings that finally appeared were 'embarrassingly bad' (Branden 1987, 209). The stakes of this failure were considerable, since Rand had signposted that Roark's architecture needed to convey the sense of exceptional genius that we are consistently told he embodies—where genius, in Randian terms, bears quasi-Nietzschean moral qualities as well as intellectual or artistic ones. Accordingly, in this context, as Schleier puts it in a book on architecture in American film, for Rand: 'a mediocre, stylistically retrogressive building is not merely aesthetically objectionable, but constitutes a moral affront' (Schleier 2009, 124). If Roark's buildings fail to fulfil their purpose in the film, the principles they are called upon to uphold are no more able to stand than Cortlandt Homes after application of a stick of dynamite.

Film critics writing of the making of *The Fountainhead* have tended to focus on the book as an unlikely choice for a film project by Vidor. In their book on Vidor's cinema, Raymond Durgnat and Scott Simmon have written of the director's 'ambivalence about elitism', since previous films included such titles as the pro-collectivist *Our Daily Bread* (1934) and *The Crowd* (1928), and since Hollywood cinema, by definition, requires a crowd to make it a success (this being a key reason for Rand's rubbishing of cinema's achievements in the passage quoted above) (Durgnat and Simmon 1988, 259). It was certainly unusual for a film with an explicitly political message to be so very obviously anti-populist as *The Fountainhead*. This critical focus on Vidor's ambivalence reflects an apparent unwillingness on the part of Durgnat and Simmon to asso-ciate a director in whose left-wing agenda they appear to invest with Rand's ideology, despite the fact that, by 1949, Vidor had for some years been actively involved in the anti-Communist Motion Picture Alliance for the Preservation of American Ideals, alongside both Rand and Gary

Cooper. Indeed Durgnat and Simmons suggest that Vidor's treatment of the novel somehow tempers or moderates Randian ideology, claiming 'Rand's ultrapurist notions of selfishness as a new religion are mellowed by Vidor's notion of frustration and suffering in the real world' (Durgnat and Simmon 1988, 261). However, the only justification for this bold claim is that in the sequence that depicts the death of Henry Cameron, the camera focuses on the red cross painted on the ambulance window twice (Figs. 1 and 2), 'as if to assert a cross of compassion' (Durgnat and Simmon 1988, 261). This is thought to serve as a stark contrast to the anti-Christian morality of the path taken by Roark (and Rand).

There is also a tendency in critical writing to focus very explicitly on the struggle for control between Rand and Vidor, often in fairly explicitly gendered terms. Durgnat and Simmon write: 'when she discovered Vidor shooting his cut version of Roark's courtroom summary, she ran to Jack Warner who forced Vidor to abide by her contract terms' and 'It is surprising that the combined professionalism of Gary Cooper, Vidor and Jack Warner could do so little to modify Ayn Rand's comic-strip dialogue' (Durgnat and Simmon 1988, 263). Reading between the lines of these

Fig. 1 A cross of compassion

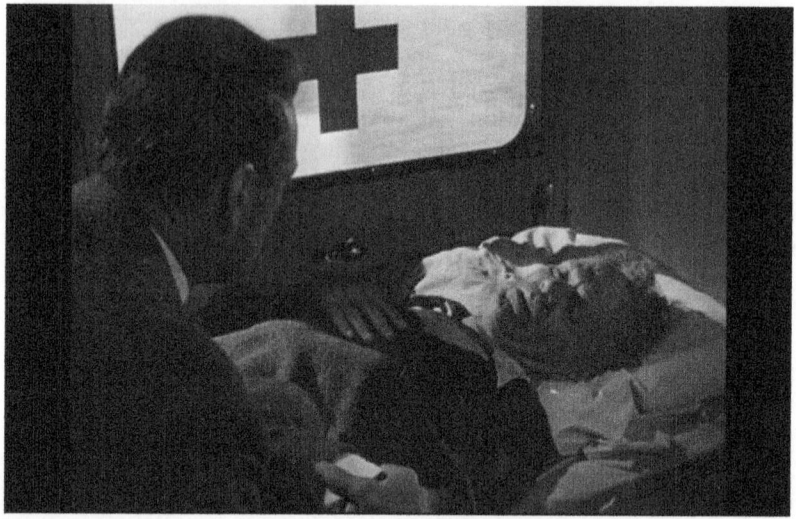

Fig. 2   The dying Henry Cameron beneath a visible cross

statements, there is a message of invidious misogyny: it is astounding that these big, important men could not squash the will of a mere woman.

Yet Vidor himself reported little discomfort with his arrangement with Rand and little tension between them, commenting: 'I got along great with her'. He also described the favourable effects of her insistence on keeping control over her script:

> If they changed any lines, she wanted to be telephoned and called to the studio. That was a great help to me, because actors always want to change lines. So I used that as a prop. I'd say to Gary Cooper, 'Okay, you'll have to phone Ayn Rand'. And he'd say, 'How long will it take her to get here?' 'Oh, it'll be about an hour.' And he'd say, 'Oh God, let's go, I'll read the line'. (Vidor 2012)

Durgnat and Simmon also assert that 'Vidor would dearly have loved Bogart as Roark' (Durgnat and Simmon 1988, 264), implying once again that the director was thwarted by a woman's whims, since Rand had strongly been in favour of the casting of Cooper, a known Conservative. It seems, then, that there is quite a lot of investment in seeing Vidor as the wronged party in the making of this film, as well as a desire to extricate him from its embarrassingly pro-capitalist message. This is despite the fact that Vidor expressed considerably more satisfaction with the resulting film than Ayn Rand, who, after viewing the finished product, turned her back on cinema once and for all. She declared film an unfit medium for conveying philosophical messages and described herself as 'through with Hollywood. There's nothing there for me' (Branden 1987, 211).

Rand might have said that, for her, the failure of *The Fountainhead* resided in the few elements that did not adhere precisely to her vision: the cutting of Roark's key line about not existing for others and the inability of the studio to secure Wright as the designer for Roark's buildings. Yet, it is also possible to argue that if the film falls flat *qua film*, as several critics strongly hold, it has more to do with the extent to which purely cinematic concerns are subordinated to the single-minded pursuit of a political and philosophical dogma. Rand's 'selfish cinema' results in a movie that places philosophy above form, arguably compromising the proper functions of film as both an industry and a medium.

3   THE PASSION OF AYN RAND

If, in *The Fountainhead*, Rand's authorial and editorial will is everywhere visible, through Roark's words as well as in the aesthetics of the film, then in *The Passion of Ayn Rand*, filmed years after her death, we encounter a very different dynamic. This is a view of Rand, filtered through the subjective perspective of Barbara Branden—or Ayn Rand as a fictionalised character. (To avoid confusion, while discussing this film I will refer to the author as 'Rand' and her character, played by Helen Mirren, as 'Ayn'.) Barbara Branden's biography of Rand, also published after the author's death, necessarily escaped any attempt by Rand to assert control over the story of her life. The film based on the biography depicts Ayn in her personal life, repeatedly failing to assert the control that, as we have already examined, was so central to the way in which Rand conducted her creative and professional affairs.

Branden's biography and Menaul's biopic raise a number of intriguing issues about how the lives of women are depicted in life writing and on screen. Owing to conditions of historical oppression, and the limitations placed on women's public agency, 'great women' have been the subjects of biographies less frequently, and for less time, than 'great men'.[4] This set of issues is particularly pertinent when the subject is Rand, given her privileging of reason and action in the world. In gender political terms, it is an audacious decision to depict the most ruthless, self-avowedly rational female author as a spiteful, jealous, wronged woman, unable to maintain the interest of her much younger lover, and to focus mainly on her personal life rather than on her career. Indeed, it is initially readable as a misogynistic gesture of putting-her-in-her-place.

This technique of reducing a rationally selfish woman to her irrational actions and reactions—'humanising' her by rendering her more vulnerable—may remind us of the controversial biopic of Margaret Thatcher, Phyllida Lloyd's *The Iron Lady* (2011). In this film, Meryl Streep's Thatcher looks back on her rise to power, bellicose rule, and subsequent political decline from a position of old age and encroaching physical and mental infirmity. The film focuses on Margaret Thatcher's increasing dementia, and her inability to accept the death of her husband, Denis, whom she imagines to be still living alongside her. Scenes of her rise to power and events from her premiership, such as the Falklands conflict, are filmed as flashbacks, juxtaposed with scenes from the diegetic present, repeatedly reminding us that Streep's Thatcher is now a dotty, doddering old lady. This technique is at once a manipulation against the grain of audience emotional response, since many watching will feel the visceral hatred that Thatcher often provokes in the UK, and a particularly gendered *memento mori*.

Yet posthumous punishment, or misogynistic humiliation, is not *all* that is at stake in *The Passion of Ayn Rand*. In many ways the adulation that Barbara Branden felt for Rand, as both a woman and as the author whose books changed her life, translates in numerous ways into the film. Via a range of visual themes, the film reifies Rand's iconic status—her *brand*—and accords to her personal narrative the status of a legend. The film is littered with visual references to the iconography of Rand's story and philosophy. The dollar sign that Rand identified as the mark of freedom is introduced in the film's opening images over which the credits roll, as a large, golden dollar sign stands beside Rand's coffin in an establishing flash-forward by means of which the narrative can begin at the same diegetic temporal moment as that at which it will also end. The dollar sign is subsequently traced by Ayn's finger in a steamed-up shop window in one sequence, while the gold dollar brooch Rand wore as her signature piece is visible in many close-ups of Mirren throughout the film. Similarly, where the script includes details of stories from Rand's childhood and development, especially in intimate scenes between Mirren and Stoltz in which Ayn and Nathan grow closer, totemic Randian objects are visually brought into focus, such as the Remington Rand typewriter which allegedly provided inspiration to the young Alisa Rosenbaum in choosing her own name.

The film is emotionally ambivalent about Rand. It sets up these shiny talismans of her persona—Randian McGuffins—the better to contrast these enduring objects with the human failings of the (anti-) heroine. Moreover, when we examine the physical depiction of the individualistic protagonists of both films—Roark in *The Fountainhead* and Ayn in *The Passion of Ayn Rand*—the ways in which the respective directors position Cooper and Mirren render visually obvious the gendering of their heroism. Cooper's Roark consistently stands as erect as one of his buildings, often filmed during physical or intellectual activity, and even wielding power tools in the sequence filmed at a quarry (Fig. 3). Mirren's Ayn, meanwhile, is by contrast depicted largely in domestic and private spaces, writing or conducting meetings of her followers, the ironically named 'Collective', in her home. (Fig. 4)

Similarly, where Roark defends selfish individualism as the highest form of heroism in a courtroom—the public sphere (Fig. 5)—it is at a surprise dinner party to celebrate the completion of the writing of *Atlas Shrugged*,

Fig. 3 Cooper as Roark: wielding a power tool

Fig. 4 Mirren as Rand: wielding the power of philosophical conviction

Fig. 5 Roark's courtoom speech

in the company of the Collective, that Mirren's Ayn speaks in parallel terms of heroism (Fig. 6). Subtly, then, the chosen settings in much of the biopic reinforce interiority and domesticity for the female public intellectual.

Yet my reading of Rand and Roark as equivalents so far is, in fact, itself a reading against the grain of Rand's intentions. While Rand, on the one hand, often admitted that she saw herself as the heroic ideal being of Objectivism, on the other, her dubious gender politics got in the way of that self-assertion, such that the kinds of gender conformity we see in the way Ayn is portrayed in *The Passion of Ayn Rand* echo features of her own anti-feminism. One could indeed argue that to some degree, by dint of both her sex and the way in which Rand talked about heterosexual female desire, the obvious *Fountainhead* counterpart for Rand and for Mirren's Ayn is Patricia Neal's Dominique. Indeed, Rand has described the Dominique of the novel in her journals as 'myself in a bad mood' (Branden 1987, 134).

Barbara Branden suggests in her biography, and it is suggested too in Menaul's film, that Rand was unable to admit to herself— or to anyone else—that her handsome, creative, but objectively non-intellectual husband Frank O'Connor was very far from the Roark-esque masculine hero of Rand's personal, sexual, and philosophical fantasies.

Fig. 6 Ayn's dinner-time speech

Rand had apparently stated many times 'I could only love a hero' (Branden 1987, 88). According to Branden, a friend of Rand once reported that she had said of Frank 'I married him because he was so beautiful', and yet also then went on to claim that they shared an intellectual affinity (Branden 1987, 87). According to Branden, this was not visibly the case: 'Although he would listen quietly to her discussion of philosophical concepts, he could bring little to the conversation' and 'the man Ayn spoke of in such extravagant terms had little to do with the real human being who was Frank [...] she responded, instead, to the heroic virtues he did not possess' (Branden 1987, 88).

This romantic disingenuousness is dramatised in sequences of *The Passion of Ayn Rand* that directly addresses the issue. As Mirren's Ayn and Stoltz's Nathan walk arm-in-arm along a New York winter street, the dialogue is as follows:

Ayn: The man must have the woman who reflects his deepest vision of himself. And in her surrender is his happiness.
Nathan: And the woman?
Ayn: Must worship the hero!
Narthan: Is that how you feel about Frank?
Ayn: Yes, of course!

In creating Howard Roark and Dominique Francon, Rand had attempted to construct the ideal heroic couple. Barbara Branden in her biography recalls: 'She has said, discussing Roark and Dominique, that theirs was to be the ideal romance, "so of course it had to start with violent antagonism"' (Branden 1987, 300). That Branden juxtaposes this anecdote with speculation on Rand's relationship with her husband is not incidental. An aim of both the biography and the biopic is to suggest that Rand felt some frustration with her own romantic situation which compared starkly to her much vaunted ideal. Indeed, in a love scene between Ayn and Frank O'Connor, played by Peter Fonda, we see the degree to which Frank and Ayn fall short of the sadomasochistic, male-dominance/female-surrender model that Rand holds up as her erotic ideal, and that Roark and Dominique so perfectly embody. 'Topping from the bottom', Ayn demands that Frank handle her roughly. 'Not so gently! Must you always ask my permission?', Mirren spits as her eyes flash. That Ayn Rand was disappointed by the beta masculinity of the beautiful actor Frank

O'Connor is an implication that Branden's book and Menaul's biopic very much want us to take away.

The 'passion' evoked in the title of the biography/biopic is, in fact, a key theme of both *The Fountainhead* and *The Passion of Ayn Rand*. In one of the most melodramatic scenes in *The Fountainhead*, enhanced by overwrought, extra-diegetic music, Dominique strikes Roark across the face with her riding whip in frustration at his having failed to come to her house, nominally to repair the marble fireplace she has deliberately damaged (Figs. 7 and 8). And in *The Passion of Ayn Rand*, Ayn strikes Nathan as a reaction to his betrayal of their love in beginning a new affair with a younger woman (Figs. 9 and 10).

The composition of both shots is strikingly similar. Both women are reduced in this sequence to emotionally manipulating the objects of their desire and responding violently when their wishes are frustrated. And Roark and Nathan both operate as agents who can choose whether or not to bestow sexual attentions on their wilful, lustful, yet masochistic female partner. Yet in Rand's neat, ordered, controlled, fictional world, Dominique's desperate frustrated whiplash leads to the extremely problematic healing and redemptive seduction/rape (which Rand has defended, in response to criticism, with the words 'if it's

Fig. 7 Dominique: a woman scorned

Fig. 8   Dominique's whiplash

Fig. 9   Ayn: a woman scorned

Fig. 10 Ayn's slap

rape—it's rape by engraved invitation';[5]), whereas in the biopic, Ayn's assault on Nathan leads to his final, devastating, abandonment of her.

4   Some Concluding Remarks

It is perhaps not surprising that the conceptualisation of female heroism was a sticking point for Rand given that our culture is one in which heroism and agentic individuality have historically been the lot of males. As psychologist of women Carol Gilligan asks in her book *In a Different Voice*: 'Were the *Odyssey* and the *Iliad* or other versions of the hero legend—stories about radical separation and violence—exemplary stories for men to tell themselves?' (Gilligan 2003, xiv). If we agree that these legends are a priori gendered masculine, we might ask if the figure of the *singular heroic female* is even thinkable in a culture that imagines women's identity as precisely constituted via connection and relatedness, and as located in the domestic or private sphere.

In writing *Atlas Shrugged*, Rand would come closer, with her protagonist Dagny Taggart, to creating a Randian female hero understandable in classic heroic terms, than her previous work had allowed for. Yet, for all Dagny's emancipated strength as COO of a railway, her affairs with several characters in the book, culminating in her love for the ideal hero, John Galt, mark her as, in Rand's words, no less a 'consummate man-worshiper' than either Dominique Francon or Ayn Rand. When we compare Ayn Rand and Howard Roark (and—onscreen—Mirren's Ayn and Cooper's Roark), the equivalence initially suggested between two heroic individualists, espousing their being-for-the-self, is fatally complexified by sex. This lack of perfect equivalence is not only rooted in Rand's dubious ideas about What Women Want, but also in the structural institutions that shaped those very ideas, in the versions of gendered heroism that are culturally available to us, and in the kinds of narratives that can be thought, written, and screened about men's and women's lives.

NOTES

1. Randian thought is very little referenced in film scholarship. A notable recent exception is the work of Kyle Barrowman (e.g. Barrowman 2017; 2018) who has attempted, in a number of essays, to use Objectivist principles and Rand's writing on aesthetics to ground a philosophical and aesthetic theory of cinema.
2. Chapter 9 is focused on an extended discussion of this text.
3. For more on Rand and race, including an analysis of 'Racism', see Chapter 10.
4. See, for example, Painter (1997).
5. Rand's words are cited in Branden (1987, 134, n.2). See also Brownmiller (1999). For an excellent assessment of the convoluted logic of desire and rape in *The Fountainhead*, critics' assessments of it, and Rand's responses to them, see Love Brown (2015). See also Chapter 4 for further discussion of this issue.

BIBLIOGRAPHY

Barrowman, Kyle. 2017. Philosophical problems in contemporary art criticism. Objectivism, poststructuralism, and the axiom of authorship. *Journal of Ayn Rand Studies* 17 (2): 153–200.
———. 2018. The future of art criticism: Objectivism goes to the movies. *Journal of Ayn Rand Studies* 18 (2): 165–228.
Branden, Barbara. 1987 [1986]. *The passion of Ayn Rand*. New York: Anchor.
Brownmiller, Susan. 1999. Ayn Rand: A traitor to her own sex. In *Feminist interpretations of Ayn Rand*, ed. Mimi Reisel Gladstein and Chris Matthew Sciabarra, 63–65. Pennsylvania: The Pennsylvania State University Press.
Brown Love , Susan. 2015. Ayn Rand and rape. *The Journal of Ayn Rand Studies* 15 (1): 3–22.

Crowther, Bosley. 1949. The screen in review; Gary Cooper plays an idealistic architect in film version of *The Fountainhead*. *New York Times*, 9 July. https://www.nytimes.com/1949/07/09/archives/the-screen-in-review-gary-cooper-plays-an-idealistic-architect-in.html.

Downing, Lisa. 2019. *Selfish women*. London and New York: Routledge.

Durgnat, Raymond, and Scott Simmon. 1988. *King Vidor, American*. Berkeley, Los Angeles and London: University of California Press.

Gilligan, Carol. 2003 [1982; 1993]. *In a different voice: Psychological theory and women's development*. Cambridge, MA and London: Harvard University Press.

Painter, Nell Irvin. 1997. Writing biographies of women. *Journal of Women's History* 9 (2): 154–163.

Rand, Ayn. 1961. Check your premises. *The Objectivist Newsletter* 1.

———. 1971. The age of envy, part II. *The Objectivist*. August.

———. 1988 [1968]. About a woman president. In *The voice of reason: Essays in Objectivist thought*, ed. Leonard Peikoff. New York: New American Library.

———. 1992 [1957]. *Atlas shrugged*. New York: Signet.

———. 1997. *Letters of Ayn Rand*, ed. Michael S. Berliner. Introduction by Leonard Peikoff. New York: Plume.

———. 1999 [1997]. *The journals of Ayn Rand*, ed. David Harriman. Foreword by Leonard Peikoff. New York: Plume.

———. 2000. *The art of fiction*, ed. Tore Boeckmann. Introduction by Leonard Peikoff. New York: Plume.

Schleier, Merrill. 2009. *Skyscraper cinema: Architecture and gender in American film*. Minneapolis: University of Minnesota Press.

Shaw, Dan. 2013. *The Fountainhead. Senses of Cinema* 68. August. http://sensesofcinema.com/2013/cteq/the-fountainhead/#10.

Vidor, King. 2012. King Vidor on *The Fountainhead. Cinemagumbo: Random musings on the art of classic film*. March 28.

CHAPTER 7

At Home with Marx and Rand: Returning Man in Pre-history

Bonnie McGill

Dear Sir,

Perhaps at *this* outset, to head off what could well collapse into *unreasonable* protest, I should begin by explaining my *reasoning* for this protest. Letter. It is only *right* that I say, here, quite clearly, that this letter is mine and mine alone, that is, Ayn Rand in *Capitalism: The Unknown Ideal* contends that '[a]n individual has no right to do a 'sit-in' in the home or office of a person he disagrees with – and he does not acquire the right by joining a gang' (Rand 1967, 256). Disagreement must be done from afar, and is already bound up in certain strictures demanding what is and is not proper, or *right* in the display of such disagreement. There cannot be a confrontation between the opposing parties. There are clearly demarcated limits. Perhaps I could not call this freedom of speech, or even perhaps a freedom of protest, if the rules are already set by what is (not) *right*.

The right to disagree—a gang cannot justify the 'sit-in' despite there being an alternative order at work in the gang; it is not the *right* kind of order. What would be right, by this account? Although perhaps, reasoning

B. McGill (✉)
Ipswich, UK

© The Author(s) 2020
N. Cocks (ed.), *Questioning Ayn Rand*,
Palgrave Studies in Literature, Culture and Economics,
https://doi.org/10.1007/978-3-030-53073-0_7

it out *now*, I have started off, headed off, on the wrong foot: 'But in order to be heard, one must have something to say. To have that, one must know one's case. One must know it fully, logically, consistently, all the way down to philosophical fundamentals' (269).

'One' cannot simply be heard. There is a necessary history to the hearing, or the hearing which is promised—there are certain strictures which involve what is already prepared, a possession which is displaced over and over. And this route which returns (to) the origin, the baseline, the 'philosophical fundamentals' is itself that which is already being returned to, along its peculiar mapping: 'fully, logically, consistently'. Although, I would like to *reason* it out, that is, logically, although this logic will be somewhat tangential, a detour perhaps to root out what is at stake here, to pursue the (dis)possession of that which is logical and consistent and what this relationship is to the knowing of 'one's case'.

What is my case? I would like to sit-in on an idea of (pre)history in which I read both Marx and Rand to be invested.[1] I say sit-in because Marx and Rand could well be viewed as occupying opposing sides and yet I would like to (protest,) trace out their joint investment in an idea of man as self-producing and therefore pre-historical, which then guarantees history as history. I say sit-in on because this is something I read to be already at work in the texts. Can I know it all the way down? Chris Matthew Sciabarra would contend that I could, having himself read Marx and Rand together in *Total Freedom: Toward a Dialectical Libertarianism* because of an investment in dialectics. He frames this as a context-keeping, allowing thinkers a complete grasp of the situation; dialectics (context) also being trans-temporal (Sciabarra 2000). To have a particular context across time would be to forward an idea of an absolute history. And indeed, Sciabarra's position is then akin to Rand's Objectivist stance. *However*, it is this grasp of a totality which is of issue—for in both Rand and Marx's constitution of man, there is a necessary (e)lapse of time within which man is re-produced, brought back to himself, and this must occur, or at least be *claimed* to occur, *outside* of time. I will then turn to read the implications of this constitution of man in an episode of the comic *Amazing Spiderman,* not least because the comic book artist Steve Ditko subscribed to Rand's philosophy, but also because I read the constitution of man to be bound up with an idea of silence and secrecy.[2] Do I know this all the way down? Only if I could know myself in my (complete) context. But then I think I am perhaps getting ahead of myself.

I have said root out, dig up, some sort of revelation of the 'philo-sophical fundamentals' which 'one' could (possibly) already have in one's possession—or at least, projected to have, at the end of the root. 'One' would already have to be within the space of revelation, outside of all history—of the 'case'—in the *post* of history. This root would be a closure to one's case. Can I say that however and maintain it? Consistently? Fully? Logically? That is, in all its guises? Although, *since* the revelation, 'one' knows what the case is by all these routes of knowing. The order of the case would be framed by these particular ways of knowing. I cannot *therefore* reasonably claim that logic is within the bounds, on the same route, as what it is to know the case 'fully'. Or even 'consistently' for that matter. *Hence,* can 'one' know the close of the case? Can 'one' have possession of the 'case' as a closed system? Put another way, is this pre-history pre-requisite to making oneself heard about a totality? If there are different ways in which to know the case, is it such that 'philosophical fundamentals' are specific to the 'fully, consistently, logically'? Or is it that 'philosophical fundamentals' are here as the root, at the close, which is reached regardless of the route taken or known?

To have it 'fully, consistently, logically, all the way down to philo-sophical fundamentals'. I have said that there are three routes—'fully, consistently, logically'—and that if these are the knowing of the 'case', this is to know the 'case' in various incarnations, but nevertheless to know the 'case' in its difference as the same—it nevertheless *remains* the 'case'. These three knowings *of* therefore constitute possession of the 'case', the being-able-to-make-oneself-heard, its pre-history, as that which is framed and constituted by the loss of any other ways of knowing. But this loss would not be an absolute loss—indeed, the list by which the 'case' is prescribed to be known recalls the loss within the exclusion. Logically, therefore, what is excluded from the readying of possession, of the moment at which one can make oneself heard would have to (re)call, listen to, the silence which frames its becoming.

What, then, about 'philosophical fundamentals'? At this point, at the reaching of 'philosophical fundamentals' there is a knowing to stop, to cut off the need to know of the case. Here one must pause. Except, if 'philo-sophical fundamentals' play at the root of the case, which is necessary to be known (to have), this is something of an arbitrary end in that 'philo-sophical fundamentals' are known to be ('fully, consistently, logically'?) sufficient to *have*. Their being the moment of termination facilitates the return of the case into a possession which *subsequently* can be said. *That said*, it must be lost in the others' hearing—'in order to be heard, one must have something to say'.

Yet if these 'philosophical fundamentals' are what is to be (re)gained, 'all the way down', not only would the knowing 'fully, consistently, logically' have to be reaffirmed, assured, at every moment, 'all the way down', so what it means to know in these ways, routes, is under question continually, and is as such then indebted to their own histories, respectively, and together, but also then, *where* or what is the 'case'? What would it mean to (re)affirm that this is still *it*? To know it, to know it, but to nevertheless not admit the 'case' into the history outside of the 'fully, consistently, logically'? The 'case', that which one has, or perhaps (now) should have, but by all (un)reasonable logic, does not have, is that which cannot be possessed, except in a knowing as a knowing in negation—to the list— to this list of routes to know which cannot close the 'case'. What would it mean to (re)call the 'philosophical fundamentals'? It would be to do with a (re)calling, a readiness to listen to that which has already escaped as itself, that a bringing back of 'philosophical fundamentals', for one has already been all the way down this, *these*, route(s), is to reconstitute the case, the object, the goal which was left and returned to because the 'case' cannot be fully known. The case remains, and remains because its close, the possession of it, its object and it as object has to be dispossessed, this history of readying to be heard has to break with it fully to begin again—to *make* oneself heard, to be heard. *Not yet.*

So now that there has been read out a case for the state of revolution, I would like to turn, in my turn to another phase, step, another sequence of what it means to be beginning again. 'The first step is to make oneself heard [...] There are many civilized ways to do it: protest meetings, public petitions, speeches, pamphlets, letters-to-editors' (Rand 1967, 269). Hence the address. The history was not a step, not a movement which in any way goes *towards* making oneself heard. Yet since I now find myself between history and its beginning, or perhaps rather prehistory and history, *once more*, I would like to think about what is at stake in making oneself heard. It is, by this account, both a continuation—the first step to be taken is already known to be necessary, it is necessary as a response—but is also an intervention, this 'step' is to do with a transition, a difference, but in sequence. 'The first step', not forgetting that disagreement cannot trespass on another, but must be done in one of the 'many civilized ways'.

I said earlier (am I making myself heard?) that this letter is mine and mine alone, and yet I headed off with Ayn Rand, and by so doing, have read out a possession which is displaced over and over—*is* there possession? What can I lay claim to as rightly mine? Especially as I am *sitting in* in some way (by way of protest) to all that I am reading, writing, here? I am not quite where I said I was.

Possession of what is mine, or the negation of such. I am thinking of a claim now by Karl Marx in his 'Economic and Philosophical Manuscripts'. I might just (dis)possess it here, *at length*:

> But since for socialist man the *whole of what is called world history* is nothing more than the creation of man through human labour, and the development of nature for man, he therefore has palpable and incontrovertible proof of his self-mediated *birth*, of his *process of emergence*. Since the *essentiality [Wesenhaftigkeit]* of man and of nature, man as the existence of nature for man and nature as the existence of man for man, has become practically and sensuously perceptible, the question of an *alien* being, a being above nature and man – a question which implies an admission of the unreality of nature and of man – has become impossible in practice. *Atheism,* which is a denial of this unreality, no longer has any meaning, for atheism in a *negation of God*, through which it asserts the *existence of man.* But socialism as such no longer needs such mediation. Its starting-point is the *theoretically and practically sensuous consciousness* of man and of nature as *essential beings.* It is the *positive self-consciousness* of man, no longer mediated through the abolition of religion, just as *real life* is positive reality no longer mediated through the abolition of private property, through *communism.* Communism is the act of positing as the negation of the negation, and is therefore a *real phase*, necessary for the next period of historical development, in the emancipation and recovery of mankind. *Communism* is the necessary form and the dynamic principle of the immediate future, but communism is not as such the goal of human development – the form of human society. (Marx 1844, 357–358)

Having had that *tête-à-tête* with Marx, although perhaps rather more *mit jemandem unter vier Augen sprechen,* I hope now I can (re)turn and head off again. That is, if one of the implications read out of Ayn Rand's formulation of how to make oneself heard undermines what it is to have possession of something, then I would like to now think through the similar claims made around communism as 'the act of positing as the negation of the negation', and how this is bound up with a continued reformulation of what man is, that is essential, or, to borrow a word from Rand, what is 'fundamental', *philosophically*.

Possession and its whereabouts are bound up with time frames—equally I could say history. This is not a new observation (more eyes than four here), and indeed playing off the history of the article, consigned to context, I would like to read out, slowly, somewhat akin to O'Malley, but probably, *no doubt,* in cahoots with Jacques Derrida's *Spectres of Marx,* what it is about history which has to be done away with, *interrupted,* for man.[3]

I see I have begun already, and at the turn of the formulation 'But since'. What is to be read, or rather reread, begins by bringing back to itself what is past; that a history is reformulated here as that in which what is to follow is in distinction to this. But this is not that history is by any means universal—there is more than one *being* of history, and *this* history, that is, what is 'for socialist man' is proof of something other and nothing more than this. Absolute proof, with the frame; there is no excess here of the one supplementing the other. Yet the history of proof is in its transformation, and has the corollary that there nevertheless *remains* (the 'case' again, 'all the way down', having resurfaced), history.

Is it history? That is, is history history? I could say yes—'[b]ut since' being the break, I could say yes because 'the *whole of what is called world history*' is already dealing with a (re)calling of a '*what*', this is not '*world history*'. World history is necessarily and already, in its own history, beyond that which it is called into being to follow. It already re-establishes its own history, not that there was a teleology which arrived at world history as world history, but because it is necessary to have this '*whole of [the] what*' which wholly escapes its calling. I could then say that this would be a case of mistaken callings, identities, in that this is not to do with '*world history*', but rather the '*whole of what*'. This '*what*' is put into circulation as already other to itself. Yet this otherness, the otherness of '*world history*', is nevertheless required in the framing of yet another turn of difference. This (re)naming, or rather the move of (re)naming that is the 'development of nature for man', has to *wholly* displace the '*what*' since this would be a move which (re)claims what it is to be. I could say (re)claims essences—the *what-ness*—which is already bound up in being other to itself. I could say *alienation*, if I did not fear it might be Marx's property.

So it is a case of, here, Marx rethinking the framework out of which there *is*, and if this is the case, then it is not so much that what is 'for socialist man' is a clean break from the past, from history, or even so much history as modified, whether by the *world* or the *what*, but rather that there is an indebtedness to this displacing. This system has to *recall against* the '*whole of what is called world history*'. All that has been (re)named *is* because it cannot return as such—that there is an essence which is put into circulation as produced, and this system is *not* a system as such, that is, cannot be the very *thing* therefore which is, because it would be to stop the creation and development. It can no longer be *recalled*—not in its difference as difference within what is '*for* socialist man [my italics]'. Whatever is 'for socialist man' is already to do with a separation from a transcendental history, this is not History, if I could put so much weight on a capital letter, but rather that the being of 'socialist man' is already a mode of being which can be known to be that which *re*opens the case for what it means to be. No longer a calling, the '*whole of [the] what* [...] is nothing more than the creation of man through human labour'.

It is perhaps this 'nothing more' which turns world history absolutely into 'the creation of man through human labour'. For it would be something of a double move, I could say a returning move, the 'negation of the negation', which in one stroke would have to account for, *recall* the whole (of what (?)) to be 'the creation of man'. If this is *all* 'for socialist man', what *is* already (whether called, recalled, mis-called), has to be within this system, but *also*, that 'socialist man' cannot be a part of this history, is already beyond this history of becoming. This history—creation and development—is 'for' him. Being positioned outside of 'his *process of emergence*', he can then know 'the creation of man through human labour, and the development of nature for man'. He, by this account, has already *emerged*, fully present. Which would be both the end of history and its beginning—that 'socialist man' has 'proof of his self-mediated *birth*, of his *process of emergence*', he would have to return to himself, know his origin, be witness for himself. P(l)ay double-time.

The investment in the being of 'socialist man' is such that *his* being would have to already have been established. The circularity involved in this self-proof, the *knowing* of existence, 'palpable and incontrovertible proof' is already 'his' possession. Yet here with the self-possession I can see (or at least the shadow of a seeing) Derrida (re)turning with the *Spectres*. This proof would have to have already occurred for 'socialist man' *without* time. This is a move which cannot be traced: the establishing of 'socialist man'. Why? If the 'proof' is 'palpable and incontrovertible', the turn of *world history* absolutely to be 'nothing more', and here I am reading a claim *to* absolute transformation, that is, a complete break from any history which would frame the transformation as transformation, would necessarily have to be claimed by another and *not* 'socialist man'. *Hence* 'socialism as such no longer needs such mediation'. The process of proof, which would be the establishing of a socialism which deals in absolutes, the *present*, would have to be consigned to pre-history. And this doubly—for not only does pre-history begin with the being of 'socialist man', but this pre-history must then begin again, return to justify, head off (again) *this* beginning with the proof of that emergence and origin. That is, return to being *world history*.

World history in the sense of a universalism.

In the nature of protest, to continue the address, I would like to pose some questions—firstly, why is it that despite the manoeuvrings of socialist man to drop out of history to guarantee man, mankind is lost and requires recovery? Would this not make mankind itself, and the investment in its being man qua man, also a passing phase? And perhaps a further question: if communism is a real phase, and part of a history to recover mankind, and man and nature have already been established as essential beings, does this not equate to recovery? What is it about mankind which is nevertheless *outside*; what is to be recovered, what is *alien* as yet to this history of presence? Is there not bound up in this an idea that there is something about mankind which cannot be accounted for? That is, of the future (and arguably pre-history where it was lost to then be recovered), which goes beyond presence? That is, beyond presence and into the 'next period of historical development'?

To read out these issues with Marx's constitution of 'man', I would like to stage a reply from Rand, since, knowing what follows, there is in her philosophy a paradoxical investment in presence which works against her own claims to individualism and privacy.

> Since religion is a primitive form of philosophy – an attempt to offer a comprehensive view of reality – many of its myths are distorted, dramatized allegories based on some element of truth, some actual, if profoundly elusive, aspect of man's existence. One of such allegories, which men find particularly terrifying, is the myth of a supernatural recorder from whom nothing can be hidden, who lists all of man's deeds – the good and the evil, the noble and the vile – and who confronts a man with that record on judgment day.

That myth is true, not existentially, by psychologically. The merciless recorder is the integrating mechanism of a man's subconscious; the record is his *sense of life*.

A sense of life is a pre-conceptual equivalent of metaphysics, an emotional, subconsciously integrated appraisal of man and of existence. It sets the nature of a man's emotional responses and the essence of his character. (Rand 1975, 25)

What would be terrifying is to relinquish a claim to privacy—to have another know everything: 'from whom nothing can be hidden', but also that the list, or 'record', 'confronts a man [...] on judgment day'. Not only is there a fear of another knowing the self, but this is then bound up with the self as 'deeds', as a 'record' returning, confronting 'a man'. What is set up as terrifying is a confrontation with the self, the self in writing, the history of the self.

What is it which constitutes the history of the self? And further, if the history of the self is here the self as list, record, what is it about lists and records, *writing*, which is to be feared? Somewhat ironic, in a philosophy of literature. There is a witness, that this history is something to which a man can be held accountable, judged by, and crucially, judged by another. If I was to dig up etymologies, I could perhaps play around with the Latin roots of protest—that of witness, assertion, publicly. What of the witness? '[A] supernatural recorder from whom nothing is hidden, who lists all of man's deeds'. I said something earlier about staging a reply from Ayn Rand, I could equally have said a protest, a witnessing of Marx by Rand, for here is 'man' as returned, 'man' as excessive to an idea of self as a totality for the 'supernatural recorder' becomes '[t]he merciless recorder [which] is the integrating mechanism of a man's subconscious; the record is his *sense of life*'. I could equally turn this protest about again and say that Marx is protesting the *alien* of the self, the supernatural, thinking through the moves by which man can go *forth* from this, that Marx is a witness to this same move of Rand, where the alien is exorcised as subconscious—that the externality is turned to become an external internally. It is no longer terrifying.

I might protest myself, against this last point. In part, because if the terrifying is to do with the 'supernatural recorder from whom nothing can be hidden, who lists all of man's deeds [...] and who confronts a man with that record', the terrifying would be the corollary not only of 'that record', but 'that record' as that which reduces the 'nothing' which is everything to 'all of man's deeds'. That is to say, there is some*thing* about this 'from whom nothing can be hidden' which nevertheless *hides* that which is not 'man's deeds'. The terrifying therefore would be that the self is returned within a particular framework—that of the list, and that list is only the 'deeds'—but terrifying especially because the everything of the nothing which can(not) be hidden is that which is *not* returned.

Rather like Marx in regard to man in the sense of a promise of absolute presence—no longer negation of negation—Rand would be arguing for the possibility of the lack of a lack in man; there is no loss of his history, his self, rather this is what is his 'essence'. But I would like to think this through further, for although there would *seem* to be a shift in that what is 'recorded' and 'record[ing]' (itself already to do with replacing, displacing) changes from a 'supernatural recorder' to 'man's subconscious', there is nevertheless an uncanny repetition of the myth of the supernatural. Before I read this out, however, I would like to say this is not to position Rand as 'supernatural', but rather to think about how the claims made to 'man's subconscious', which would, by implication *not* be known to man, are nevertheless able be traced by Rand ('from whom nothing can be hidden'), and that further, if a 'sense of life is a preconceptual equivalent of metaphysics' how is Rand able to know what is before it (?) is thought. Or to turn it another way, before its being, but before its being as *nevertheless being*.

This framing rehearses how the proof of existence for socialist man must already have occurred, and this is not 'socialist man' speaking for himself, but rather a formulating by Marx of what has occurred. To follow Marx's claims, what has already occurred for socialist man, within the negation of the negation, could not, strictly speaking, be thought, and this cannot be thought as happening *in time*. A 'sense of life', Marx's proof, cannot be *thought*, reasoned, in time, for this would mean that if it 'sets the nature of a man's emotional responses and the essence of his character', there would be no 'nature of a man's emotional responses' nor 'essence of his character' as already established—that is to say, without this pre-conceptuality, both would be subject to the same reasoning, logic, *production*: essence and nature would not *be* so much as be *to be*. Time frames in the claims of both texts are subject to perspectives, respectively, which must necessarily disrupt, interrupt, *protest* the claims being made in their very formulations.

The subconscious therefore becomes the site at which there has already been the integration; 'the merciless recorder is the integrating mechanism of a man's subconscious; the record is his *sense of life*'. There are two things which I would like to raise here, one being a question as to the merciless, and whether this is a continuation of the claims around what was terrifying in relation to the supernatural, and the other being what is at stake in the claim to the 'integrating mechanism', for the 'of' would be to position it *not* as wholly the subconscious, but something belonging to it.

To take up the question of the mercilessness in relation to 'the integrating mechanism' is to come up against an idea of the infinite. What is merciless about this is that it threatens, if not disrupts, any essential idea of man. Put another way, it demands a thinking which refuses closure, for the mercilessness of 'the integrating mechanism' is both unsparing in this venture for it records all, and yet this 'all' nevertheless calls into question, by it being (always) 'integrating', what it would mean to claim such an (in)finitude. The time invoked by the 'integrating' means that *being* is already divided within itself. There is no *being* at *a* moment. The claim to 'man's subconscious' plays out this impossibility of closure and challenges the grounding of man's essence as essence for this is what cannot of itself be accessed; it is not self-defining but claimed by another.

Would this then be socialist man? 'Its [socialism's] starting-point is the *theoretically and practically sensuous consciousness* of man and of nature as *essential beings*'? But also, that if the integration is to do with his '*sense of life*' and this in itself is 'a pre-conceptual equivalent of metaphysics, an emotional, subconsciously integrated appraisal of man and of existence' this requires a subconscious which exists prior to the man, before life, before thought, and yet already knowing 'man and [...] existence'.

This subconscious has already *lived*, although perhaps not bodily, by this account; is this terrifying? Or I could start perhaps thinking of the alien, Marx coming back round. There has already been formed a judgement, an 'appraisal', the subconscious is the witness. The witness to *what* however? Have I not already said '[a] sense of life is a pre-conceptual equivalent of metaphysics, an emotional, subconsciously integrated appraisal of man and of existence'? Well maybe I said Ayn Rand said it. And while I am here chasing origin(ator)s, this ghost of a judgement, appraisal, is not then subject to logic; it is subconsciously integrated. It cannot be held to account, this judgement is excessive to reason, it *is*, and *is* having been integrated as what is alien to this system (yet more *tête-à-têtes*). There is, bound up with this integrating system an idea that whatever it is to be integrated, or what has been integrated, indeed, by all accounts I am not sure exactly *where* I am in the time frame, *post*, marker, (somew)here, is nevertheless that which is already set up as different.

This '*sense of life*' is that which grounds as entirely with*out* grounding, is alien to the system of logic, or rationality which Rand elsewhere advocates, and yet necessary:

> A sense of life represents a man's early value-integrations, which remain in a fluid, plastic, easily amendable state, while he gathers knowledge to reach full *conceptual* control and thus *drive* his inner mechanism. A full conceptual control means a consciously directed process of cognitive integration, which means: a conscious *philosophy* of life. (ibid., 29)

I would like, now, to think through this dichotomy of conscious/unconscious and read Rand alongside the claims made by Marx which I left hanging some time ago, for both are invested in consciousness, whether as a '*philosophy* of life', or a beginning for socialism, as what constitutes man.

There is a difficulty in asking the question again, or pursuing what a 'sense of life' is, for I would be replaying the moves, in a *sense*, that Rand is—perhaps it is because this, *or that*, 'sense of life' is bound up with representation, allegories, myths, the pre-conceptual; a *list*. I could very well re-start this question with the question of what is at stake in the list? Or even again, the list which I have just now constructed. What is it that I am trying to say here? That there is something about the integration which is indebted to the construction of the list. Here is another: 'a man's early value-integrations [...] remain in a fluid, plastic, easily amendable state'. This is supplementary, or I could say here that the 'early value-integrations' are themselves already *not*. For this is a system of representation which for Rand can be known, always in a state of revelation, despite its revolutions; the history of man is for Rand its own mechanism, or perhaps meta-mechanism. What I want to say—have I dug it up from some subconscious? Impossible to trace—is that the 'value-integrations' are already caught up in a system which revolves on a relationship of worth for which there is no justification; or at least these 'value-integrations' are not reasonable. I could say, are out of control 'while he gathers knowledge to reach full *conceptual* control and *drive* his inner mechanism'. It would be a case, *still the case*, of gaining control of value—that is, a control of the means by which 'man and [...] existence' are known; a control of the mechanism, of the production, a control of the system. I see Marx, or at least his writing returning here.

'A full conceptual control means a consciously directed process of cognitive integration, which means: a conscious *philosophy* of life'; this goal to be (re)achieved. But here I could say that the list reasserts itself—if I could ever claim the close of the list, if I could claim the *itself*, and not be bound up in a deferral of what *is* (yet another list)—in that if 'one must not express "intentions, opinions, objectives or motives" without stating one's reasons for them – i.e., without identifying their basis in reality', the reasoning is to do with a grounding in reality (ibid., v). I said that the goal is to be (re)achieved, this would be because the integrating system must be replayed itself as itself. There is a move from the 'integrating mechanism', the record of which is 'his *sense of life*' to the 'sense of life [being an...] *integrated* appraisal of man and of existence [my italics]'. It is this which requires some doubled time frame, or perhaps a pre-history. To put it another way, integration must be reworked therefore—consciously, as itself, already being, for integration is always *to be* integrated (itself).

But what is it that is being (re)integrated? If reason is the taking control, a 'consciously directed process' and 'opinions, objectives, or motives' are based in reality, but cannot of themselves be known to be *in reality* without reason, would it not be that reality is the very site of (re)integration; or put another way, that what justifies 'opinions, objective, or motives', *reason*, (another list), is not reality? 'Man's need of precise definitions rests on the Law of Identity: A is A, a thing is itself' (ibid., 78). *Socialism's starting point...* How to know this? It would be that in an effort to ground what is known, the pre-conceptual, what is *already* integrated, but not as itself as being, but as a value-judgement, would have to, on the one hand, *promise* reality. The integrated relies on the idea that the 'external' has been made 'internal'. This has already occurred, but to *know* this, to be sure of the reality, pre-historically and this in the sense of a personal history, there has to be a re-integration of what was integrated—although, as in the claims of Marx, only another, I could say Rand, can know this—that is, can trace the (re)integration.

Why is this important, or *necessary*? Partly because 'A is A, a thing is itself'. It is already integrated. It can be reasoned, because it is *already*, and being already, man can put it at a distance, walk around it, identify it, trace it back to its origin, its 'basis in reality'. *The thing is*, if this loop is reasoned out, there never was a thing in reality—there were 'value-judgements', there were 'appraisal[s]', there was already a system by which there was not reality proper but an *ex*change. And I mean here that the change cannot be traced, the object, thing, opinion, objective, *goal*, the *pre-* is already in the *post*.

On its way to—

'[O]nly Man is an end in himself' (ibid., 164). If Rand were going for universalisms, the whole of world history, *reality, maybe*, then man would have to put himself on the table, be up for questioning, and yet, '[m]an, by his nature, cannot refrain from generalizing; he cannot live moment by moment, without context, without past or future' (ibid., 26). In general, then, 'A is A, a thing is itself', *specifically*, I could start by saying that 'A' is *not* an end in itself. It may well be 'itself', but 'itself' only in the repeat, and therefore would reiterate the loss of the goal, *within* itself, the thing is the thing, and yet 'Man is an end in himself', does not go towards anything but himself, and here perhaps ethics would come into play, that 'Man' must stand apart from all else, value is premised in this difference. Hence that 'Man' cannot be subject to reiterations, 'he cannot live moment by moment', which would be too much of a specificity, that is, would require a continual rethinking of what it is to *be*. '[P]ast' and 'future' are both *in general*, as 'context' is. There has to be a time frame in which man lives, and yet this would be to reduce difference *in general*. Living 'moment by moment' would disrupt the thing *being* itself, the *is* which would guarantee existence over time, history as an ordered unity, reality which has been derived from the 'sense of life', and has formed the 'essence of this character'. Moment by moment, this would have to be re-thought, re-integrated. If such were the case it would not only, by implication of Rand's claims, prevent the gaining of knowledge, and knowledge therefore is *in general*, no need to think it through further, but also that what has been already integrated by the subconscious, the 'sense of life' would no longer be the grounding which returns reality as what is reasonable and reasoned: which *is*. Indeed, the subconscious which for Rand is both that which cannot be traced further, that is, has already integrated, and that which must be traced, read by her as the site which has already integrated difference, is what would, if life is to be thought moment by moment, be that which could no longer be thought as that which knows, beyond being, reality, which, until 'full *conceptual* control' is reached, 'remain[s] in a fluid, plastic, easily amendable state'. For, the 'value-integrations' are the reality, or at least, the reasoned reality once knowledge has reiterated, ordered, them; re-ordered the 'inner mechanism'. Driving the (sub)conscious mechanism—there is nothing hidden from Rand, or man, by these claims; nothing excessive.

Except man.

Man must already be at an end, in himself. Man, and only man, must be that which is already. Already *post*, in the post to himself.

Marx: 'Its [socialism's] starting-point is the *theoretically and practically sensuous consciousness* of man and of nature as *essential beings*. It is the *positive self-consciousness*'.

Rand: 'A is A'.

There is nothing lost here. Having held Marx in suspense for some time, I think I might pass over into the next phase of mankind, but first: 'Hegel remarks somewhere that all facts and personages of great importance in world history occur, as it were, twice. He forgot to add: the first time as a tragedy, the second as a farce' (Marx 1973a, 96).

A series of doublings, the remark of which is itself doubled. Somewhere. Which would be perhaps that whatever is doubled cannot *rightly* be put back in its proper place.

I said earlier (so twice now, which is the farce? Although perhaps the standard of greatness will save me), that there is something about man, for Marx, which cannot be accounted for, despite communism being to do with mankind as essential beings, and the knowledge of this: it is conscious knowledge. Somewhere Rand said –

I wonder, then, in all its revolutions, doublings, whether it is to do with *how* reality is thought, that is, there is something at work with '*communism*', being to do with a 'through', and 'Communism' being an 'act' and '*Communism*' being 'the necessary form and dynamic principle of the immediate future.'

Somewhere Rand said something about a record of deeds.

'[C]ommunism' in its first outing (at least, here, this time) is a mechanism by which there was the being of '*real life*'—the frame for this 'positive reality', albeit 'mediated'. Arguably this is also an act in it being to do with 'the abolition of private property', but it is also a mechanism by which 'positive reality' (or would that be '*real life*'?) can exceed it. '[C]ommunism' is, or can be, history. Indeed, the time frame is required at each revolution of what is communism, so although 'through *communism*' there is '*real life*', the latter is not indebted to '*communism*' for its being over time. Or at least, *no longer*.

There is something about this no longer; 'socialism as such no longer needs such mediation'—of history, of its coming into being. At some point, it was necessary. I could equally well question whether this was *ever* a necessity, if the mediations can be read as mediations—does not, to take up Marx's claims, *real life* remain, despite its (non)mediation? So would this not come back to an investment in an absolute?

Marx writes to P. V. Annenkov:

> M. Proudhon, incapable of following the real movement of history, produces a phantasmagoria which presumptuously claims to be dialectical. He does not feel it necessary to speak of the seventeenth, the eighteenth or the nineteenth century, for his history proceeds in the misty realm of imagination and rises far above space and time. In short, it is not history but old Hegelian junk, it is not profane history – a history of man – but sacred history – a history of ideas. (Marx 1973b, 661)

In his dismissal of Proudhon, Marx claims an ability to see, or know, 'the real movement of history', and how this should be thought—that is, across centuries, *in* 'space and time', and also that it should be 'a history of man'. But if this is what it means to be 'following the real movement of history', which is, more or less, 'a history of man', how man moves, this would require the movement to be stilled, man to be still(ed). This 'real movement of history' has, by this account, already gone ahead to be followed, and this following is universal—Proudhon's failure to follow, does, by implication, position 'the real movement' as open to being traced. Indeed, what is set up here are two dichotomies, one between the real and the phantasmagorical, and another between 'profane history' and the 'history of ideas'. Man, by Marx's account, is not an idea; real, and in space and time, man should therefore be located within this movement.

Where within this movement? Although perhaps 'movement' would be better, since this 'movement' is absolute, does not move from itself, has already *made* the move. What would be the *right time* to locate 'man'? Arguably one has to speak of centuries, but then *no longer*. Here is perhaps the interruption of this trans-century move. I said something about communism being a mechanism, the frame which mediates, but *no longer*. If this is to do with what brings into being, what happens to this system when the being is being? If, as Marx claims, there is *no longer* a need for mediation, that there is presence—what would happen to history then?—although latterly this presence, '*real life*', 'positive reality', the '*self-consciousness* of man and of nature as *essential beings*' required communism, but no longer, what then is communism?

It is not 'the emancipation and recovery of mankind'. Communism is *no longer* to do with a bringing into presence; these lists of what is *no longer* the case ironically play out the difficulty, if not impossibility, of claiming '*positive self-consciousness*'. Perhaps a charge could be levelled that Marx already claims to be dealing with a negation of a negation, this is not about 'having' something—'private property'—*but*, this is *no longer* about a freeing from value systems *if* '[i]t is the *positive self-consciousness* of man, no longer mediated through the abolition of religion, *just as* [my italics] *real life* is positive reality'. To say that 'positive self-conscious' is a knowing of the self to be essential is here *no longer* the case because of the equivalence. The equality of the 'negation' of the 'abolition of religion' and 'private property' would be to disregard difference and take up a position by which these two things are (in positive reality?) the same, despite the route—or indeed, because there is a root: some system according to which these two can be exchanged. So, perhaps, *in reality*, to answer the question, what is communism, is to consign it to the history books because it takes its being from what is *no longer*. Communism is (the) *no longer*. There cannot be both communism and presence because communism as the framing by which there is the bringing into presence would be to position presence as already lacking its ability to be itself. It cannot then recover mankind.

I want to say that communism breaks all of history as a teleology which *recovers* mankind; I want to say this because it is the negation of the negation. It has to double the move of all that has gone previously— all the mediations and negations which require a supplementation, which require *time*. I want to say this, but *no longer*. *No longer* because all the phantasmagoria, all the non-truths, non-realities or realities which were mediated, *negative* realities, are constituting the need for the freeing of mankind. The freeing and the recovery. So where is man? Somewhere above space and time.

Communism is an act and a form and a principle. (T)here is another list. It is not the goal. This is not to do with what was, but what is *right now, no longer*.

Here is another list: '[c]ommunism is the act of positing as the negation of the negation'. There are acts at play. And this is the real; a '*real* phase'. So it is not that there can be a revelation as such in the revolution, or even that the presence is an end in itself ('Only man is an end in himself'), but that there can be, at this time, known to be 'the next period of historical development'. History, in its heterogeneity, is this list of acts, phases, whether real or not, phantasmagorical or not. Because communism would be the opening onto the next, 'the act of positing as the negation of the negation', plays *itself* out as act, acts as the grounding, and the grounding as an act.

What does it mean, to be 'necessary for the next'? This is perhaps 'the negation of the negation' again in the 'next', I could perhaps say *right now, no longer*, because whatever this 'next' is, 'communism' would have to be that which is always its own pre-history. What is 'next' would itself have to double, to be that which follows, 'the next period of historical development', but also that which is already known to be here as 'next'—it is 'the necessary form and dynamic principle of the immediate future'. There is a prescription for its starting point, it is a *'real* phase', but the reality of this phase is not for itself, that is, not an end in itself. It cannot be 'the goal of human development' because this stopping, and a stopping as the 'form of human society', would fix what it is to be 'human', or at least, 'human development'. That is, Marx has an investment in man as excessive to the 'form' and the 'structure' of society, of history. To stop history would therefore be to stop man, even in the same move in which there must already have been a pre-history for man, hence the 'emancipation and recovery of mankind' is always what is to come, after a sequence of 'next[s]'. There has to be an idea of the 'next' already in place because for Marx, man would have to have already exceeded his own history to be recovered, and cannot thus be *governed* by communism as the ultimate 'goal of human development – the form of human society'.

There is nothing alien about history post-communism—post 'the negation of the negation'. But it is the implications of essentiality to nature and man, and consciousness, which I would now like to think through further in relation to *The Amazing Spider-man* comic, 'Face-to-face with... The Lizard!' The section I would like to start with has Dr. Curtis Connors, who has lost an arm, and subsequently turns into The Lizard, explaining why he is experimenting with reptiles:

> *Dr. Connors*: If a lower order of life, such as certain types of lizards,
>   lose a leg, or any base extremity, they often simply
>   grow a *new* one! If only I could learn how this is done,

and apply the secret to **humans**... think what it would
mean! (Lee and Ditko 1963, 10)

Mrs. Connors as the framing narration then recounts how, after
producing a serum which works on animals, Dr. Connors tries it on
himself.

> *Mrs. Connors*: He drank the bubbling serum before I could stop
>   him! And then...
> *Dr. Connors*: My right shoulder...such a strange sensation! I – I feel
>   *life* returning!
> *Mrs. Connors*: And then...
> *Dr. Connors*: I've **done** it! **I've grown a new arm**! This is the
>   greatest medical feat of all time!
> *Mrs. Connors*: But, the change didn't end there!! No – – the hand,
>   the arm, **all** of Curtis Connors began to change
>   until...
> *Dr. Connors*: What has **happened** to me? What have I **done**? (ibid., 10)

Whatever it is to question what it is to be human, for Dr. Connors at least,
this is not at first jeopardised by the application of the reptile secret of
regeneration. The human is considered that which can be brought back,
or at least part of it, and this would necessitate the human *remaining*
human despite the addition of the reptilian secret of regeneration. The
secret of regeneration is desirable, but this is not a complete regeneration—this is only to do with 'a leg, or any base extremity'—there is,
then, a core which cannot be regenerated. Or should not; for this secret
serum would be such that the change does not stop at the appropriate
time; regeneration would turn on its orderability, that it is not excessive
to what is promised by the secret.

What would be the secret? It has something to do with 'a strange sensation! I – I feel *life* returning!' A sensation of life, Rand returning, but here
life is not something which is familiar. Life is at odds with itself, not least
because I can read a difference in the bold and italics, but also because 'I
– I' would double *doubly* life as that which is excessive to itself. But this
is strange. Life is not about a totality, but rather can be reduced to particular parts—the base extremities, '[m]y right shoulder'—what is felt. But
equally this is also to do with the return of life *as* the problem 'I feel *life*
returning' is then what should not be felt. At least, not consciously, not
knowingly—it could be consigned to the subconscious—so if the 'strange

sensation' is '*life* returning' then this latter would have to be already known to be known as '*life* returning'. And by yet another turn, the 'strange sensation' is (right now) no longer strange as such, that is, can be claimed as what 'I feel', is comprehensible even in its strangeness. Life is uncanny—I think I have been skirting around this. Or at least, the return of it is. This is life returning upon life. There is an 'I' claiming the return of life, so ghosts notwithstanding, this '*life*', even if this is arm-life specifically, would have to be a life claimed from a position of difference, even if that difference is nevertheless life. 'I – I'.

Life, '*life*', would, in the return, be a recuperation of a loss, or the production of the new (arm). It is just this; there is, in the return a completion, 'I've *done* it!' There is a sufficiency to which anything further is beyond what it is to have returned life. But in this, the return is also to do with an idea of control; that what was expected and hoped for has happened. Returning life would be the goal, and the control therefore would rest on the ability to (re)create a whole. The return of life would be to fit within particular limits. Yet '[w]hat have I *done?*' undermines, or perhaps rather, re-opens the question of the 'strange sensation' which was felt. If the return of life was something which could be read as an explanation of the 'strange' because the arm regrew, this is only an explanation of the 'strange' at a particular point. That is to say, an idea of life returning within this system is only at a certain moment. It is not to say that the life returning is explanation of the 'strange sensation' for all time, but rather has a particular history, a time frame to which it is indebted.

Would life be able to return then, in a strict sense? That is to say, if 'I – I feel *life* returning' is a reading of a 'strange sensation', and this is because later Dr. Connors says 'I've *done* it!' then '*life* returning' as explanation is explanation suspended until the future. That is, explanation as justified, as itself, is *itself* indebted to a claim by the 'I' that his action has achieved its aim. So it may be that what is felt can be explained and justified later, but the question would be at which point in time to stop the return, the question of *later*, for this is '*life* returning'. At what point would it be right to stop the return? Having gone all the way down to the root? Whatever is *right* remains waiting. Is not right, right now, not the right secret, but later. Indeed, the return(ing) would be that which otherwise would continue indefinitely. To know it to the root would require a greater infinity. So it would rather be that the stopping of the return at a point in time would be arbitrary, 'I've *done* it!' for this moment. But '*life*' remains 'returning'.

Since Rand invested much in man's deeds, it is interesting that in both cases, 'I've *done* it!' and '[w]hat have I *done?*' are in italics and bold type. The action constitutes the difference, in the sense that it is not a questioning of the '[w]hat', the outcome as such, although this is a reading, but that the question questions that an action, which the 'I' has undertaken, '*done*', has gone awry—that is, there is a questioning now of the lack of (self) control; that the 'I' cannot account for its *own* actions. How to record the secret of returning life when it is still returning? Life has been consigned to history to have the possibility of a return, and yet 'the change didn't end there!! No – – the hand, the arm, *all* of Curtis Connors began to change until…' There is a sequence, 'the hand, the arm, *all* of Curtis Connors began to change'. The body (parts) reconstitute(s) the time frame in which there is the change, but for the '*all*' to be known as 'change', 'Curtis Connors' would have to not change to be that which orders this sequence. If this is '*all* of Curtis Connors', this '*all*' would go some way to supplementing what would be '*all*' in a strict sense. Indeed, in the comic, the picture below the writing shows a hand, albeit green with scales, the lower arm cut off by the frame and in a white lab coat. This reptilian hand is not '*all*', but the beginning of the sequence of the 'change' according to the narration by Mrs. Connors. It *heads off* the sequence, stands in the place of this sequence as sequence, as the history of change. It cannot be arrested. There is, in 'the hand, the arm, *all*' an idea that the 'progression' of change, the *history* of change is not constituted by a continuum, hence then the necessity for the quotation marks of 'progression'.

I have read it as a sequence, but I would like to think about why this is the case, for I can read in the sequence a separation from the different body parts and the commas. If this is progression, a time sequence (*another list*) then it is bound up with an ability to separate, to demarcate specifics *while* knowing the whole. I am thinking of two quotes by Walter Benjamin, from his essay 'Theses on the Philosophy of History', the first being '[h]istory is the subject of a structure whose site is not homogeneous, empty time, but time filled by the presence of the now' and the second being '[t]he true image of the past flits by. The past can be seized only as an image which flashes up at the instant when it can be recognized and is never seen again' (Benjamin [1950], 255, 260). Both ideas of history within Benjamin's claims play out the idea of a separation,[4] that '[t]he past can be seized only as *an* image [my italics]', a different image to what is the 'true image of the past'. The distinction would come from a difference in representation—there is a 'true image', within which representation *is*, indeed, the past is already lost if this 'true image' is '*of* the past [my italics]', and yet what is 'seized' is '[t]he past [...] only as an image which flashes up at the instant when it can be recognized'. This is not the past as objective; the past already has to be within a space of recognition, the appearance on the scene of the past is because the past is already known as such. But this knowing is not transcendental, indeed, rather like the claims around the explanation of the 'strange sensation', this 'flashes up' is that the past, or rather the image of it, cannot be held, brought to a stand-still; there is not the *persistence* of the past. The image of Dr. Connors' transformation is the image of the reptilian hand; this is the *all* of that past.

And yet, like Marx, there is an investment in an idea of presence, a presence which is not homogeneous. History would then be to do with a difference from itself, a returning relationship which does not return, is 'strange' because it cannot return to itself because itself, itself *as* itself is already lost. A series of nows. Up in a flash, then lost.

Can the human return?

> *Mrs. Connors*: Trembling, sobbing like a man possessed, the
> creature who had been Curtis Connors raced
> out into the night [...] He returned the next day! He
> tried to work on a new serum, one which would
> make him human again...but it was hopeless! His
> brain had been too dulled – – too changed!

The human is retrievable, provided that the brain is not 'too dulled – – too changed!' The brain would be that which guarantees (the return of) the human, or at least, its level of dullness, how 'changed' it is, for 'the creature' is nevertheless able to try to (re)produce the human. To whom does the brain belong? Man is now something which is being imitated— 'like a man possessed'—and if '[h]e tried to work on a new serum, one which would make him human again', then the 'he', and the 'him' are not human, and 'Curtis Connors' is now a point of history for 'the creature'. Who, then, is the '[h]is' of '[h]is brain'? For if the '[h]is' is the brain as belonging to 'the creature', this would mean that the dulling and changing happened to the creature's brain, *not* Dr. Connors'. There was no change from Dr. Connors to the creature whereby the brain negotiates and traces this change. There cannot then be a history.

The return to the human is equally headed by the brain, and the help of 'the compound I [Spider-Man] created' (Lee and Ditko 1963, 13). The picture shows the Lizard holding his head saying 'My head! My brain! What – – what is *happening* to me?' (ibid., 19) The narration then frames as 'a fantastic change takes place' Dr. Connors's saying 'I – I'm *human* again!' (ibid.) The return of the human is as a production by another, not a self-production, and by means of science. The 'fantastic' would be the triumph of the human over the animal—that the brain can be turned back; indeed the brain is here that which prefaces the '*happening*' of the change to be '*human* again!' The 'I', always 'I', is also that which cannot be accounted for as either Lizard or Dr. Connors as such, but rather has to be supplemented by the image(s). If the 'brain' *is* what it means to be the Lizard or Dr. Connors—stands in the place of, heads off what it mean to be either, there is nevertheless, in the claim 'My head! My brain! What – – what is *happening* to me?' a 'me' which cannot be reduced to the brain; is excessive to it. Where then would consciousness be? Indeed, there is something about the move of the return of Dr. Connors via 'test tube' which threatens—he 'tampered with forces of nature which must not be tampered with!' such that, at the close of the story, Spider-Man suggests 'we just keep this whole affair a *secret*' (ibid., 13, 20). The transgression as nature, that the human is not absolute, but can be returned, reproduced by science, would then threaten the very doctrine of logic promoted by Randian philosophy even as it is that same reason and intellect of Spider-Man as a scientist, creating the antidote, which saves Dr. Connors. *This* must be the secret. Indeed, to bring Marx back into it—that there is no alien, no mediation—no excessive 'I' by which 'I' cannot account for itself; no self-history within history. It cannot be timed.

But am I all the way down? Down to philosophical principles? Who owns the brain? Which is the 'his', the 'I'?

Yours Faithfully,
Bonnie McGill

NOTES

1. Besides, J. Hillis Miller has already claimed dibs on 'host'.
2. For discussions of the influence of Ayn Rand on Ditko and his comic-book art, see Pineda and Jimenez-Varea (2013), Brühwiler (2014).
3. See, for example, O'Malley (1966, 508–527), specifically 523–524 for his reading of human pre-history.

4. Indeed, the 'Theses' itself plays out the sequence, separation in it being written in numbered sections.

Bibliography

Benjamin, Walter. 2007 [1950]. Theses on the philosophy of history. In *Illuminations*, ed. Hannah Arendt, 253–264, trans. Harry Zohn. New York: Schocken Books.

Brühwiler, Claudia Franziska. 2014. 'A is A': Spider-Man, Ayn Rand, and what man ought to be. *PS: Political Science and Politics* 47 (1): 90–93.

Lee, Stan, and Steve Ditko. 1963. Face-to-face with...The Lizard! *The Amazing Spider-Man*, 6 November.

Marx, Karl. 1973a [1852]. The eighteenth Brumaire of Louis Bonaparte. In *Karl Marx and Frederick Engels, selected works*, 96–179. London: Lawrence and Wishart.

———. 1973b [1846]. Letter: Marx to P. V. Annenkov, December 28, 1846. In *Karl Marx and Frederick Engels, selected works in one volume*, 659–668. London: Lawrence and Wishart.

———. 1992 [1844]. Economic and philosophical manuscripts. In *Early writings*, trans. R. Livingstone and G. Benton. London: Penguin.

O'Malley, Joseph J. 1966. History and man's 'nature' in Marx. *The Review of Politics* 28 (4): 508–527.

Pineda, Antonia, and Jesus Jimenez-Varea. 2013. Popular culture, ideology, and the comics industry: Steve Ditko's objectivist Spider-Man. *The Journal of Popular Culture* 46 (6): 1156–1176.

Rand, Ayn. 1967. *Capitalism: The unknown ideal*. New York: Signet.

———. 1975. *The Romantic manifesto: A philosophy of literature*. New York: Signet.

Sciabarra, Chris Matthew. 2000. *Total freedom: Toward a dialectical libertarianism*. Philadelphia: University of Pennsylvania Press.

PART III

Politics and Economics

CHAPTER 8

The New Left: Rand, Pedagogy, and 'the Cure'

Jerome Cox-Strong

1   THOUGHT, ACTION, AND NOVELTY IN THE NEW LEFT MOVEMENT

The New Left: The Anti-Industrial Revolution was Ayn Rand's fifth non-fiction collection. Published in 1971, it marked the end of a period of relatively prodigious regularity in Rand's non-fiction publishing; her first such collection, *For the New Intellectual* (1961) was followed by *The Virtue of Selfishness* (1964), *Capitalism: The Unknown Ideal* (1966) and *The Romantic Manifesto* (1975 [1969]), prior to the publication of *The New Left* itself.[1] The four initial collections offer titles of vague positive endorsement—the first, for example, is *for* 'the new intellectual'; the third pronounces capitalism to be 'the ideal'. The title of *The New Left*, however, forms a pejorative description of the enemy. The newness on offer is not hopeful or exciting, but, as can be read from the sub-title, negating. The Industrial Revolution, for Rand, was an 'absolute necessity', a genuinely path-breaking moment, one that went further than any other in the realisation of capitalism's potential and thus, it is argued, in

J. Cox-Strong (✉)
University of Manchester, Manchester, UK

© The Author(s) 2020
N. Cocks (ed.), *Questioning Ayn Rand*,
Palgrave Studies in Literature, Culture and Economics,
https://doi.org/10.1007/978-3-030-53073-0_8

the promotion of freedom.[2] It is such freedom, therefore, that the 'New Left' is set against.

With *The New Left* encroaching explicitly on enemy territory, it is helpful to first map this territory beyond and outside Rand's purely antag-onistic formulation. The decade prior to Rand's publication was critical to the New Left's ideological development, yet the boundaries and lineage of this ideology are contested. Where Maurice Cranston (1970, 7) contem-poraneously declared that 'both the importance and *novelty* of New Left thinking are acknowledged by all the present contributors' to his collection also titled *The New Left*, Kevin Mattson (2002, 87) considers that the 'New Left' developed by C. Wright Mills—seen by Dan Geary (2009, 1) as having a 'particularly significant impact on [the] New Left'— 'sounded, at times, quite old', and that 'what Mills meant by a "left" was [...] not that different' from what had gone before'.

There is greater consensus regarding the centrality of the group known as the Students for a Democratic Society (SDS) to the wider 1960s New Left movement. Rebecca Klatch describes the SDS as 'one of the primary organisations of the New Left', and, similarly, Jack Newfield argues that 'by October of 1965 [...] SDS had become the largest and most respected of all the campus-based groups on the New Left' (Klatch 1999, 1; Newfield 1966, 84). Peter Levy, however, suggests that, alongside a broader 'cooperative spirit' amongst a range of left-leaning groups—including the SDS, but also the American Jewish Congress, National Association for the Advancement of Colored People and League of Industrial Democracy, among others—it was another campus-based grouping, the Berkeley Free Speech Movement (FSM) who were ultimately critical in 'ushering in a wave of campus unrest that did not subside until the 1970s' (Levy 1994, 26). In the wake of the FSM, Levy argues, 'student radicals would serve as the primary agents of change, not as adjuncts to other people's struggles' (117).

While the abiding image of the FSM today perhaps remains that of Mario Savio's 'Bodies upon the Gears' speech, given from the steps of Berkeley's Sproul Hall on December 2, 1964, it represented neither the beginning nor end of the movement. The beginning is generally seen to have come on October 1st, when the arrest of then-Berkeley graduate student Jack Weinberg led to a spontaneous demonstration numbering, according to the contemporaneous estimate of Michael Miller and Susan Gilmore, 'more than 2000 assembled students', who surrounded the police car escorting him. January 4, 1965, meanwhile, saw *an* end

arrive—if not, given its open-ended influence and adjacent campus movements that followed, *the* end—with Berkeley's new acting Chancellor,
Martin Meyerson, provisionally agreeing to designate the Sproul Hall
steps as a free discussion area, among other concessions (Miller and
Gilmore 1965, xxv). While this caused some 'dissatisfaction' amongst
the FSM, Savio, conversely, suggested the developments to be 'hopeful',
anticipating, as Levy noted, the wave of campus activism that would soon
follow at Berkeley and elsewhere.[3]

As is explicit in 'The Cashing-In: The Student "Rebellion"', this
outcome was to Rand's horror; she describes it as 'an almost complete
capitulation to the F.S.M. [...] includ[ing] the right to advocate illegal
acts' (Rand 1971, 14–15). 'The Cashing-In' formed Rand's direct
response to the FSM, and thus it is largely unsurprising that the essay
is republished as the headline act of *The New Left*, having been first
published soon after the FSM's critical period.[4] Moreover, Rand's return
to 'The Cashing-In' and the FSM in *The New Left* is supported by her
central focus on education and pedagogy later in the collection in 'The
Comprachicos', the second essay, in turn, that this chapter shall primarily
engage with. All of which suggests that Rand's writing in response to the
Free Speech Movement was not *merely* in response to the Free Speech
Movement. Rather, just as she accuses the FSM of being a 'trial balloon,
a kind of cultural temperature-taking' (35) pre-empting a wider Leftist
uprising, Rand was writing towards a far wider target.

2   Diagnosis and Treatment

In responding to the FSM, the essay covers familiarly Randian ground.
Villains enter from stage left; Rand enters from stage right. The central
thesis of the essay concerns the degradation and diminishment of education: 'the consequence, today, is a chaos of subjective whims setting
the criteria of logic, of communication, demonstration, evidence, proof,
which differ from class to class, from teacher to teacher' (Rand 1971, 31).
Such chaos is sustained through 'the moral cowardice of most university administrations' (32), who lack the 'proper attitude [...] of firmness,
dignity and uncompromising severity' (49–50). It becomes quite clear,
quite quickly, however, that the essay is turning on the question of pedagogy itself. More specifically, it is Rand's construction of the pedagogical
ideal, absolutely critical to Objectivism as a universalising, secular belief

system. While some philosophies direct attention to 'single issues', Objectivism does no such thing.[5] While some manifestations of ideology seek to excuse themselves from certain debates, Objectivism is intended to impose itself upon all issues as 'the answer', and to figure all issues in terms of a construction of 'reason' as 'man's only means of grasping reality and of acquiring knowledge' (84). Thus, if 'reason' is key to Objectivism, it follows that education and pedagogy are inherently key to this sense of 'reason', as they represent the means of imparting and 'acquiring knowledge', the quantifiable, all-important Randian base unit of Objectivist reason. Rand's claim is that 'The rejection of reason means that men should act regardless of and/or in contradiction to the facts of reality' (ibid.). Elsewhere, in *For The New Intellectual*, she writes that reason is 'his [man's] only tool of knowledge' (Rand 1961, 156). Thus, the overriding principle of Objectivist pedagogy is an educational structure that imparts upon a 'student' these 'facts of reality', and that causes that student to acquire that core 'tool of knowledge'.

Rand touches upon pedagogy and spheres of education throughout *The New Left*; indeed, her foreword establishes such subjects as the very purpose of the collection, declaring that 'this book is intended for college students—for those among them who *are* seeking '"a voice of reason to turn to" [...] [and] for all those who are concerned about college students and about the state of modern education' (Rand 1971, viii). Yet while Rand regularly returns to the language of education—student, teacher, professor—what is striking is the connections she makes to that of *medicine*—to diagnosis, patients, doctors, plagues, health, disease and, as this chapter shall ultimately examine, 'the cure'. This medical language emerges first within the text through quotation; in beginning her response to the FSM, Rand cites a 1965 article by Berkeley sociology professor William Peterson criticising the movement, in which Peterson concludes on what Rand terms 'a note of warning': '"By my diagnosis [...] not only has the patient [the University] not recovered but he is sicker than ever. The fever has gone down temporarily, but the infection is spreading and becoming more virulent"' (19).

In configuring the University as the patient, Petersen thus positions the student protests as the symptom, an attack on the body-pedagogy that therefore must itself be attacked lest it continue to spread. In *Neoliberalism's War on Higher Education*, Henry Giroux quotes from a protest banner of the 2012 Quebec student protests, that '*this isn't a student strike, it's the awakening of society*' (Giroux 2014, 155); Petersen's antag-onism towards the FSM, meanwhile, is sustained by an inverse form of reconfiguration: this isn't a student protest, it's the spreading of an infec-tion. Where Giroux suggests that in 'speaking out', students 'are using their voices and bodies to redefine the boundaries of the possible' (ibid.), Petersen instead relies on a medical framework in which such 'redefinition of boundaries' is 'virulent', and becoming more so; a framework in which the protest-infection is not encountered as a marker of political participa-tion, of the political energy of a new generation, but as *dangerous*, even fatal.

This connection between pedagogy and medicine is indeed one that Rand increasingly employs herself as an analogical and imperative frame-work. She later argues that:

> To declare – in such circumstances – that politics is not the concern of philosophy is so unspeakable a default that it can be compared only to the stand of a doctor declaring, in the midst of a bubonic plague epidemic, that health or disease is not the concern of medicine. (Rand 1971, 108–109)

Just as Petersen relies on an analogous framework that can sustain the necessary binarism of his perspective, so too does Rand revert to the very same medical antagonism. While writing on a more general note, the sense of foreboding remains present, identifying a position 'so unspeak-able […] that it can be compared *only*' to a medical scenario. And, again as with Petersen, the medical emergency is not under control; rather, the doctor's fabricated declaration comes 'in the midst' of an ongoing threat.

The link is drawn further towards the end of 'The Cashing-In'. Where Peterson conceives of 'the University' as 'the patient', Rand generates a distinct, yet no less medical analogy of her own:

> It is obvious that a student who demands the right to run a university (or to decide who should run it) has no knowledge of the concept of knowledge, that his demand is self-contradictory and disqualifies him auto-matically. The same is true – with a much heavier burden of moral guilt – of the professor who taught him to make such demands and who supports them.
>
> Would you care to be treated in a hospital where the methods of therapy were determined by a vote of doctors and patients? (47)

That it constructs a clear procedural overlap between therapy and pedagogy, between patients and students and so on, is problematic: where the former builds around an exclusive, private relationship among equals, the latter, within typical structures of education—discounting, that is to say, teaching practice developed within private tutoring and via other structures of financial intervention—builds around curriculum and hierarchy. That is not to say that it *should* do so, but rather that Rand seeks to perpetuate the construction of hierarchy within the analogy in her initial argument against the student as involved in 'run[ning]' the university. That is precisely the connection Rand draws, employing in service of a critique of pedagogy an analogy directly correlated to medicine, an analogy in which professors and teachers are 'doctors', administering pedagogical 'therapy' to students who are 'patients'.

There is a faux-impartial, performative deference to etiquette at work in the phrasing within Rand's analogy, in asking 'would you care to be treated[...]?' It is, after all, a question that, if one were to follow Rand's own model of black-and-white thinking, is reducible to a statement followed by a binary response. Phrased accordingly, it could simply be: 'A hospital where the methods of therapy [are] determined by a vote of doctors and patients: yes or no?' Care doesn't really come into it. The 'answer' is, of course, meant to be a resounding *no*, delivered by Objectivism, those who identify as Objectivists. But by phrasing it as 'would you care to be treated', Rand strips away her own self-imposed urgency and gravity—a sense that this is a threat rather than a choice—and turns the analogy into not just a choice—whether you 'would care to' or would not—but into an act of choosing that is itself voluntary, the choice of whether to participate in the choice posed.

'Would you care' is to an extent reminiscent, in the contemporary political sphere, of the faux-civility employed as a form of false-equivalence by factions of the right, alt-right and far-right—that 'freedom of speech' means the left must share platforms with the right, that it is the left's rejection of right-wing politics that represents a bad-faith, totalitarian discourse, and thus, in opposing and contesting right-wing ideology and discourse, it is the left who employ censorship and transgress the bounds of civility. There is only one answer, as above, that Rand expects in response, yet the question remains one prompted by a language of professional deference and affected formality, in spite of a constructed scene in which the lunatics have, in effect, taken over the asylum.

This opening also constructs a 'you', and renders the 'you' as a participant of the analogy. The 'you' is being 'treated'; to an undefined extent, the 'you' is affected by the 'vote'. Yet there remains a separation between the 'treatment' of the 'you' and 'the methods of therapy'. The 'you' is not receiving 'therapy'. The 'vote of doctors and patients' is not 'determining' 'the methods of' 'treatment'. In the sense that one might assumptively contextualise it, the 'you' is recognised and designated as a 'patient', because they are being 'treated' at the 'hospital'. But the analogy does not make that distinction by itself. There is a 'you', a 'hospital', 'doctors', and 'patients'—the precise relationship of the 'you' to the other entities is largely undefined.

Further, the 'methods of therapy' are not just 'determined by a vote', but by a vote, specifically, of 'doctors *and* patients' [emphasis added]. This 'and' carries the foreboding of Rand's horror at the concept; the very idea of 'and' runs counter to the essence of Objectivism. 'Reason' demands synthesis and singularity; 'reason' demands that there can only be one, that there can only be Objectivism. The supplementary 'and', following Objectivist logic, entails the addition of the unreasonable. If there is an 'and' involved, then it must either connect the reasonable to the unreasonable, or, even worse, the unreasonable to the unreasonable.

Voting itself carries similar issues for Objectivists, for if a correct, rational, reasonable answer always exists, a vote can only allow for the possibility of 'voting for' the wrong option, while also representing the precise opposite of individualism. Rand alludes to this in an issue of *The Ayn Rand Letter*, writing that '"democratic" in its original meaning [refers to] unlimited majority rule [...] a social system in which one's work, one's property, one's mind, and one's life are at the mercy of any gang that may muster the vote of a majority at any moment for any purpose' (Rand 1972, 4).

In this specific case, however, a vote of doctors alone might be vaguely palatable to Rand—at least a professional demographic such as doctors might be a 'gang' that Rand deems knowledgeable or reasonable. Perhaps, in that 'doctors-only' scenario, all a 'vote' would serve to do would be to act as a drill, to remind the 'doctors' just how reasonable they are. A vote of doctors and patients, however, is the crux of the rhetoric, mirroring and matching up to Rand's angst at the idea of students going beyond the confines of their imposed intellectual inferiority, and being involved in the conception of pedagogy in a localised form.

What might seem peculiar here, in the context of the preceding paragraph, is the challenge Rand makes to the monolith of the professor, of the 'doctor', as an incorruptibly reasonable figure. The professor is not the model Objectivist—far from it. But the professor who carries the 'much heavier burden of moral guilt', the professor who 'teaches the student' to make such absurd demands as Rand claims, is still written, still defined, as 'the professor'. This is, however, to be expected, is indeed *necessary*; Rand's argument rests on the claim of a deterioration of quality, of deviants dragging the system down by abusing or failing in their roles, rather than the misapplication of job titles altogether. Her crusade is to reveal the sentient, devilish cracks in the system, to identify the sirens of 'the New Left' who cause would-be Objectivists to crash on the rocks. That necessarily relies on the cracks *still being* cracks, and the sirens *still being* sirens, rather than something else entirely. It relies, then, on the unreasonable professor *still being* the professor. In this, Rand's predilection for analogy becomes even more problematic, as does, indeed, that of Petersen, whose own medical language sits, as cited by Rand, awkwardly alongside his separate description of the FSM as an 'efficient, almost military organization' (Rand 1971, 17). Rand and Petersen's contention thus shifts furiously and impatiently: the 'student rebellion' is anarchistic, and yet militaristically efficient and hierarchical; the problem is implied to be both in a pedagogical structure too much like that of medicine, and yet, a structure that must be framed through medicine to glimpse the necessary solution.

Even where sustained, the 'doctors and patients' analogy is further complicated. Rand claims that all the flaws of the student are the fault of the professor, for it is the professor 'who taught [the student] to make such demands'. If these 'professors' and 'doctors' are 'teaching' and administering the 'absurd demands', then they become patients themselves, in that they require as much therapy—according to Rand—as the nominal 'patients', as the students themselves. All of which disrupts the analogy further: the doctors are unreasonable, the patients are unreasonable, the vote is certainly unreasonable, the hospital itself, then, is unreasonable. This, Rand could hypothetically argue, makes things easier: *burn it all down.*

All that perhaps remains salvageable for Objectivists is the idea of the 'methods of therapy'. If what is at stake is the threat of a 'vote', then the threat is that the *wrong* methods will be chosen, rather than that *all* the methods on offer are inherently wrong. There is, in other words, a light at the end of the tunnel, just as long as you look the right way. What these methods are, however, remains shrouded. Rand rails against the FSM on the grounds that it cannot convey what it stands for, that its activists cannot identify what they are building—'organizers—of what? Of "deprived people." For what? No answer. Just "organizers"' (19)—yet it is her own discursive inadequacy that comes to light, her own methodology that falls short of providing answers to *how to find* the answers Objectivism promises. The 'therapy' itself can broadly be gleaned from elsewhere in *The New Left*. In 'The Left: Old and New', Rand declares that 'the goal of an ideological battle is to enlighten the vast, helpless, bewildered majority in the universities—and the country at large' (54), and in 'The Comprachicos', that 'the only purpose of education *is* to teach a student how to live his life—by developing his mind and equipping him to deal with reality' (196–197). As contextualised within the analogous framework of students as patients, this process of 'develop[ing] his mind' can thus be construed as the 'therapy'.

The methods, however, remain undefined. They are simply 'the methods'. Yet such ambiguity is entirely the point, as it performs a gatekeeping role. Objectivists do not need to be told what the 'right' methods are, because within their own system of logic, they already know. Objectivists know that a vote is unnecessarily damaging, that a vote allows the 'guild socialists' and other cartoon malcontents to put a foot in the door (47–48); they know that the goal is a quasi-divine 'enlighten[ment]' of the 'majority'. The uninitiated, the 'helpless'—the left—do not know this, but, I would suggest, are not meant to: this absence, this void, defines their 'helplessness', and validates the Objectivist's sense the left is getting it wrong. Conversely, for Rand's reasonable Objectivists, the goal is a matter of intuition; of knowing, believing, feeling. The latter sense is described later as 'the Progressive nursery graduate's last link to rationality—the feeling that there is something wrong with him' (194); to reach the goal of Objectivism is to return to this purportedly natural state. The 'methods' are not just amorphous—they do not exist. There is only one true method: to cling to and retain that feeling, 'the feeling that there is something wrong'.

3   COMPRACHICOS OF THE MIND

Rand expands upon this further in 'The Comprachicos', an essay that connects an argument that the 'progressive nursery schools' […] view of a child's needs is militantly anti-cognitive and anti-conceptual' (Rand 1971, 155) to the titular neologism, a nightmarish villain form conceived of in Victor Hugo's novel *The Man Who Laughs* (1869).[6] Hugo's text, much like Rand's pedagogical thesis, places the figure of the child under threat, conceiving of the Comprachicos as a force who not only buy, sell, and trade children, but do so towards the ultimate aim of making them into 'monsters' (Rand 1971, 152).

Further, this threat is given a sense of exoticised distance through the Orientalist lineage given to the Comprachicos' 'monstrous practices' (152), but also through the constructed etymology of the term 'comprachicos' itself; in his historiographical critique of Hugo's novel, John Boynton Kaiser notes 'comprachicos' to be an entirely fabricated, albeit broadly linguistically accurate, 'compound Spanish word signifying Child-buyers' (Kaiser 1913, 249)—one that is, moreover, used in place of the broadly equivalent French, *acheteurs d'enfants*, as would perhaps be more appropriate to a text written *in* French. 'The art of moulding a living man', Rand translates Hugo to declare, has been 'practiced in China from time immemorial' (Rand 1971, 153). Through this practice, 'the Comprachicos did not merely remove a child's face, they removed his memory. [...] [he] was not aware of the mutilation he had suffered. This horrible surgery left traces on his face, not in his mind' (ibid.). It is this fable, rather than the contemporary Comprachicos that Hugo imagines, on which Rand ends her extended quotation: concerning the critical matter of 'how the monster is made', 'one breaks the vase, the child comes out, and one has a man in the shape of a pot' (154).

Even before the connection is explicitly drawn, Rand signposts her intentions:

> [Hugo's] exalted mind could not conceive that so unspeakable a form of humanity would ever be possible again. The twentieth century proved him wrong.

> The production of monsters – helpless, twisted monsters whose normal development has been stunted, goes on all around us. (ibid.)

Where Hugo's Comprachicos specialise in physical mutilation, Rand's are the aforementioned 'progressive nursery schools', 'today's educators', whom she dubs 'comprachicos of the mind' (155). The effect, however, her argument claims, is the same: the production of 'helpless, twisted monsters whose normal development has been stunted'. Much of this claim rests, again, on Rand's typical mode of attack, creating a sensational scenario around what she claims her opponents are against, rather than critiquing what they are explicitly and nominally in favour of. To these pedagogical opponents, Rand claims, 'the development of [a child's] conceptual faculty […] is an unnatural burden that should not be imposed on him', rather 'he should be free to act on his spontaneous urges and feelings in order to express his subconscious desires, hostilities and fears' (ibid.). This further returns to the territory of 'The Cashing-In', drawing a direct contrast between a pedagogy of reason, rationality, and naturality, and a pedagogy of chaos, irrationality, and general anarchy, a pedagogy of deliberate *anti*-reason. A further scenario develops this anti-reason of the 'comprachicos of the mind' as another active, engaged threat:

> A mental dwarf must be started when he is small. […] At the age of three […] a child is delivered – by a Progressive nursery school – into the midst of a pack of children as helplessly ignorant as himself […] He wants to learn; he is told to play. Why? No answer is given. He is made to understand […] that the most important thing in this peculiar world is not to know, but to get along with the pack. Why? No answer is given. […] He picks up a toy; it is snatched away from him by another child; he is told he must learn to share. Why? No answer is given. He sits alone in a corner; he is told he must join the others. Why? No answer is given. He approaches a group, reaches for their toys and is punched in the nose. He cries, in angry bewilderment; the teacher throws her arms around him and gushes that she loves him. (162)

This, Rand declares, is the 'art and science practised by the comprachicos of the mind' (ibid.), one that is indeed constructed as performing both distinct functions. The clinical nature of the scenario's refrain—'Why? No answer is given'—and methodical violence—which is subsequently exacerbated by the declaration that this child 'is expected to court the hounds and seek their love while they tear him to pieces' (163)—is linked inextricably to the outpouring of faux-emotion attributed to the teacher. While the particular medical language identified elsewhere in the text is absent, the concurrent medical imperative is nonetheless retained, the conceptualisation of an active and artificial pedagogical methodology, an artificial method that, as outlined at the beginning of this chapter, can be framed in Rand's own medical language as a pedagogical 'cure'.

This scenario further serves to demarcate the effective founding myth of Objectivist philosophy and pedagogy. Objectivism—as child—asks 'why', seeks only to *learn* 'why', yet is met by an 'understanding' that 'the most important thing in this peculiar world is not to know, but to get along with the pack'. The unwavering rigour, resilience, and verisimilitude of Objectivism, however, is met by a pedagogy that is set adrift, the teacher's language unanchored, and always changing. This again underpins Objectivism's alleged naturality while highlighting the scenario's impossible, 'win-win' construction. If the teacher answers the Objectivist child's question, the child is, surely, led astray by virtue of this being 'a Progressive nursery school'. Yet, as is said to happen, 'no answer is given', an 'outcome' that is, in its own way, critical to the mental mutilation of the child.

This phrase, 'no answer', or 'no answer is given', appears three further times throughout *The New Left*, with Rand employing it also in 'The Cashing-In', as well as in 'The Left: Old and New' and 'The Anti-Industrial Revolution' (19, 85, 133). Indeed, it epitomises Rand's approach to discourse, rhetorically asking nominally fatal questions of her antagonists, before declaring their failure and lack of answers in the very next instant. It is a framework, according to which Objectivism stands alone in having answers to 'the big questions', or indeed, to any questions at all, even merely 'why?'.

4   KNOWING BEFORE KNOWING: PRETERNATURAL RATIONALITY

In spite of the myriad declarations to this effect, Rand contradictorily claims just prior to the 'mental dwarf' passage that 'at birth, a child's mind is tabula rasa; he has the potential of awareness [...] but no content [...]' (Rand 1971, 155). Furthermore, she writes earlier in *The New Left*, in the essay 'The Anti-Industrial Revolution', that '[Man] is born naked and unarmed, without fangs, claws, horns or "instinctual knowledge"' (136). Yet, I would argue, it is precisely such an 'awareness' and sense of 'instinctual knowledge' that Objectivism otherwise makes a claim towards; an inaugural, immediate spirit that Objectivism claims to be the ideological manifestation of. To claim that in being born naked, 'man is born [...] without [...] instinctual knowledge' would thus be to cast Objectivism *itself* as fundamentally unnatural, and would be to position the philosophy—irrespective of how *reasonable* it claims to be—as no less an artificial force than those Rand opposes.

As the scenario develops, so does a sense that the foundations of knowledge—a base knowledge, however base it may be—are there in advance, presenting the child as knowing the concepts underpinning words *before* he is said to know the words themselves, even while he is claimed, once more, to know the concepts from which such words develop:

> A small child senses whether an adult's emotions are genuine, and grasps instantly the vibrations of hypocrisy. The teacher's mechanical crib-side manner— the rigid smile, the cooing tone of voice, the clutching hands, the coldly unfocused, unseeing eyes—add up in a child's mind to a word he will soon learn: phony. He knows it is a disguise; a disguise hides something; he experiences suspicion—and fear. (Rand 1971, 162)

'Phony' is 'a word he will soon learn', a word he has therefore not yet *learnt*—yet, a word he can nonetheless already, *instinctively* conceptualise. What 'he will soon learn', then, is cast as that of which he has already learnt the *basis*; as Rand lays out pages beforehand, 'his next, *conceptual* task' is to learn 'to organise' 'the chaos in his mind' (157). Phony is 'a word he will soon learn', and yet the different elements listed are already there, and already 'add up in [his] mind' to the word itself. Tension abounds: he is Objectivist, 'he *knows* it is a disguise' [emphasis added], because he already 'knows' pure right and wrong, and yet he must 'add up' to determine this, drawing the scenario towards the sense of 'and' inherent in such addition, the very sense of 'and' that, as before, runs fundamentally counter to base Objectivism, an 'and', the presence of which introduces the unreasonable and irrational to a reduced, quantifiable kernel of knowledge and rationality. Yet with his preternatural Objectivism otherwise established, the scenario builds to a necessary conclusion: the success of the 'comprachicos of the mind'. The child 'adjusts': 'he cannot know by what imperceptible steps he, too, has become a phony' (165). He has been moulded into a 'monster'; he has, in Rand's medical language, become infected by the disease.

As such, we are returned to the central conceptualisations *of* such a pedagogical 'disease', and 'the cure' that Rand connects it to—'the cure' that, she declares, 'is worse than the disease' (175). 'The comprachico technique' that is 'the disease', Rand argues, results in 'half-illiterate college freshmen who are unable to read a book (in the sense of under-standing its content, as against looking at its pages)' (174). It is this 'disease', in turn, that is in Rand's view subsequently usurped by 'the cure' of theme learning—'the teacher of physics discusses the machinery required to make shoes [...] the teacher of economics discusses the production and consumption of shoes [...] the teacher of English reads stories involving shoes (or the plight of the barefoot) and so on' (175). This, too, is itself followed by a description of 'the "discussion" method of teaching' as 'still more evil' (ibid.).

One could question whether it matters which particular pedagogical structures and techniques are cast as the disease, the cure, or 'still more evil', or rather, whether the critical element is simply the medical artifice Rand employs as the central frame, given the targets themselves are largely interchangeable in their unerring abhorrence according to Objectivism. Yet it perhaps remains significant that it is theme learning, discussion learning, and the concepts of altruism and empathy largely underpinning the 'comprachicos of the mind' scenario that are given precedence. The latter, after all, forms a core antagonist across all of Rand's philosoph-ical perspective, while the former two pedagogical concepts develop a pedagogy of context and dialogue, of learning as a connective, discursive process—if it is a 'process' at all, given the linearity of such a term—as opposed to a firmly hierarchical process of delivery.

Rand's critique decries, ironically, the supposed absence *of* 'context or earlier preparation' (175) from such methods, yet this aversion can be understood to bring to light Rand's basic pedagogical principle, that of facts *as* facts. Even as Rand elsewhere declares that 'concepts are not and cannot be formed in a vacuum [...] all conceptualization is a contex-tual process' (Rand 1979, 55), the thesis of her writing in *The New Left* and more widely belies an unavoidable antagonism to the concept *of* context. Context moves one away from all that Rand holds dear, away from quantified reason, from logic, from rationality, in so much as an acknowledgement of context is thus also an acknowledgement of the structures that propel and sustain the very 'knowledge' that Rand holds up to be unerring: structures of dialogue, structures of communication, structures, that is to say ultimately, of collaboration.

In amongst this wider pedagogical discourse, however, the base analogy of medicine remains prominent. In particular, turning to focus explicitly on this idea of 'the cure' that Rand employs further exposes the tangled, problematic, contradictory chaos of Rand's pedagogical discourse. It remains significant that 'the cure', as it is encountered *in* Rand's writing, is used as an unequivocally negative framework. That is not to infer any kind of surprise that the pedagogical structures that are so antagonised in these passages of *The New Left* are indeed cast as antagonists. Rather, it is only where one places these passages into the wider context of the collection that this surprise might develop.

As this chapter has examined, medical lexis forms a critical backbone to the essays featured in *The New Left*—it is present in William Petersen's 'diagnosis' of the health of the University, in the inference of protest as being symptomatic of the virus afflicting that same 'patient', in Rand's analogous reference to a 'bubonic plague epidemic', in the use of 'doctors and patients' as a model for the horror of collaborative approaches to learning, and beyond. Yet in all such examples, there is a consistent appeal to medical protagonism and antagonism. The patient that is the University, a potential force for rationality, is afflicted by the virus that is student interference and protest; the analogous hospital that is undermined by, again, the interference of student-patients, and by the dereliction of duty of professor–doctors; even, indeed, the fact that the techniques and 'mutilation' of the so-called 'comprachicos of the mind' comes to be termed 'the disease'. Where anti-Objectivist forces appear according to medical frameworks, they appear as *threats*: viruses; plagues; diseases. Except, that is, for this conceptualisation of 'the cure', the cure that is *worse than* the disease, the cure that is itself, then, no less of a threat.

Such basic contradictions are not what set 'the cure' apart, given, indeed, the myriad other contradictions one can draw from Rand's work. What sets 'the cure' apart is that it encapsulates what Objectivist pedagogy is said to be:

a. 'The cure' is quantifiable, in content and in purpose;
b. 'The cure' is not to be discussed or debated, but instead to be delivered by a medical professional, and absorbed by the patient;
c. 'The cure' is expressly artificial, yet restores what is claimed to be a wholly natural prior state.

In the context of such persistent medical language, one begins to encounter 'the cure' as a framework for Objectivism itself. Just as Objectivism claims there is only the rational or irrational, 'the cure' leaves little to no room for uncertainty; just as with the nursery child, the cure is either genuine if it works, or clearly a 'phony' if it does not.

The concept of *a* cure more generally is, of course, supported by a number of other concepts—naturality, equilibrium, restoration—that are themselves problematic. However much it elsewhere might resist the move, I take Objectivism here to cast itself as a philosophy that is natural, and that seeks, in a sense that repeats *laissez-faire* principles, to restore a natural equilibrium; an ideology that projects as the singular and ultimate way *of being*. Thus, within such a framework, and amongst such unerring reliance on the analogy of medicine, it is precisely the idea of 'the cure' that defines *Objectivist* pedagogy, over and above any pedagogical structure Objectivism opposes. Objectivist pedagogy seeks to cure the masses, to suppress those 'helpless, bewildered students' who dare to discuss and who dare to speak out of place; it is Objectivist pedagogy that ultimately moves to restore an educational hierarchy in which one must fulfil a particular rigid role, the student who must learn 'the cure', or the professor who must deliver it. The difficulty for Rand, of course, is that even as such a cure would surely represent the apex of science and rationality—indeed, science and rationality in a deliverable form—its single mention comes instead as an apparatus of and analogy for the left, and thus as much as the cure *might* be seen as a force of Objectivist rationality, it comes to devour the narrative, to turn the ultimate medical solution into yet another sickness, drawing to mind Derrida's *pharmakon*: 'this medicine, this philter, which acts as both remedy and poison' (Derrida 2004 [1981], 75). The cure, as with the disease, is cast as an artificial attack on the body that represents the natural reasonability of the Objectivist rationale, and in doing so, the narrative solution Rand might seek to find amongst her repeated return to the language of medicine is lost altogether.

5   OBJECTIVIST ECHOES: CONTEMPORARY PEDAGOGY AND RAND

While *The New Left* is contextually aligned to its contemporaneous period across the 1960s, the echoes of Objectivism and Objectivist pedagogy remain critically relevant in the present day, and can be read within contemporary higher education and academia. The now-standard neoliberal projection of a service-consumer relationship onto academic 'participation' is tied closely to Randian ideals, as is a drive towards knowledge that can be autonomously delivered and acquired, knowledge as conceptualised by the very model of 'the cure' examined in this chapter. The language of academic consumerism is further anticipated and conceived of in Rand's writing. While considering the so-called 'comprachico mentality', Rand pauses to add the following in parentheses: 'This [...] is one of the reasons to question the motives—and the compassion—of those unemployed busy-bodies who flitter about, protecting consumers from oversized breakfast-cereal boxes. What about the consumers of education?' (Rand 1971, 185). Rand's question is one that fixes students as 'consumers of education', recipients of the conceptualised 'cure'. Or rather, according to Rand's account here, there *are* no students, only hard-done-by consumers. This certainty is symptomatic of what Henry Giroux identifies as 'a common set of assumptions and practices driving the transformation of higher education into an adjunct of corporate power and values' (Giroux 2014, 30): student-as-consumer, as with broader consumerism elsewhere, now stands as an unquestionable business model. This transformation, Giroux suggests, represents 'a full-fledged assault [...] being waged on higher education in North America, the United Kingdom, and various European countries' (ibid.).

The assimilation of higher education into this new, yet utterly familiar 'neoliberal paradigm' (31) is further alluded to by Caroline Jackson, who declares, in an article on 'Class Struggle University' for the quarterly leftist magazine *Commune*, that 'academia has effectively accepted that universities now represent a site for consumption rather than intellectual endeavor' (Jackson 2020). But such a conclusion, while broadly accurate in identifying academia's 'effective acceptance' of the Objectivism-led consumptive model, is mistaken in suggesting that this model has *replaced* intellectual endeavour. Rather, the concept of intellectual *endeavour* is central to the Randian 'cure', to neoliberalism, and thus also to contemporary academia. As Bill Readings famously argues in *The University in Ruins*, far from being replaced, intellectual endeavour lives on, reanimated as a critical component of 'academic excellence':

> Today, all departments at the University can be urged to strive for excellence, since the general applicability of the notion is in direct relation to its emptiness. Thus, for instance, the Office of Research and University Graduate Studies at Indiana University at Bloomington explains that in its Summer Faculty Fellowship program 'Excellence of the proposed scholarship is the major criterion employed in the evaluation procedure.' This

statement is, of course, entirely meaningless, yet the assumption is that the invocation of excellence overcomes the problem of the question of value across disciplines, since excellence is the common denominator of good research in all fields. (Readings 1999 [1996], 23–24)

Just as Rand's 'doctors and patients' analogy in *The New Left* moves to construct a sense of insanity inherent in allowing student-patients to vote on their own 'methods of therapy'—to participate in the development of their own pedagogy—the principle of excellence operates similarly. 'Excellence', as Readings notes, 'appears here as uncontestable grounds' (23): in Randian phrasing, 'would you care to be' taught in a university that *does not* "strive for excellence"?. Who, in other words, could possibly stand *against* academic excellence? And just as Rand's fiction and non-fiction each serve to prove one another 'right', so too is this sense of excellence similarly self-evident and self-serving. 'Existing' academic excellence guides the designation of subsequent academic excellence, according to criteria that exist purely to assign such designations, a rabbit hole whose end can only be that academic excellence *simply is* excellent, *because it is* excellent. Yet this assimilation is also paradoxical. According to the critical perpetuity of neoliberalism, whereby, as Giroux remarks, 'the future replicates the present in an endless circle' (2014, 31), academia can always be *more* excellent; 'all departments of the University', as Readings notes, 'can be urged to strive for excellence' (1999 [1996], 23). This perpetual drive towards 'more' and yet also, 'more of the same' is, I would argue, familiar from a reading of Objectivist arguments. Further, as Neil Cocks argues in the concluding chapter of this book, the claimed newness of broader Randian discourse and practice is always oddly lifeless: repetitious, deathly; pointless.

It is my contention that in returning to Rand, and in drawing together much of what this chapter has sought to engage—the student protests of the Berkeley FSM, the sense of rigid pedagogical hierarchy inherent in the concept of 'the cure', and the pedagogical structures that Rand opposes in the name of rational thought—one encounters an uncannily contemporary model, one that might at this point be identified as academia's New Objectivism. This model, as above, retains and is propelled by the familiar hallmarks of Objectivist pedagogy more generally, the ideological imperatives of certainty and rationality, and the language of delivery and consumption. It is, however, marked also by the sense of 'novelty' that Maurice Cranston was earlier quoted as associating with the

New Left, a novelty that is in and of itself critically resonant with the assimilative nature of neoliberalism, in which alternative ideologies and political models are absorbed and reconstituted. Traces of this lexical and visible malleability as regarding 'the student' are present in *The New Left*; Rand's foreword credits an unnamed 'graduate student in sociology' with inspiring the collection (1971, vii–viii), even while the collection itself develops a thesis that *rejects* student participation. Rand is, it would seem, not averse to *doing it for the kids*.

New Objectivism, too, does not reject student participation. Instead, and in the name of the aforementioned 'protection', it projects a cognitively dissonant façade of the language and appearance of student activism, student participation and the very models of pedagogy to which Objectivism remains so ideologically opposed. Thus, the empty imperatives of contemporary academic managerialism—learning that is student-centred, flipped and flexible; learning that strives towards 'student impact'; learning that is formulated as a result of 'the process of engaging and listening to the student voice'[7]—form a nominal fulcrum in which the student is not only apparently empowered, but where such empowerment is not suppressed, as it was with the Berkeley FSM, and alongside all educational activism that seeks to challenge any aspect of the equilibrium, but instead is actively *embraced*. And indeed, this carries a practical secondary benefit to the contemporary academic institution: the gradual—or not-so-gradual—erosion of the role of the professor or lecturer; a volatile force in an otherwise increasingly slick machine, who *can* strike, resist managerialism, and work *with* students in precisely the manner that Rand casts as a fundamental dereliction of duty.

The spread of New Objectivism is, then, carried primarily by its explicit adoption by existing proponents of 'old' Objectivism. But this spread is further underpinned by the manner in which it has, to again employ Rand's medical lexis, infected the language of mainstream critical *opposition to* the neoliberal model. Giroux's analysis, for example, is scathing in its critique of neoliberalism's impact on higher education. Yet his *solutions* are defined in much the same terms *as* neoliberalism and New Objectivism:

> We need to address what the optimum conditions are for educators, artists, activists, and so on, to perform their work in an autonomous and critical fashion. In other words, we need to think through the conditions that make academic labour fruitful, engaging and relevant. (Giroux 2014, 194)

Having interrogated the intersectional and sociocultural frameworks of neoliberal academia and academic discrimination, Giroux adopts the familiar phrasing through which such frameworks are perpetuated: relevance, 'optimum conditions', 'autonomous performance', 'academic labor' that is 'fruitful'; conditions, performances, and labour that he uncritically celebrates in the language of 'excellence': 'the distinctive role that faculty play in this pedagogical project [...] must be defended in a broader discourse of excellence, equity and democracy' (150).[8]

Relevance also finds a root in *The New Left*. Rand suggests that it is a *lack* of 'relevance'—the failure of higher education to provide 'the training he [the student] needs [...] to be taught to think, to understand, to integrate, to *prove*'—that produces the central issue of students 'decid[ing] that they were qualified administrators, without knowledge, preparation or experience', student demands, then, for 'the power to run the universities' (Rand 1971, 196–197). 'What they are teaching today has no relevance to anything' (ibid.), she declares, and thus, the students' demand that their courses be 'relevant' to their actual lives has a badly twisted element of validity—the demand for relevance is invalidated only by virtue of it originating with 'the students'.

As Giroux exemplifies, avoiding the simplistically quantifiable narratives of solutionism in which Rand revels is difficult, just as it is difficult to avoid lapsing into the critical language of quality or accuracy, value or expertise, especially where one engages with a subject as ideologically indictable and critically contradictory as Rand herself. Perhaps, then, what is critical in engaging with Rand and Objectivism—both in its base form, and as part of contemporary academic 'New Objectivism'—is, instead, an explicit *acknowledgement of* such difficulty. It is precisely such an acknowledgement that distinguishes radical, deconstructive, or even merely 'progressive' pedagogy from the Objectivist pedagogy of 'the cure'; it is precisely such an acknowledgement, in other words, that distinguishes Randian pedagogical models that seek to eradicate difficulty in the name of quantified linearity from models that ultimately embrace and accept the notion that such difficulty is unavoidable, and indeed, perhaps *desirable*. Thus, it is not enough to simply reject the *kind* of 'cure' that one critically encounters in pedagogical discourse. Rather, one must reject the narrative allure of 'the cure', regardless of the pedagogical model to which it is applied.

NOTES

1. After five collections in ten years, it would be eight years before the arrival of the sixth. That collection, *Introduction to Objectivist Epistemology* (1979), was the last to be published in Rand's lifetime. She began work on a seventh, *Philosophy: Who Needs It*, but died in March 1982, six months before its eventual publication in September 1982, under the guidance of Rand's legally-anointed heir, Leonard Peikoff.

2. For Rand, to oppose the 'absolute necessity' of the Industrial Revolution was also to oppose the 'truth [...] that reason leads to (and is the foundation of) individualism and competition, i.e., capitalism. Capitalism's enemies know it. Its alleged friends are still twisting themselves into double-jointed pretzels in the struggle to evade that knowledge' (Rand 1971, 83).

3. This quotation, and the chronological accounts not attributed to Miller and Gilmore are taken from an online text reproduction of the February 1965 issue of the *California Monthly*, a magazine published by the California Alumni Association. Parts of this chronology can also be found as reproduced on the *Free Speech Movement Archives* website (fsm-a.org).

4. 'The Cashing-In' was first published in three parts across the July, August and September 1965 issues of Rand's first periodical, *The Objectivist Newsletter*. Following this first instance, the essay was reproduced a year later in *Capitalism: The Unknown Ideal*, before its appearance in *The New Left*, which was itself finally subject to a posthumous expansion in 1999 as *Return of the Primitive*, thereby giving 'The Cashing-In' its fourth separate appearance—three of which were in newly published materials. This does not itself signify the importance of the article, but it does indicate its *insistence*.

5. The vacillation here between different categorical terminology in reference to Objectivism—from belief system, to philosophy, to ideology—reflects the malleability of the idea propagated by its conceptualisation as something universal, and universally applicable.

6. *The Man Who Laughs* was first published in French as *L'homme qui rit*, in addition to later being published in English under the alternative title *By Order of the King*, itself a translation of *Par ordre du roi*, a title Hugo used in correspondences prior to publication.

7. From the webpage 'Top tips for engaging the student voice', an article on the website of The British Council, a UK-based cultural and educational organisation.

8. Giroux also invokes excellence elsewhere: 'How do we understand and incorporate into classroom pedagogies the ongoing search for equity and excellence, truth and justice, knowledge and commitment?' (Giroux 2014, 39); 'One such measure of the degree to which higher education has lost its ethical compass can be viewed in the ways in which it disavows any relationship between equity and excellence' (87).

BIBLIOGRAPHY

British Council. 2017. Top tips for engaging the student voice. British Council. https://www.britishcouncil.org/education/skills-employability/what-we-do/vocational-education-exchange-online-magazine/july-2017/top-tips-eng aging-student-voice. Accessed 20 March 2020.

California Monthly: Vol. LXXV, No. 5, *Online Archive of California*. https://oac.cdlib.org/ark:/13030/kt196n983c/?brand=oac4. Accessed 20 March 2020.

Cranston, Maurice. 1970. *The new left: Six critical essays*. London: Bodley Head.

Derrida, Jacques. 2004 [1981]. *Dissemination*, trans. Barbara Johnson. Reprint, London: Continuum.

FSM-A. Chronologies of the conflict. *Free Speech Movement Archives*. fsm-a.org/stacks/FSM_chron_index.html. Accessed 18 February 2020.

Geary, Dan. 2009. *Radical ambition: C. Wright Mills, the left, and American social thought*. Oakland, CA: University of California Press.

Giroux, Henry A. 2014. *Neoliberalism's war on higher education*. Chicago, IL: Haymarket Books.

Hugo, Victor. 1869. *L'homme qui rit*. Reprint. Paris: Gallimard, 2002.

Jackson, Caroline. 2020. Class struggle university. *Commune*. https://communemag.com/class-struggle-university/. Accessed 18 February 2020.

Kaiser, John Boynton. 1913. The comprachicos. *Journal of the American Institute of Criminal Law and Criminology* 4/2: 247–264.

Klatch, Rebecca E. 1999. *A generation divided: The new left, the new right, and the 1960s*. Berkeley, CA: University of California Press.

Levy, Peter B. 1994. *The new left and labor in the 1960s*. Urbana, IL: University of Illinois Press.

Mattson, Kevin. 2002. *Intellectuals in action: The origins of the new left and radical liberalism, 1945–1970*. University Park, PA: Penn State University Press.

Miller, Michael V., and Susan Gilmore. 1965. *Revolution at Berkeley: The crisis in American education*. New York: Dial Press.

Newfield, Jack. 1966. *A prophetic minority: The American new left*. New York: New American Library.

Peikoff, Leonard. 1990. Assault from the ivory tower: The professors' war against America, *The voice of reason: Essays on Ayn Rand's thought*, ed. Leonard Peikoff, 186–206. New York: Meridian.

Rand, Ayn. 2007 [1957]. *Atlas shrugged*. London: Penguin.

———. 1961. *For the new intellectual*. New York: Random House.

———. 1964. *The virtue of selfishness*. New York: New American Library.

———. 1966. *Capitalism: The unknown ideal*. New York: New American Library.

———. 1975 [1969]. *The romantic manifesto*. Revised edition. New York: New American Library.

_____. 1971. *The new left: The anti-industrial revolution.* New York: New American Library.

_____. 1972. How to read (and not to write). *The Ayn Rand Letter,* 1/26.

_____. 1979. *Introduction to Objectivist epistemology.* New York: New American Library.

_____. 1982. *Philosophy: Who needs it,* ed. Leonard Peikoff. New York: Bobbs-Merill.

_____. 1994 [1990]. *The Objectivist newsletter volume 1–4, 1962–1965.* New York: Second Renaissance Books.

_____. 1999. Schwartz, Peter, ed. *Return of the primitive: The anti-industrial revolution.* New York: Meridian.

Readings, Bill. 1999 [1996]. *The university in ruins.* Cambridge, MA: Harvard University Press.

Savio, Mario. 1964. Sproul Hall sit-in speech. www.americanrhetoric.com/speeches/mariosaviosproulhallsitin.htm. Accessed 18 February 2020.

CHAPTER 9

Topographies of Liberal Thought: Rand and Arendt and Race

Stephen Thomson

1 RECEPTION IN THE PUBLIC REALM

Rand and Arendt: the assonance is tempting. Yet these are two names rarely if ever voiced in the same breath. There are also some teasing circumstantial resemblances in their trajectories. Disembarking in the United States as bourgeois European Jews in flight from the totalitarian persecutions of early twentieth-century Europe—the one from Bolshevik Russia in 1926, the other Nazi Germany in 1941—both go on to enjoy sorts of philosophical prominence unusual for women in the 1950s and 1960s. Yet these parallels count for so little that the same biographer may write a life of each without mentioning the other (Heller 2009, 2015). Only, it seems, the contrarian genius of *Spiked* magazine has felt moved to unite them in print, under the deliciously paradoxical banner of an anti-feminist feminism (Holdsworth 2016). Otherwise, they might as well inhabit parallel, non-communicating universes. Or at least, since they did inhabit the same public sphere, it seems they occupy distant, maybe even radically dissymmetrical, areas of it. For while Rand addresses

S. Thomson (✉)
The University of Reading, Berkshire, UK

© The Author(s) 2020
N. Cocks (ed.), *Questioning Ayn Rand*,
Palgrave Studies in Literature, Culture and Economics,
https://doi.org/10.1007/978-3-030-53073-0_9

only the narrow, shady margin of the libertarian/neo-con right, Arendt has the run of the sunlit agora, commanding the respect of thinkers of widely diverging interests. It is not just a matter of appealing to distinct constituencies or sides. Rather their audiences are constituted in ways that are incommensurable, by an address that is either homogenising or capable of diversity. If Arendt remains good to think with, even indispensable, in spite of whatever differences we may have with her, it is because she invites us to think in a way that is nuanced, capacious and multifaceted. But Rand has only one side, offering a single point of entry, and a uniform issue; wearing ever deeper, with relentless trenchancy and driving tendentiousness, the same narrow furrow. This, then, would be why, in the city of political philosophy, one meets Arendt at every turn, and Rand hardly at all.

In the last analysis, I cannot honestly say I demur from the broad outline of this account. I would be only too happy never to have to meet a Rand; and, although I have been aware of her since she was namechecked by Margaret Thatcher in the 1980s, I have hitherto managed to avoid the assignation with the greatest of ease. For this, I suppose, I am indebted to the topography outlined above. There are, nevertheless, some problems arising out of its common-sense appeal to the public sphere as a coherent urban space. For one thing, as some recent swellings seem to confirm, a Rand's narrowness may not preclude a certain power of amplification. There are pronouncements that proliferate in an algorithmic continuum whose most respectable (which is to say normalising) instances would be Jordan Peterson or Douglas Murray, that must remain all but incomprehensible without reference to Randian reason. And it does not matter if this 'reason' seems scarcely reasonable. This only means that the task of understanding how it functions as reason has yet to begin. Can the agora, which likes to think of itself as encompassing all reason, simply disown this dark reserve? The Murrays and Petersons, after all, like to insinuate that they *are* the agora, the real one that has been unjustly put in the shade. It may be vexing for the well-thinking that a lack of expansiveness should prove no impediment to expansion. But can the answer be to treat what is effectively a growing constituency of the public sphere as an alien invasion?

Here, then, is another problem with the topography outlined above. It effectively works to *ensure* that an Arendt and a Rand never meet. But it cannot thereby ensure that there is never at any point any overlap in their thinking, only prevent its discovery. And yet there is at least one salient instance where their thinking does, to a troubling degree, align. Both Arendt, in 'Reflections on Little Rock' (1959), and Rand, in her essay on 'Racism' (first published 1963), oppose the tactics of the Civil Rights Movement, and for similar reasons. For while both claim to despise racism as much as any prejudice, they argue that one cannot, and must not, legislate for integration since law and politics are forbidden to interfere in what are properly social or individual matters. Equally (and not quite coherently in either case), both take a dim view of direct action tactics, particularly those that target public schools and that seek to mobilise schoolchildren politically.[1] Despite what seem compelling prima facie grounds, however, no comparative analysis is ever made. The sole exception to this would seem to be Shane Moran who, in an article questioning Arendt's usefulness to the critique of globalisation in light of the limitations of her racial politics, alerts us to some suggestive 'parallels', not least in the 'careful distinction between economic and political rights' that both Arendt and Rand draw (Moran 2013, 293, n.18). These remarks are, nevertheless, confined to an undeveloped footnote. This too may be an effect of the dissymmetry outlined above. For, while no one would be surprised to learn that Rand takes such a reactionary stance, the Arendt article tends to be seen as a problem in an otherwise impeccable œuvre; one that must be finessed, excused, or relegated to the margins (Morey 2014). Even in the growing critical literature on Arendt's problematic views on race, some are still reluctant to call her 'racist' in spite of the evidence of racism they find in *The Origins of Totalitarianism* (Moruzzi 2000, 97–98). And while others have more recently moved the question towards the centre of the œuvre, this never, with the exception of Moran, brings Rand into the picture (Burroughs 2015; Owens 2017; Gines 2009, 2014). This is a pity because many of these critiques are concerned with the topographical dimension of Arendt's politics implicit in Moran's remark on the 'distinction between economic and political rights'. For the landscape of separate realms and spheres around which *The Human Condition* is ordered, stands accused of schematic rigidity, an over-preparedness to universalise, and consequently an insensitivity to the specific landscape of American racism. And this notion of schematic rigidity potentially poses, for Arendt, a problem even more fundamental than the stain of racism. What is supposed to distinguish Arendt is a nuance and complexity that stand above, and can survive, occasional lapses or disagreements. But what if nuance was but a veil cast over a set of concepts no less driven towards their own self-serving goals than those of a Rand? Could it be that Arendt is simply a more sophisticated version of a Rand?

I would not, ultimately, go this far. Certainly, one can have great fun at the expense of Rand's bug-eyed trenchancy. She does not simply lack nuance: she openly despises it. She fetishises an idea of clarity exemplified by the law of identity ('A is A'), and loathes whatever she sees as the 'fog' of arbitrariness and relativism (Rand 1975, 31). For these are obstacles in the way of the individual will of 'man', who must be helped in his titanic struggle towards self-realisation by an art that shows him at his square-jawed best. It is thus in the name of heroism that her rare concessions to qualified judgment are made. This is why she loves Victor Hugo despite his political leanings (31 and passim); or (rather less plausibly) Vermeer because, despite the sordidness of his subject matter, his style 'projects clarity, discipline, confidence, purpose, power—a universe open to man' (39). This is a landscape for heroes, akin to Rand's (rather artless) epitome of art: 'a heroic man, the skyline of New York, a sunlit landscape, pure colors, ecstatic music' (16). And if this reminds us of Gary Cooper in the closing shot of *The Fountainhead* (King Vidor 1949) as discussed in Chapter 6 of this book—erect, chiselled, dwarfing the tall buildings that are his work—this is no accident. 'A is A' means 'A is A', and Rand is absolutely unafraid of tautology as she trawls her own novels for examples of good art. On one occasion she even rewrites the opening of *The Fountainhead* to show how bad it would have been if a weak-wristed liberal, and not she, had written the character of Roark (Rand 1975, 81–84). It never seems to occur to her that the 'real' Roark might also be awful in his way. Naturally, for he is awful the way Ayn Rand is awful. Her prose moves quickly, decisively, heroically from one slab of assertion to the next. The assertions may be odd, and the leap from one slab to the next vertiginous, but the sheer speed and momentum carry her across the abyss, with a tempo that evinces an undeviating will, even as it deviates wildly. Presumably, this is part of the thrill of reading her. But what Rand builds, slab by slab, is the mausoleum of what Arendt calls, in *The Life of the Mind*, 'thinking': that is, non-instrumental deliberation, a debate of the self with the self that follows no goal, and whose capacity to entertain 'unanswerable questions' may be an essential condition, not just for ethical being and art, but even for the possibility of posing answerable questions (Arendt 1981, 62). If Rand ever deliberated in an open-ended way, or tolerated a moment's disagreement with herself, there is no trace of it in her writing, only this single tumescent 'I' that lives by decree.

But it is also important to note the extent to which Arendt's *The Human Condition* (first published 1958) is also guided by an heroic vision, and one that is not wholly immune to satire. What she offers is, in large part, a lament for the passing of 'the public realm' in which alone 'the shining brightness we once called glory' was possible (Arendt 1998, 180). Her heroism seems thus to belong in a distant, bygone, and possibly Athenian age. Now, in modernity, we are stuck with the homogenising force of 'society' which, because it has dissolved the boundaries between private and political, 'excludes the possibility of action' and replaces it with mere 'behavior', subject to mindless, statistical, technocratic management rather than politics (40–43). So, in the end, 'individual life' will be 'submerged in the over-all life process of the species' (322). If this sounds grim we should note that, even in its Athenian heyday, the public realm scarcely guaranteed 'glory'. One could count oneself lucky to get as far as 'disclosure of self' through speech and action. And if we were foolish enough to attempt action without speech, we would be revealed as 'robots'. For in such a case we have to do with a 'what', not a 'who' (178–179). Since the barest personhood is not, thus, guaranteed even in the public realm, what hope is there for the subjacent realms of 'Work' and 'Labor'? 'Work' at least has the dignity of providing 'world' by 'erecting' durable objects. But the private realm of 'Labor'—the (Aristotelian) sphere of mere reproduction, of tasks that disappear in the doing and produce nothing—is so bound up with the merely physical life of the organism as to barely qualify as human. Indeed, to 'live an entirely private life means above all to be deprived of things essential to a truly human life' (58). But Arendt seems to accept this as a price worth paying for a thriving political realm. At one point she does at least express some passing sympathy for servants and 'the violent injustice of forcing one part of humanity into the darkness of pain and necessity' (119). But mainly she shares the Greek 'impatience with every effort that left no trace, no monument, no great work worthy of remembrance' and tends to overlook the dependence of such things on a host of non-monumental efforts (81). For, after all, not even the greatest of men can stride into the agora without a good breakfast and clean socks.

Arendt's discourse is nothing like as aggressively individualistic as Rand's, and it goes some way to account for the interdependencies that structure the whole. Even so, it is ultimately the loss of public man that exercises her, so that it is not at all clear that she sees the loss of individuality implicit in maintaining his existence as a structural injustice. From the point of view of the hegemon, it is natural to identify the polis with the limited, exclusive fraction of full citizens privileged with political life. But where, then, does this leave the wholeness of the topography of different spheres and realms? Just by producing such problems, Arendt's schema is infinitely more nuanced than Rand's. And yet, I am going to suggest, both alike circumnavigate the same abyss. If this claim seems dubious, the name I will give to the terrain in which this abyss is situated will seem even more so. I will call it liberalism.

2 REFORM AND EDUCATION

It is a label Rand would emphatically reject. She despises 'liberals' as wrong-headed do-gooders whose appeal to 'society' only serves to shackle her heroic individuals. She has, it is true, been an inspiration for some of the heralds of the brand of laissez-faire political economy that we have come to know as 'neoliberalism'. The liberalism I want to evoke, however, is an expansive category that incorporates all manner of 'social' and 'economic' liberals and much else besides in a single problematic field; a field that can neither split nor unify because its protagonists are at once bound together and rent by a single aporia. A liberal, then, would be anyone who posits each and every human as *de iure* individual, yet who is constantly exercised by the difference between the individual in fact, and the individual worthy of their individuality. One of the names for this abyss, and the one in which we are all caught, is education. For education is at once the force charged with making all individuals worthy, and the currency in which their present deficit is calculated. In its most hopeful, moderately progressive versions, it is a means of speculatively flattening hierarchy by rotating it through ninety degrees and projecting it forward into time. In time, with sufficient education, everyone will ascend the ladder. But in the meantime this meliorism is also a medium of delay. And who is to say this delay may not prove eternal, and the ladder just another pyramid in disguise? It may be that the degree of commitment to ensuring that the delay really is only a delay constitutes one of the most important political differences among 'liberals'.

To take a classic example, the essence of liberty for John Stuart Mill is that each is the best judge of his course of action since 'no one but the person himself can judge of the sufficiency of the motive' (Mill 2006, 109). Yet, he also deplores the fashionable idea that we should 'search in our own minds and hearts for laws of conduct binding on ourselves and on all others' (95). The appearance of contradiction here is a function of the extreme rarity of minds able to interrogate the 'grounds' of their opinions (43), sufficiently 'capacious' to reconcile both sides of a question (55), or possessed of the 'judicial faculty' (60). And the only way to bridge this gap is to cultivate the 'soil' in which a 'small minority' can 'grow', who will serve the rest by 'opening their eyes' (74). The project of equality demands this stratification. And in the meantime, the 'honour and glory of the average man is that he is capable of following', but 'with his eyes open' (76). This, then, is the problem that has shaped education's equivocal mission since at least the inception of bourgeois liberal democracy, and that has tended, at least since Condorcet, to ensure that it is equal and universal only insofar as it is elementary. But it is important to note also that the idea of education may bear a certain liberalism into the most revolutionary thinking. If Rosa Luxemburg rejects the claim that the German proletariat in 1919 is 'unripe' or 'immature' (Luxemburg 1918), it is partly *because* they have outgrown the 'children's seven-league boots' of pre-Marxist socialism (Luxemburg 2006, 70). Structurally, temporally, education just is reform, even if it is the reform necessary to enable revolution. Now that it is a very long time since the revolution has not arrived, any educator with transformative pretensions must live this delay as an agony and reckon, in the meantime, with their own involvement in reproduction.

I make this last point because it suggests why my own argument cannot absent itself from this problematic landscape or presume to adjudicate between Rand and Arendt from a place that is quite free of either. The preceding steps of argument also, I hope, suggest why it might be that the two converge on the matter of the education of African American children. The mere presence of such a parallel population, who must be said to be individuals, but not perhaps the same sort of individuals—worthy of education, but not in the same space—sheds a deeply unwelcome light on some topographical anomalies that otherwise pass as normal. The case of African Americans in the 1950s and 1960s (but not only then) illustrates in a spectacular way what it might mean to inhabit the same city, yet not inhabit the same city. The physical architecture of segregation enforces in a brutal and literal way a division of space within itself, erecting everywhere borders that paradoxically keep the fact of separation ever-present. Rand and Arendt alike struggle to reconcile this with an ideal of free association whereby space ought to accommodate a comfortable spread of groupings determined by nothing but their own preference. But they can only do so by accepting the hegemon's preference as predetermining the whole field of preferences. The school poses an acute problem for this logic of choice. For it is, even in the most normal circumstances, the place par excellence where the state by rights sequesters a form (albeit a curious form) of private property. Its standing in any topography of public and private, political and social, is thus profoundly equivocal.

3   Rand's Racism

Rand's essay on 'Racism' ends by declaring the leaders of the Civil Rights Movement, notably in their battles over education, the real racists. Since this reversal is currently enjoying considerable success in alt-right messaging, not the least interest of reading Rand's essay is to work out how she gets there. She starts with a typically idiosyncratic and tendentious definition: 'Racism is the lowest, most crudely primitive form of collectivism' (Rand 1964, 147). If this is unorthodox, it is also entirely predictable: anything Rand deems bad *must* be a manifestation of 'collectivism', if only to ensure that 'capitalism' is the solution. But how is the thing to be argued? The essence of racism, it transpires, is the abdication of individual responsibility and 'rationality' to 'chemical predestination', such that the racist asks to be judged not 'by his own character and actions', but rather by those of 'a collective of ancestors' (147). Seen in this light, families that derive either shame or pride from their forebears, or 'the celebrity who starts his autobiography with a detailed account of his family history', are essentially engaged in the same enterprise that culminated in the 'wholesale slaughter of Nazi Germany' where the same 'racism' achieved 'full expression' (147–148). In case one has any doubts about this rather bold teleology, Rand then doubles down on it, suggesting that all talk of 'blood' must inevitably lead to 'torrents of blood' (148–149).

It may seem, thus, that mass violence is the terminus towards which Rand is driving. But her argument is ultimately much less invested in racism's 'full expression' than in the essence presented by the family historian. True, she cannot resist lingering a little over the horrors of the Soviet Union. But the prime instance of 'racism' with which she will perorate is famously non-violent. It is also not a mass phenomenon, because in Rand's world there is no such thing. There are no masses, only aggregates of individuals. Even *qua* fantasy, the collective cannot be a collective fantasy. The appearance of mass phenomena is thus a potential distraction that must be reduced to the individual level of the family historian. We should not be misled by talk of 'the greatness of the German (or French or Italian or Cambodian) race': any attempt to bolster '"tribal self-esteem" by alleging the inferiority of some other tribe' must be tracked back to each member's 'sense of his own inferiority' (148–149). For there are no 'tribes', and no 'self' that could feel 'esteem' except individuals lured from their capitalist vocation by the 'quest for the unearned'.

It is on these grounds, then, that the 'Negro leaders' are the most notable racists of their time. They are quite right to protest against 'government-enforced discrimination' insofar as it impinges on their individual rights. But as soon as they make collective demands, they become racist (153). As racists, they naturally proceed to collectivise others and attack their individual rights. Thus 'quotas' (one of Rand's bugbears) effectively demand 'that white men be penalized *for the sins of their ancestors*' (154–155). Here we see how pivotal the instance of the family historian is. The only thing that can link 'white men' across history is genealogy, and it is racist. Rand's individuals are thus as disparate in time as they are in space. Whatever property anyone holds at any given point is theirs and theirs alone. This is their prime individual right, and any attempt to question it is an assault on individual rights. From this perspective, then, the 'Negro leaders' are making a tragic error: it is 'suicidal' that those 'who need the protection of individual rights most urgently— the Negroes—are now in the vanguard of the destruction of these rights' (156–157).

For all its maniacal fidelity to the logic of individualism, this account cannot help but make a couple of pretty hefty concessions to obviously systemic phenomena. For it would seem hard to parse 'discrimination' emanating from a 'government' in purely individualistic terms. And if, as it seems, the 'Negroes' really do need 'protection' *as a group*, it must surely (on Rand's own terms) be in response to some prior 'racism' that had already cast them as a collective. The history implicit in all of this seems glaringly obvious and hard to dismiss as the sins of ancestors. Indeed, it would be hard to imagine a process of collectivisation more massive, coercive and brutal than the slavery of the middle passage and the plantations, not to mention their massive, ongoing, structural effects, from Jim Crow and redlining to mass incarceration (Alexander 2019). Rand does, in other contexts, and in more general terms, manage to gloss 'slavery' as an individual wrong, by determining it as the expropriation by one man of the sweat of another's brow (see 'Man's Rights', in Rand

1964, 113). But how can this massive, systematic, racialised appropriation of human beings be conjured away as the mere aggregate of individual sins of individual ancestors?

The short answer is 'capitalism'. Rand is obliged to admit that the 'major victims of such race prejudice as did exist were the Negroes'. But it was confined to 'the noncapitalist' or 'feudal-agrarian' South, and it was 'the capitalist North that destroyed' it (Rand 1964, 151–152). Thereafter, in 'its great era of capitalism, the United States was the freest country on earth—and the best refutation of racist theories', welcoming and integrating men 'of all races', many of which had been at each other's throats for generations in the Old World. For capitalism is 'the only system that functions in a way which rewards rationality and penalizes all forms of irrationality, including racism' (150–151). So it makes sense that 'the Negroes' were doing rather better for themselves *before* the 'clamor for racial equality, propagated by the "liberals"' made them disastrously 'race-conscious' (152). For this race-consciousness reintroduced a racism that capitalism would otherwise, left to its own devices, tend to repel.

Crucial to this picture is the conceit of capitalism as an immaculate conception, a new order that wipes the slate clean. Rand's account of 'a free market' where nothing counts except 'productive ability', which is to say 'individual ability', coupled with 'ambition' (150), reads like an uncritical, irony-free recapitulation of Marx's skewering of the exchange relation in which individuals A and B are 'indifferent' to each other 'as breathing individuals', and 'the general interest is precisely the generality of self-seeking interests' (Marx 1993, 242–245). But nothing highlights more clearly the extent to which Rand's economic thought lacks economic thought than its application to 'the Negroes'. For them, in Rand's terms, the price of admission to the intrinsic rationality of capitalism is forgetting the *hurt* of slavery. For this too is a *prejudice* that must be left at the door if capitalism is to realise itself in an aggregate of individuals who reciprocally accept that they have no one but themselves to thank for their success or failure. What this account conveniently forgets is accumulation; or, more specifically, that it must have a past and not just a future. Even more specifically, Rand has no concept of primitive accumulation. For it is not just that African Americans had had practically no chance to accumulate for themselves under Jim Crow; or that they were now being ushered onto a playing field that, far from being level, was riven with structural exclusions, built on the back of their own labour; or that, in the bitterest of ironies, they were thus obliged to struggle against their own, but radically alienated, fixed capital. More than this, when Africans were first appropriated and brought to America en masse, it was as pure instruments of accumulation, and through an act of pure accumulation.

Rand is not, of course, obliged to think the thing in such specifically Marxian terms. It seems, nevertheless, that she thinks primitive origins are something she has to reckon with. Curiously enough, this is where the very genealogy she otherwise seems to forbid comes into play. Thus racism is cast, from the very start, as a sort of atavism: it is the 'lowest, most crudely primitive'. As such, it tends to deal in 'brute force', and to arise in more primitive people: it is 'more prevalent among the poor white trash than among their intellectual betters' (147–149). The genealogy at work here, the only one she will allow any deductive force, is an alien genealogy. It is the genealogy of collectivism; that through which 'statism [...] rises out of prehistorical tribal warfare' (149–150). Capitalism, which knows no genealogy, is thus locked in a Manichean but asymmetrical struggle *with genealogy*. The problem with this baroque fix is that, if it relieves capitalism of any responsibility to the past, it also renders it curiously impotent, defenceless against alien, atavistic incursions. Maybe this is why, as Rand concedes elsewhere, 'capitalism has never yet existed' in its pure state, but is rather 'the system of the future' ('The Objectivist Ethics', Rand 1964, 37). For while it is always already perfect in itself, capitalism's perfection *in fact* must await the achievement in each individual of the heroic struggle to overcome irrationality and realise themselves, individually. Herein lies the pathos of the hero, who can only bitterly resent those primitives whose unwonted apparition in actually existing capitalism withholds from him full enjoyment of the ideal state.

And so Rand's anti-racism arrives, through an elaborate detour, at exactly the same target as a more conventional American racism. She has, we are to understand, nothing against 'the Negro leaders' as 'Negroes'. It is just that their incorrigible refusal to understand how individual rights are bound up with private property makes her sad. But we have not quite done with the malice and duplicity of Rand's notion of 'private property'. For it would seem the category is sufficiently capacious to include *public* schools. She argues, in line with her general hatred of 'quotas', that 'racial quotas in schools' are 'pure racism' (156). And she is quick to add that such legislation would be 'evil' whether in the cause of 'segregation or integration'. But she also argues *on the same page* that it is only in 'privately owned establishments' that one must never legislate: in 'government owned facilities' it is quite 'proper to forbid all discrimination' (156). It seems to follow, then, that public schools really are, in some way, private. But how? The evil of quotas, remember, is that they operate a zero-sum game: what they give to one has to be taken from another. And the paragraphs following Rand's remarks on schools are peppered (not entirely coherently) with indignant protests against any 'claim to the property of another man' or anything gained 'at the expense of others' (156). It would seem that the issue of school places is drawn into this topic such that a black child seeking to attend a 'white' school would *deprive* a white schoolchild of something that belongs to her by rights. Assuming an overall sufficiency of school places, this thing can only be the right of a white child to a place in a 'white' school, or its corollary, the exclusivity of the 'white' school. Of course, such exclusivity may indeed be construed as a form of social capital, or even a sort of property, but a sort whose value lies primarily in *depriving* others; in this instance, what is more, of a public good. Then again, is this not the secret of all 'private property'?

This casts a baleful light on the 'private means' of protest of which Rand does approve: 'economic boycott or social ostracism' (156). Even leaving aside structural imbalances in economic 'means', how are the already-ostracised to practice ostracism? In terms of schools, Rand's advice amounts to this: stay in your allotted place and pretend anyone cares. But we might also think of more fundamental ways in which the sacrality of 'private property' and 'individual rights' limits the terrain of protest open to those who started life in America *as* property. Rand reserves her most extravagant 'outrage' for 'the mere idea of using children as pawns in a political game' (156). Indeed, she rather grandly arrogates the outrage of 'all parents' in view of parental dereliction, and so assumes a right over the children, in the name of their individual rights. But to take this stance she must also forget that it concerns children whose great-great-grandparents might not even have enjoyed the right to keep their children because they were legally the property of the slave-owner. Even now, it seems, the children are exposed to a rhetorical appropriation that, denying them agency, consigns them instead to a pathos of the individual that exhausts itself in the bare expression of their barest rights. Reduced, thus, to 'the smallest minority on earth' (154), there is literally nothing anyone can do for them.

4 ARENDT'S LITTLE ROCK

The pathos of childhood plays an even more pivotal role in Arendt's 'Reflections on Little Rock'. But before we come to this, there is much ground to cover. The terms of Arendt's argument, which bear a close though not exact relation to the topography of *The Human Condition*, are by no means identical to those of Rand. Instead of the language of private property and individual rights, there is a more fine-grained consideration of the balance of power between political, public, social, and private realms. And these terminologies do not translate smoothly into each other. The social, for instance, stands in the place of Rand's individual at some points, and has slightly different implications. The overall topography nevertheless attempts to legislate, and ultimately fractures, along similar lines, and betrays analogous anomalies, notably on the status of public schools.

Expressed as a thesis, the thing may seem rock solid: equality belongs solely in the political realm, not at all in the social; conversely, discrimination, which ought never to appear in the political is the very law of the social. And, so long as Arendt's illustrative examples oblige these categories, all is well. Only, as in Rand, they founder on the rock of the very thing they are meant to legislate: racial difference. Let us start with 'society' because, as the realm where exclusivity is the norm, it is crucial to Arendt's argument. Here, everyone must be free to associate and form groups according to whatever criteria they choose. There can thus be no right to go to any hotel of one's choosing because hotels clearly lie within the social. But there is no loss in this so long as society is ultimately inclusive at the level of mutual respect. Thus, Jews who claim the right to holiday in resorts that cater exclusively for Jews cannot complain if other groups wish to do the same with regard to their own kind (52). The perfect balance of the example evinces a self-evident clarity and justice. And Arendt's argument unfolds with a sort of confidence in common sense that she might suspect in a more philosophical context (Arendt 1981, 52).

The problems begin, however, when exceptions and grey areas are determined with the same confidence. So, Arendt says, the same principle of exclusivity 'obviously' does not apply to hotels 'in business districts', or to theatres and museums, or to buses and trains. For these 'are in fact public services', even if they are privately owned (52). But is this really so obvious? And what sort of 'fact' is at stake when we might just as well say that the hotel is *in fact* privately owned? The common-sense notion of fact seems unable to settle the question. And so too, it seems, is Arendt. For, only a couple of pages earlier, she has paired the right to sit on a bus with, precisely, 'the right to go into any hotel', in a list of rights that she declares 'minor indeed' compared with the 'elementary human right' to 'marry whoever one wishes' (49). So is there a right to choose your hotel after all? Or is it, as a 'minor' right, really no right at all? The answer certainly matters in the case of the right to sit on the bus. For this had surely ceased, since 1955, to be in any sense 'minor'.

To be fair, Arendt does seem to clarify the matter of buses in the later passage: '[t]hough not strictly in the political realm', she says, buses 'are clearly in the public domain where all men are equal' (52). But this clarity comes only at the price of a further equivocation. For, it seems the 'public' can institute equality where it does not 'strictly' belong. Can we quite trust this 'domain' that has a habit of occupying portions of other realms, or acquiring their prerogatives? Or might the judgment of what is 'clearly [...] public' start to look like a matter of ad-hockery? Indeed, despite this claim to apodictic certainty in any given instance, the 'public' has no consistent force throughout Arendt's article. And this is pivotal when we come to her astonishment that the Supreme Court should have started its attempt to legally compel integration in 'of all places, the public schools' (50).

Where and what is the 'public' in this instance? These schools are surely rather more *strictly* 'public' than the buses that might be privately owned, and rather more *obviously* places 'where all men are equal'. Indeed, one might even contend that, as legally-enforced expressions of the will of the state, they are already somewhat more *strictly* political. And Arendt more or less concedes this last point later in the article when she singles out 'compulsory education' as the only matter in which the private rights of parents are 'legally restricted' in deference to the state's 'unchallengeable right to prescribe minimum requirements for future citizenship' (55). But she immediately pivots to consider the school, not from the point of view of its legal and political constitution, but as it is *for the child*. It is 'the first place away from home where he establishes contact with the public world that surrounds him and his family'. And, as Arendt is quick to add, *this* 'public world is not political but social' (55). With this change of perspective—to the child, and to the school as lived experience—the pendulum of the 'public' thus swings all the way back to the opposing pole.

It may be tempting to see, behind this seeming desire to keep politics out of education, the shadow of totalitarianism. In 'The Crisis in Education', the essay she explicitly flags as the undeveloped backdrop for 'Reflections', Arendt tells us, 'Education can play no part in politics, because in politics we always have to deal with those who are already educated. Whoever wants to educate adults really wants to act as their guardian and prevent them from political activity' (Arendt 2006 [1954], 173). And it is easy to infer the corollary, that politics should not interfere in education lest it end in dragooning youth as the cadre of a new order. Here we might think of the 'jeering and grimacing mob of youngsters' that escorts Elizabeth Eckford off the premises of Little Rock Central High School in the famous photograph (Arendt 1959, 50), and of Arendt's warning, towards the end of 'Reflections', of the possible 'rise of mob and gang rule' (56), not to mention the part played by mobs in *The Origins of Totalitarianism* (1951). Yet if 'Crisis' traces the genesis of the mob to a sort of politicisation, it is emphatically not in the form of indoctrination effected by a totalitarian entity positing itself as 'guardian'. The fault, indeed, lies with the *abdication* of adult authority promoted by 'Rousseauian' progressive education, and its propensity to leave each child 'a minority of one confronted by the absolute majority of all the others' (Arendt 2006 [1954], 178). The sort of tyranny that concerns us here is thus a Tocquevillian tyranny of the majority. Whatever dire political potential this may have, it is to be understood in the first instance as a properly social phenomenon. Moreover, the framing of this argument, in 'Reflections', in terms of familial or quasi-familial relations takes us into an area of the social that is markedly private. And this ultimately means that even the mob is thoroughly depoliticised.

In 'Reflections', the scene of mob violence, which Arendt reads as 'a fantastic caricature of progressive education', is thus to be understood in private-social terms, as a matter of wrongs 'adults' have perpetrated on 'children' by abdicating authority. Even political intervention is drawn haplessly into this paradigm. Since Federal anti-segregation legislation simply cannot legislate such things, its only effect is 'to burden children, black and white, with the working out of a problem which adults for generations have confessed themselves unable to solve' (50). Law takes effect, thus, in the form of a cascade of smaller, more private abdications, dividing the scene by age rather than colour. Thus the prime wrong done to Elizabeth Eckford is that she 'obviously, was asked to be a hero' by adults who did not feel able to be heroic in their own persons. Her experience at the hands of the mob is secondary, contingent upon this since the mob itself is likewise the product of adult abdication. Arendt, indeed, expresses sympathy for those of the jeering youngsters who will look back in shame when they 'outgrow their present brutality' (50). Axiomatically, for Arendt, none of the child actors can be a political subject, so that their actions, however grave, must be attributed to the misguided tutelage of their parents and other adults around them. The jeering youngsters of the mob are thus covered by a weird version of childhood innocence whose realisation is deferred until adulthood. But this convolution points to a problem in the whole adult-child schema: why are we to imagine that they will reach this point just by growing into *adults*? It is almost as if they were to grow into the children they ought to have been, had they not in fact grown up in the vast ambient racism of 1950s Arkansas, a racism that surely reaches into every realm and sphere. In other words, all this juggling of 'adults' and 'children' only serves to obfuscate the continuum of racism in which all stand.

There is, nevertheless, one more question we need to ask about 'adults': how exactly *should* they exercise their authority? Arendt is adamant that politics must not intervene in the social. This is why the Federal legislation is so misconceived. Our task is not 'to abolish discrimination', but rather 'keep it confined within the social sphere, where it is legitimate, and prevent its trespassing on the political and the personal sphere, where it is destructive' (Arendt 1959, 51). But if legislation is limited to policing the borders of the social, preserving it as a sort of homeland of discrimination, who or what is to protect the 'personal sphere', adrift in the social? Is this not an abdication on Arendt's part? If, as the case of Elizabeth Eckford would seem to suggest, there really is no protection in the social, is it entirely responsible to consign schoolchildren to this Wild West? Can the answer really be to take refuge in the placid equilibrium of Jewish hotels for Jewish holiday-makers?

The picture of 'society' painted in *The Human Condition* is rather less neat. And, unsurprisingly, some of this makes its way into 'Reflections'. For, defined as 'that curious, somewhat hybrid realm between the political and the private in which, since the beginning of the modern age, most men have spent the greater part of their lives' (51), society does seem to involve the political in some way. The question is, in what way? Arendt is clear that the principle of 'equality' obtains only in the political realm proper, so that neither legislative interference nor activism can be justified.

Yet it seems none of this can prevent things that belong properly in the political from popping up in the social. And the net effect of this may be that politics proper is powerless to protect us from informal political attack.

Arendt's account of the political right of 'eligibility' (for political office) is a case in point. Although 'an inalienable right of every citizen', its 'equality is already restricted' by 'personal distinction' and other qualities on whose nature and genesis Arendt expatiates at some length, but in the vaguest terms, before concluding that they concern 'things in which all are equals to begin with' (50–51). Somewhere in this remarkably garbled stretch of exposition is the unwelcome thought that access to this universal right must be anything but equal because it passes through markedly politicised areas of the social. What, after all, is 'personal distinction', and how does it come into being? And if lacking this sauce, one's social being is confined to 'things in which all are equals to begin with', does this not seem to point in the direction of the awful dissolution into the 'over-all life process of the species' prophesied in *The Human Condition*? At the very least, the 'hybrid' nature of the social would seem to offer wildly different possibilities of access to the political to different subjects, including the possibility of being restricted to the private end of things, prey to more or less occulted forms of political power.

To seek refuge in the personal and the private would thus seem a catastrophe. Yet it is in precisely this direction that Arendt seems to urge African Americans. Rather than (mystifyingly in her view) fastening onto the cause of education, they should be demanding instead the 'elementary' right to marry whom they choose (49). Seemingly they are advised to secure their private realm *before* they even think about ascending the steps of social and political power. At work here is an equivocation over whether the private realm of home offers refuge from the social, or is entirely encircled, and perhaps even infiltrated, by it. Arendt speaks of the 'protective four walls' beyond which we step into the 'public world' meaning, in the first instance 'the social sphere' (51), and at one point evokes a rather sentimental view of a 'private life' that few now, under the onslaught of society, 'know the rules of and live' (53). And a little later she eulogises the home that is 'strong and secure enough to shield its young against the demands of the social and the responsibilities of the political realm' (55). But this refuge certainly will not work for the 'mixed marriage' which, since it 'constitutes a challenge to society', must expect to be challenged by it in return. Indeed, 'the partners to such a marriage have so far preferred personal happiness to social adjustment that they are willing to bear the burden of discrimination. This is and must remain their private business' (53). This, then, is the consequence of asserting the 'elementary' right to marry, at least for this couple. They are on their own, beaten back into a private realm that offers no protection of any sort since it includes as 'private business' the hatred of the world they have been obliged to renounce.

One of the most remarkable aspects of this analysis is that Arendt does not pause to ask what this might mean for the children of such a couple. They have, it would seem, voluntarily forfeited any right to a home 'strong and secure enough to shield its young'. And one must ask if this dreadful state of affairs applies uniquely to the mixed-race couple. Arendt, like Rand, assumes that Elizabeth Eckford's parents *chose* to expose her to a baying mob that she might otherwise have avoided. But it beggars belief that the anger of the mob could be entirely alien to an Elizabeth Eckford. Even supposing she enjoys a well-insulated home, she is liable to it in some form the moment she takes a step beyond its 'protective four walls'. For the landscape that meets her is everywhere cleft by lines indicating spaces she may enter, and spaces she may not, on pain of being met with a rage that may differ in number and intensity from that of the mob, but not in kind. This is segregation. And supposing she avoids the explosion of rage by toeing the line, does this mean she is free of it? Or is she swallowing it, and storing up a disquiet of her own that must be borne back into the home before it can be voiced in safety? In which case, just how well insulated can her home be?

What we see here is the collapse of all these 'realms' and 'spheres' into the soup of 'society', where their negative instances continue to roam unchecked like zombies, ready to devour those whose last bastion is the 'private'. To put this another way, any subject that utterly lacks political power also lacks social power and is ultimately unable to defend their private life, perhaps even their mere existence, against whatever social and political power is in the field. This is, indeed, more or less what Arendt prophesies in *The Human Condition*, only as the fate of all in a world where society will finally have swallowed all other spheres. The differential instance of race in America, however, belies the putative uniformity and indifferentiation of this nightmare. It suggests that while the political, albeit in its most etiolated, bastardised form, may continue to intervene on behalf of some, there are others for whom it never fully existed in the first place. Indeed, it reminds us that this has always been more or less the case, even in the heyday of the public realm. For it concerns a class of people whose historical role is broadly structurally analogous to that of those women, servants and slaves who, in Arendt's Aristotelian ideal, were expected to absorb the burden of labour so that 'men' could live out their properly political lives. The solidity of the realms and spheres was only ever even notionally possible at the expense of naturalising this *dependence*.

On what grounds, then, would one deny political agency to people on whom the political is nevertheless allowed to act? Why should one not decide, whenever one finds oneself on the sharp end of politics, that here and now are the time and place to act politically? And why should this question not extend *even* to children whose first 15 years may have been one long apprenticeship in the politicisation of everyday life? Arendt and Rand are alike impossibly fastidious in their view of the proper bounds of political action. They take what one might call the hegemonic view, awarding to the already-constituted power the right to determine the decorum of protest. But the thing shows, if anything worse, in Arendt. For while, in Rand, this stance evinces an unshakeable faith in the justice and solidity of the political structure, Arendt is at this very time already announcing its decline and eventual disappearance. Surely, when summary justice is making a mockery of any attempt to assign legitimate spheres of action, no one should have to wait for the spheres to realign themselves before determining to act. But it seems Arendt finds it easier to imagine a society abandoned by politics, and the dissolution of her own schema, than the emergence of new political spaces.

To find out what this might look like, we might turn to Arendt's later essay *On Violence* (1970). Here, the whole business of different realms and spheres has vanished, and Arendt seems almost nostalgic for the tactics of 'boycotts, sit-ins, and demonstrations' which have, it turns out, proven 'highly successful'. For the focus has shifted to the 'large urban centers' where 'the basic irreconcilability of interests' has been 'dangerously exposed'. Remarkably, given her earlier contortions over the rather mild and legally-prosecuted request to attend school, Arendt is quite sympathetic to the view that the ensuing 'black riots' showed 'rationality' and 'restraint'. She also, however, understands the 'perfectly rational reaction' of the white underclass who have been 'singled out to pay the full price for ill-designed integration policies', and fears the emergence of a 'black racism' that might provoke a 'really violent white backlash' (Arendt 1970, 76–77). Arendt had already predicted something of the sort in 'Reflections', in view of the rise of the black population of the big Northern cities, and the 'special attraction for the mob' that the question of race holds (Arendt 1959, 47). And now that the mob and its violence really have moved centre-stage, it seems they have swept away all trace of the different realms and spheres, leaving in their wake the mere clash of races. It is as if analysis were obliged by circumstances to suspend its categories, declaring a sort of epistemological state of exception; and, moreover, as if racialisation were an inevitable consequence of this shift from a civil to a martial topic. The disappearance of Arendt's topography is not, thus, an unalloyed cause for celebration. Indeed, if, as it seems, it has been hustled off the stage before it could be called to account for allowing such violence to arise out of it in the first place, we may have to demand its return.

5   Colonialism in the Public Sphere

This is also, by the same token, the point at which I have to step aside from the sort of immanent critique I have attempted till now, locating where Arendt and Rand run aground in their own terms, and only adducing racism in the final instance. For the entire point of this was to avoid determining the racism at work in their essays as a merely personal prejudice supervening on an otherwise healthy structure. The point has now come to suggest what remains to be included in these structures to account for their structural racism. A key passage from Frantz Fanon's essay 'On Violence' from *The Wretched of the Earth* will help to point the way. In her essay *On Violence*, Arendt views Fanon's essay not unsympathetically, given the dim view she takes of the current glorification of violence. But she overlooks his account of the complex relations between colony and metropolitan centre, and the place each gives to violence.

> The colonial world is a world cut in two. The dividing line, the frontiers are shown by barracks and police stations. In the colonies it is the policeman and the soldier who are the official, instituted go-betweens, the spokesmen of the settler and his rule of oppression. In capitalist societies the educational system, whether lay or clerical, the structure of moral reflexes handed down from father to son, the exemplary honesty of workers who are given a medal after fifty years of good and loyal service, and the affection which springs from harmonious relations and good behaviour—all these aesthetic expressions of respect for the established order serve to

create around the exploited person an atmosphere of submission and of inhibition which lightens the task of policing considerably. In the capitalist countries a multitude of moral teachers, counsellors and 'bewilderers' separate the exploited from those in power. In the colonial countries, on the contrary, the policeman and the soldier, by their immediate presence and their frequent and direct action maintain contact with the native and advise him by means of rifle-butts and napalm not to budge. It is obvious here that the agents of government speak the language of pure force. The intermediary does not lighten the oppression, nor seek to hide the domination; he shows them up and puts them into practice with the clear conscience of an upholder of the peace; yet he is the bringer of violence into the home and into the mind of the native. (Fanon 2001, 29)

This is a key passage because it rams home Fanon's contention that, in the colonial landscape, it is not a question of approving or disapproving of violence. Here, *there is violence*. The situation imposes it. This is not to say that there is *no* violence within the political order of the metropolitan centre. Rather, it is muffled, deferred, channelled through the filters and buffers of civil institutions. But in the colony, the state of exception is the norm, such that there never was any distance between the most private realm, and the law in its most brutal instance. Likewise, this situation is intrinsically racialising even though, for Fanon, *there is no race*. It is, indeed, the crucible for the violent imposition of race, as a means to normalising violence. Crucially, however, Fanon's implied solution is not to import metropolitan civility into the colony. Rather, the violence of the colony is the privileged point from which we can engage the revolutionary hope of smashing the entire edifice. And this is ultimately because the colonised zone is not a mere extraterritorial elsewhere but a supplementary sphere or realm of the centre.

In short, what is missing from Arendt and Rand alike is a proper understanding of the part played by colonialism in the political spaces they predicate. The boundaries within which their normative rules and relations are supposed to obtain are drawn by the exclusion of another territory on which they nevertheless depend, historically, economically, and politically. So when emancipated slaves show their faces in the (metro)polis it is as the sign of the incomprehensible presence of an extraterritorial zone of subjection that was always *there*, but ought never to have been *here*. Arendt is quick to point out that the 'crime' of American slavery is distinct from the colonialism of the European nations in which America never participated, and consequently that American racism has a distinct genesis (Arendt 1959, 46). But what are we to think when she suggests that the 'visibility' of black skin in the public realm is ineffaceable and something African Americans will just have to put up with? Such visible things, she suggests, cannot be dismissed as 'mere exterior appearances', because the public just is the realm of appearances (47). But this is ultimately question-begging. What, we must ask, is it that is visible in the visibility of mere skin colour?

Arendt really ought to know better. It is not just that *The Origins of Totalitarianism* (1951) identifies imperialism as one of the sources for the political horrors of the twentieth century (Arendt 2017). Her reading of Rosa Luxemburg leads her to Marx's notion of the 'original accumulation of capital'[2] as 'simple robbery', and even to posit an 'essential dependence of capitalism upon a noncapitalistic world' (192–193). Yet in many important respects she continues to frame the outside of capitalism as radically heterogeneous. Indeed (drawing heavily on *The Heart of Darkness*) she casts the colonial world as a 'phantom world': an 'underworld' in which, without 'the delaying effect of social ethical values', men 'escaped the reality of civilization' (248). These men thus no longer operate on the same ontological dimension as capitalism. This is why the colonial financier dominates this scene: his separation from 'normal banking', never mind 'production and exploitation', already gives him a 'touch of unreality' (262). He is the part of capitalism that already embodies in embryo the willingness 'to abandon the so-called laws of capitalist production and their egalitarian tendencies' (266) that flourishes in the counter world of imperialism. In a way, then, this topic of the unreality of the colonial zone saves the honour of the capitalist norm.

But there is one aspect of the colonised zone on whose reality Arendt is curiously insistent. For while 'race' generally does not mean very much, black Africans have 'a genuine race origin' (268), according to a 'precise meaning' of the word that concerns 'not at all the color of their skin but the fact that they behaved like a part of nature, that they treated nature as their undisputed master, that they had not created a human world, a human reality' (250–251). The real race is thus the one that fails to generate reality because it fails to take the first step towards capitalism. And it seems this reality of their race is antipathetic to their reality as human beings. Otherwise, it is hard to see why the 'real crime' in South Africa, the one for which 'there could be no excuse and no humanly comprehensible reason', was the treatment of Indian and Chinese workers 'as though they were not human beings' (269). Where, then, does Arendt stand on the Boers' discovery in black Africans of 'the only "raw material" which Africa provided in abundance'? (252). And what, finally, were the 'inherent conflicts' and 'serious difficulties' that made it harder for post-abolition England and America to live together with their ex-slaves? (230–231). For all Arendt's dismissal of 'the color of their skin' as the true marker of race, it is hard to imagine that the 'visibility' of the ex-slaves, linking them back to 'a genuine race origin' and a phantom world at the antipodes of capitalism and the public sphere has nothing to do with this.

There are at any rate signs that Arendt—in spite of her commitment to 'the central pillar of genuine nationhood, the equality of all peoples' (217), and her sense that imperialism was a catastrophic deviation for capitalism—cannot quite let go of the colonial sentiment for which some 'primitive' peoples are appropriable but not assimilable; indeed, appropriable *because* not assimilable. This is a serious problem for a serious philosopher anatomising the human condition and proposing a universal schema governing the very possibility of political life. But it takes a Rand to embrace this logic and unfold its consequences to the bitter end. In the Q&A after her graduation address to West Point, 6 March 1974, published as 'Philosophy: Who Needs It', Rand reprises some of the themes of the essay on 'Racism'. Because 'the smallest minority on Earth is an individual', one best defends any human being, however categorised, by embracing individual rights. Group rights of any sort are deleterious to individuality and racist. Slavery was a great evil, but it came from the old world, and it is to the glory of America (and capitalism and individualism) that people died abolishing it. The real racists are the liberals who insist on bringing it up (Rand 1974). The remarks that have rightly received most attention, however, are those that declare the native Americans 'savages' who, because they have no concept of property, can have no right to it, and are therefore rightfully dispossessed. Do we not have the 'right to invade' dictatorships since, failing to respect individual rights, they have no rights themselves? If this analogy seems strained, we should note that, for Rand, the 'savages' are bigger criminals than the dictators. Their pretended 'right to keep part of the earth untouched, unused, and not even as property' is an offence against the tide of civilisation. Rand stops short of avowing genocide per se. But in case we were in any doubt over the general tendency of this unusually blunt version of Manifest Destiny, she immediately goes on to justify the Israeli appropriation of Arab land. This, too, is only right. Because, whether in the Americas or in the Middle East, the bringers of individual rights have always 'represented the banner of the mind' and are always 'in the right'.

This 'banner of the mind' is the standard of the only collective Rand formally recognises, just as the outrageous refusal to institute property rights is the only form of selfishness she deplores. It is sovereign, impassive and nakedly unconcerned by the violence of the moment of its constitution. This is why Rand is such an embarrassment to liberal thought. She speaks her 'mind': the mind of the individual, and the mind that gives him his rights, even unto the right to liquidate any collective that has proven its inability to divest itself of the most primitive form of collectivity. This is a little too blunt for most 'liberals', and they may all too easily be drawn into the cardinal error of making us 'race-conscious' by protesting. Fools who, since they do not acknowledge the necessary constitution of 'mind', cannot know their own.

For all the stentorian self-certainty and sheer wrongness of this position, there is nevertheless perhaps something in it to which we liberals need to attend. Are we quite sure we do not ourselves speak with a mind constituted in the secret violence of primitive accumulation? For my own part, I have been privileged to lead the life of the mind in a terrain freed of want or coercion, in cities and institutions built to a greater or lesser degree on the wealth of enclosure and plantation, and with no obligation to dwell on that fact even as I earnestly dissect the ills of these distant phenomena. Of course, this is precisely the sort of handwringing that would have the avatars of Rand hissing 'virtue signaling'. But they would miss the point, for the bleeding heart of my confession is that I am a liberal. Nothing brings home to me the basically liberal foundations of even my most radical intellectual adventures than my abiding preference, in spite of everything I have said, to think and deal with an Arendt rather than a Rand. And maybe all this means is that Arendt makes available to me a virtual world that gratifies my peculiar urges and talents, and gives my ridiculous reason a reason to exist. What is wrong with Rand, on the other hand, is not simply that I disagree with her or am offended by her, but that she seems too obvious, not worthy of the intellectual tools I want to exercise. Supposing I were standing in a burning house that Rand had set alight, I fear I would still not find her interesting enough to care. Actually, I believe I am standing in a burning house that Rand has set alight. But is this belief enough to stir me to action? And what would action look like anyway? Perhaps, at most, a chapter, a comparative critique, asking whether it is wise to deal with the pair as if they moved in separate worlds, or whether they are to be placed on the same map after all; and answering, finally, they *are and aren't*.

NOTES

1. See Chapters 7 and 8 for more on this issue.
2. 'Ursprüngliche Akkumulation', also known in English as 'primitive accumulation'. See *Capital* Vol. 1, Part 8.

BIBLIOGRAPHY

Alexander, Michelle. 2019. *The new jim crow: Mass incarceration in the age of colourblindness*. London: Penguin.

Arendt, Hannah. 2017 [1951]. *The origins of totalitarianism*. London: Penguin.

———. 2006 [1954]. The crisis in education. In *Between past and future: eight exercises in political thought*, 170–193. London: Penguin.

———. 1959. Reflections on little rock. *Dissent* 6/1: 45–56.

———. 1970. *On violence*. New York: Harvest.

———. 1981. *The life of the mind vol. 1 thinking*. New York: Harvest.

———. 1998. *The human condition*, 2nd ed. London: University of Chicago Press.

Burroughs, Michael D. 2015. Hannah Arendt, 'Reflections on Little Rock', and white ignorance. *Critical Philosophy of Race* 3 (1): 52–78.

Fanon, Frantz. 2001. *The wretched of the earth*, trans. Constance Farrington. London: Penguin.

Gines, Kathryn T. 2009. Hannah Arendt, liberalism, and racism: Controversies concerning violence, segregation, and education. *The Southern Journal of Philosophy* 47: 53–76.

———. 2014. *Hannah Arendt and the negro question*. Bloomington and Indianapolis: Indiana University Press.

Heller, Anne C. 2009. *Ayn Rand and the world she made*. New York: Nan A. Talese.

———. 2015. *Hannah Arendt: A life in dark times*. New York: Houghton Mifflin Harcourt.

Holdsworth, Candice. 2016. Don't reduce Rand or Arendt to their sex. https://www.spiked-online.com/2016/01/21/dont-reduce-rand-or-arendt-to-their-sex/. Accessed 17 March 2020.

Luxemburg, Rosa. 1918. Die 'unreife' masse. *Die Rote Fahne* 18. December 3.

———. 2006. Reform or revolution, trans. Integer. In *Reform or revolution and other writings*. New York: Dover.

Marx, Karl. 1976. *Capital: a critique of political economy vol.1*, trans. Ben Fowkes. London: Penguin.

———. 1993. *Gründrisse*, trans. Martin Nicolaus. London: Penguin.

Mill, John Stuart. 2006. *On liberty and The subjection of women*. Harmondsworth: Penguin.

Moran, Shane. 2013. Politics in dark times: Reflections on Hannah Arendt. *Politikon* 40 (2): 277–297.

Morey, Maribel. 2014. Reassessing Hannah Arendt's 'Reflections on Little Rock' (1959)'. *Law, Culture and the Humanities* 10 (1): 88–110.

Moruzzi, Norma Claire. 2000. *Speaking through the mask: Hannah Arendt and the politics of social identity*. London: Cornell University Press.

Owens, Patricia. 2017. Racism in the theory canon: Hannah Arendt and 'the one great crime in which America was never involved'. *Millennium: Journal of International Studies* 45/3: 403–424.

Rand, Ayn. 1964. Racism. In *The virtue of selfishness: A new concept of egoism*, 147–157. London: Signet.

_____. 1974. Graduation address, West Point. https://www.salon.com/2015/10/14/libertarian_superstar_ayn_rand_defended_genocide_of_savage_native_americans/. Accessed 17 March 2020.

———. 1975. *The Romantic manifesto: A philosophy of literature*, revised edition. London: Signet.

CHAPTER 10

'"Oh, that's Francisco's private joke" […]': *Atlas Shrugged*, the Gold Standard, and Utopia

Neil Cocks

1   THE GOLD STANDARD

This book is concerned with the constitutive excesses of Objectivism, what has to be in place for the 'unified identity' with 'no place of rift or loss' it celebrates to be secured (Wilt 1999, 177). In my under-standing, this philosophy of straight lines and purity finds itself committed to repressing all that muddies its arguments, or in any way sends them astray. As it can be argued that, for Rand, what stands above all else against excess is the gold standard within economics, it is to this aspect of her Objectivist discourse that I turn by way of conclusion.

Alan Greenspan makes the Objectivist case for gold in an early and influential article for the *Objectivist Newsletter*.[1] For Greenspan, 'gold and economic freedom are inseparable […] the gold standard is an instrument of laissez-faire and […] each implies and requires the other' (Greenspan

N. Cocks (✉)
University of Reading, Reading, UK

© The Author(s) 2020
N. Cocks (ed.), *Questioning Ayn Rand*,
Palgrave Studies in Literature, Culture and Economics,
https://doi.org/10.1007/978-3-030-53073-0_10

1966, 101). Gold is taken to be a commodity of 'intrinsic' or 'objective value', because it is desired by all, is homogonous, divisible, and portable, and universally acceptable as money, that is, it can act as a commodity of exchange and a store of value (Greenspan quoted by Mises Institute 2017; Greenspan 1966). Greenspan offers a traditional defence of gold that repeats David Hume's account of price-specie, maintaining that the standard allows trade imbalances to self-correct.[2] The force of his wider argument is that the gold standard system is autonomous, requiring no discretionary measures, and is thus able to free the economy from centralised interference. The idea is that when the gold standard is abandoned:

> welfare statists [...] use the banking system as a means to an unlimited expansion of credit. They have created paper reserves in the form of government bonds which — through a complex series of steps — the banks accept in place of tangible assets and treat as if they were an actual deposit, i.e., as the equivalent of what was formerly a deposit of gold. The holder of a government bond or of a bank deposit created by paper reserves believes that he has a valid claim on a real asset. But the fact is that there are now more claims outstanding than real assets. The law of supply and demand is not to be conned. As the supply of money (of claims) increases relative to the supply of tangible assets in the economy, prices must eventually rise. Thus the earnings saved by the productive members of the society lose value in terms of goods. When the economy's books are finally balanced, one finds that this loss in value represents the goods purchased by the government for welfare or other purposes with the money proceeds of the government bonds financed by bank credit expansion. (Greenspan 1966, 107)

It is an understanding foreshadowed in the celebrated 'money speech' from *Atlas Shrugged*, where Francisco d'Anconia, a wealthy and talented copper magnate, defends the good of money against 'welfare statist' criticism:

> Whenever destroyers appear among men, they start by destroying money, for money is men's protection and the base of a moral existence. Destroyers seize gold and leave to its owners a counterfeit pile of paper. This kills all objective standards and delivers men into the arbitrary power of an arbitrary setter of values. Gold was an objective value, an equivalent of wealth produced. Paper is a mortgage on wealth that does not exist, backed by a gun aimed at those who are expected to produce it. Paper is a check drawn by legal looters upon an account which is not theirs: upon the virtue of the victims. Watch for the day when it bounces, marked, 'Account overdrawn'. (Rand 1957, 413)

For d'Anconia, the destruction of gold is the destruction of money. Gold here is a precise equivalent of wealth, that is, it can be confidently exchanged with something else, because it is an objective value. In the absence of such a guarantee, there can be no money, and thus no store of value, only paper which is 'counterfeit'. An economy rooted in the imitative has no real base, according to this argument, and any claim it makes must, therefore, be backed up by violence. It is the reality of gold that is understood to make such violence unnecessary. For 'the destroyers', violence is the reality that gets things done. Far better, it is claimed, for money to be this reality. When this is the case, when value can be stored, then freedom and moral action will result. For *Atlas Shrugged*, the notion of an objective value enabling moral action is repeated in the notion of competence: being able to do something well, which, for Rand, is a question of knowledge, is also what I have described as the reality that gets things done: 'the code of competence is the only system of morality that's on a gold standard' (Rand 1957, 66).

One possible critical response to this defence of gold would return to it a history of the standard in America from the nineteenth century to the late 1950s. Already this would be to work against Objectivist practice, as Greenspan and his associates write of gold as if it were without a history, a constant across time, that, if properly embraced, will repeat its previous accomplishments, offering long term price stabilisation. The details of such histories would further unsettle arguments forwarded by Rand and Greenspan: the Objectivist investment in gold can be understood to be an exercise in nostalgia, one taking a limited 30-year history of the Western gold standard and elevating it to something more far-reaching, while in the process ignoring the wider contingencies that granted whatever success it achieved (Bott 2013; Chatham House 2012). Here the advantage of *Atlas Shrugged* as speculative fiction. The world of the novel is not quite that of America in the 1950s. It follows that there is no engagement with either World War, and thus no need to take on board the inflation that resulted from them (Eichengreen 1997). As such, Rand is left to account for the suspension of convertability in purely psychological terms: evil or misguided individuals simply decided to destroy the savings of others for their own ends. Certainly, there is no recognition of the irony of the post-war economy instability with which Rand takes such an issue being also partially attributable to the nostalgia for gold that lead to an overvaluation of currency (Bott 2013). Both Greenspan and Rand also resist addressing the difficulties the gold standard faced during the period which they see as exemplifying the economy they wish to create: the significant discretionary measures that it required; the crashes and price instability it encountered (Eichengreen 1997, 1992; Frisch 1983).

My approach calls upon another tradition of critique, however, one focused, at least initially, on the theory of gold rather than its history. For the Objectivist, gold is well suited to exchange because it is secure in its value. It can produce equivalent value, that is, it can be compared to any other thing, because it is what it is and nothing more. Perhaps the most celebrated objection to this understanding of gold is set out by Theodor Adorno:

> Like gold, genuineness abstracted as the proportion of fine metal, becomes a fetish. Both are treated as if they were the foundation, which in reality is a social relation, while gold and genuineness precisely express only the fungibility, the comparability of things. (Adorno 1974, 155)

Abstracted from wider, enabling structures of *relation*, gold can act for Objectivists as a fixed point through which to establish seemingly stable relations of value. Such abstraction is, for Adorno, a repression of what is necessary to this value. It demonstrates a commitment to a limited materialism, seeing value wholly to reside in the *substance* of gold. Here we might think about 'value' within d'Anconia's speech. Paper 'delivers men into the arbitrary power of an arbitrary setter of values' whereas in the past gold 'was an objective value'. The new values are produced by a 'setter'; they are imported. In the good old days, on the other hand, gold *was* its value. The value of gold is thus intrinsic to, and naturalised within, its substance. Even within this specific understanding, however, the problem of constitutive excess is not overcome, as gold and value can be differentiated in the confirmation of their coincidence. In being an objective value, gold is something other than itself.

To come at the gold standard's problematic take on materialism from another angle, we might return to Rand's claim about the 'gold standard' of 'competence'. I read gold in this not to keep to its assigned position: in Rand's formulation, the gold standard upon which the code of competence rests is not that holding up the system of economic exchange, in so far as it can be assumed that the materiality of gold is not a necessary condition for competence in every given field. If the gold standard is indeed applicable to both economics and general competency, then why assume that it has anything to do with the substance of gold?

There is in this an unacknowledged concession to the figurative status of the standard, a concession that introduces further questions: when we understand the gold standard to concern something other than gold, is this an extension of the reach of the yellow metal? Is this testament to the power of gold? Or might the prevalence of gold instead be understood in terms of its overextension or irrelevance?[3]

2   "'WHAT'S THAT?" SHE GASPED, POINTING AT THE SIGN'

It is, perhaps, already clear that I am reading in Rand a resistance to engage the implications of what Roland Barthes describes as the historic shift from 'index' to 'sign' in terms of money; the move from a feudal investment in origins and materiality to 'the limitless process of equivalences, representations that nothing will ever stop, orient, fix, sanction' within bourgeois society (Barthes, 40). To call upon gold might seem to counter this new world of uncertainty and displacement, but this is indeed, as I have claimed, a nostalgic enterprise. Gold, I will not be the first to suggest, is not free from the displacements of the sign it is so often set against.[4]

To begin to work through such tensions specifically in Rand's writing, I will turn to two brief quotations from *Atlas Shrugged*. The first is from the initial climatic sequence in the novel, where radical rail boss Dagny Taggart has found her way to Galt's Gulch, the hidden village where all those capitalists who have gone on strike to protest against the evils of a mixed economy dwell in prelapsarian bliss:

> close before her, rising on a slender granite column from a ledge below to the level of her eyes, blinding her by its glare, dimming the rest, stood a dollar sign three feet tall, made of solid gold. It hung in space above the town, as its coat-of-arms, its trademark, its beacon— and it caught the sunrays, like some transmitter of energy that sent them in shining blessing to stretch horizontally through the air above the roofs,
> 'What's that?' she gasped, pointing at the sign.
> 'Oh, that's Francisco's private joke.' (Rand 1957, 706)

The second is from the very end of the novel, where, with the United States in ruins due to the mismanagement of liberal 'destroyers', the hero John Galt, Taggart's eventual romantic partner, ends the strike of the mind, enabling the return of those in the hidden village to wider society: "'The road is cleared," said Galt. "We are going back to the world." He raised his hand and over the desolate earth he traced in space the sign of the dollar' (ibid., 1168).

In the first quotation, the 'dollar sign' is 'made of solid gold', while in the second the 'sign of the dollar' is traced in space. The idea, I think, is that gold has not in fact gone away at the novel's close. Rather, the gold-backed new capitalism of Galt's Gulch has been so firmly established that it can underwrite the immateriality of the final sign. Read in this way, Galt is indicating that the broken world will rise again under the sign of individuality and free trade, while tracing the yet to be realised, and thus insubstantial, profits that will be gained: in d'Anconia's formulation, the sign is a cheque that will be honoured. Transforming the sign into material success will not be a risky endeavour, however, as Galt has the finance and the 'gold standard' of competence to realise the opportunities that now present themselves. Here we might introduce also Midas Mulligan, the valley's owner and banker, who is reported to have said to a 'destroyer' who criticised his financial speculations: "The reason why you never get rich is because you think what I do is gambling" (Rand 1957, 315).

A reading such as this, dedicated to the probity of Galt's economic project, must negotiate numerous challenges, the most pressing of these, perhaps, that of establishing the precise sense in which the absence of a thing signifies and requires its continued presence. Might we not instead read the second quotation as narrating a *disappearance*, for example? If we were to understand the final tracing as exemplifying Rand's commitment to a neoliberal 'shock doctrine', with its 'signature desire for unattainable purity, for a clean slate on which to rebuild a reengineered model society', then one possible conclusion to be drawn is that there is no place for gold within this moment (Klein 2007, 20).[5] Comparing the dollar signs, the one hanging solidly over a limited utopia, the other traced above a ruin, it might be argued that gold has its place only in achieved perfection, not in the open-ended work of creation. In such a reading, there is something necessarily unbodied about capitalist futurity. It might be, for example, that the dynamism of capitalism resists the solidity of gold, and its suggestion of material closure; or that capitalism, as still an 'unknown ideal', can never be present to us; or finally, and more generally, that gold as material truth resists an unproblematic location within the text (Rand 1966). Irrespective of these various interpretations, I read the perfect society as

never accessible to the narration of *Atlas Shrugged*. In the novel, Galt
and the economy he champions are only ever on the cusp of perfection.[6]

On occasion, however, the novel can be understood to strenuously
resist such a reading. The most obvious counter-argument is that Galt's
Gulch models the world to come, and thus societal perfection is seen in
miniature in the valley. Indeed, when Dagny Taggart finds that she has to
return to the world beyond, Galt insists: 'You have seen [...] Atlantis [...]
it is here, it exists' (Rand 1957, 813). Moreover, those who think their
'highest values are not to be attained' and their 'greatest vision is not to
be made real' are elsewhere dismissed as dangerous idealists, as they lack
the grounding in the actual that is the condition for utopia to be achieved
(812). The perfection of the valley *is* its reality. There 'one dealt with men
as clear and firm as sun and rocks', men who recognise, rather than deny,
the natural order of the world, understanding that 'reality is an absolute
not to be faked', just as the reality of the gold standard is not to be faked
with fiat money (798).

From such contentions it follows that, for Galt, what differences there
are between the valley and an ideal America come down to scale, where
scale is understood to have no disruptive effects. Having seen the valley,
one has seen also the wider world in all of its perfection. Unlike the
new America Galt promises to build, however, the gulch has not been
created on scorched earth; no violent intervention against state power and
existing modes of living were necessary for its formation. It also contains
no undesirables, it is untouched by death or serious illness, and, as I shall
discuss at length below, only a handful of children enjoy the freedom it
offers, while men vastly outnumber women. The economy of the valley
is also one that cannot be elevated to a national level, let alone univer-
salised, without difficulty. To take just one example, Galt has opted for
bimetallism, in which silver and gold circulate as the only coinage, but
the valley does not have its own gold and silver mines. The discovery and
mining of metal is not factored into the economy.[7]

In this last, we can see Randian philosophy dodging the demands
of the gold standard, premised as it is on the notion of scarcity: the
economy of *Atlas Shrugged* rests on unlimited resources. In terms of gold,
Rand has no interest in accounting for the bounty necessary for expansion, or how, given the uneven distribution of metals in their raw states,
the commitment to a fully bimetallic currency would play out in terms of
international relations.[8] Elsewhere, there is an interest in explaining the
riches available to the valley, but the explanation is again indebted to the

advantages afforded by speculative fiction: it turns out Galt has created a 'motor' that generates unlimited power, and thus, presumably, unlimited wealth. There is thus a central tension in the utopian economy of *Atlas Shrugged*: one should never live beyond one's means, but there is no limit to such means if one is Galt or Mulligan.

In this concluding chapter I will be working towards a reading of the politics of the natural within *Atlas Shrugged*, and how it relates to abundance, but for now my interest is in another, and I would claim related, issue introduced by Galt's wonder-engine: how it works is never explained. In the realm of plenitude, where want has been driven out, and all, as we shall see, is immediately present, the engine that enables this miracle is inexplicable; the lack of lack premised on a lack.

The problem, then, is not simply that the perfection of the valley is not repeated in the world to come, as this would suggest that it is located solely in the failure of futurity to become present. Instead, I read presence always to be constituted through lack in the novel, and lack, when figured as pure truth, to be implicated in its other. In regard to compromised presence, we might turn again to 'a dollar sign [...] made of solid gold'. Gold is certainly necessary to this sign as it is what it is made 'of', yet, for example, this is '*a* dollar sign', an instance of a wider phenomenon. 'A' dollar sign calls upon other such signs, and thus cannot be taken as wholly constituted by what it is made of in any given instance. It follows that there is a division between 'a dollar sign' and gold. On these terms, we might argue that gold is not in excess of the sign only at the end of the novel, but from the first. In regard to compromised lack, although, as read above, the space in which the sign is finally traced might be understood to oppose the substance of solid gold, thereby taking on a sublime position, the space can also be read as a medium. It is what the sign is traced 'in', and thus the final sign might share the initial sign's materiality. Even if taken as the sign's location, space is still other to the sign. The final 'dollar sign', however free from the materiality of gold, requires something that lies beyond and in opposition to it, yet something also that is formative.

3   'But ... on Whose Authority?'

The neat opposition between a material and a traced sign can also be challenged through the introduction of additional appeals to gold, materiality, and signs in *Atlas Shrugged*. Take the following discussion between Taggart and Galt, while in the valley:

Galt reached into his pocket and dropped two small coins into the palm of [Taggart's] hand. They were miniature disks of shining gold, smaller than pennies, the kind that had not been in circulation since the days of Nat Taggart; they bore the head of the Statue of Liberty on one side, the words 'United States of America—One Dollar' on the other, but the dates stamped upon them were of the past two years.

'That's the money we use here,' he said. 'It's minted by Midas Mulligan.'

'But ... on whose authority?'

'That's stated on the coin—on both sides of it.' (Rand 1957, 727)

Although both this gold that drops from one hand to another and that hanging above the village are understood in terms of a formative materiality, there are differences between them. This gold is circulating as coin, whereas 'a dollar sign [...] made of solid gold' is statically isolated 'in space', made up of gold that cannot be spent.[9] The discs bear 'the head of the Statue of Liberty on one side, the words "United States of America—One Dollar" on the other'. These words are not a 'dollar sign', but what enables discs to be dollars: it is Galt's claim that the words 'state' the answer to a question, one concerning the authority by which coins can be minted. The 'dollar sign [...] made of solid gold', on the other hand, is not a dollar, and neither does it make something else a dollar. It follows that a dollar cannot simply be gold, but neither is it a sign.

It could be argued that this particular construction of disc and coin requires a mismatch or inequality between materiality and meaning that is problematic for gold standard arguments: both sides of the disc bear something different (the Head of the Statue of Liberty; words), yet what is stated on the two sides of the coin is the same (the authority on which minting rests), and thus material difference does not affect statements. Counter to this, it might be suggested that the division in authority does not present a problem, as what we have instead are statements concerning two different authorities, liberty and nation, for example; intertwined, yet distinct. The difference in what is borne is reflected in what is stated. I would argue that this does not account for all of the disruptive differences at play. Here we might turn to the words and the head, rather than the bearing and the stating: both state in the same way, a disappearance of difference that also has implications for a gold standard discourse invested in the necessary separation of money made of material and by decree. Even if we remain with stating and bearing, there is a difficulty in keeping them distinct, where the result is disrupting, rather than, say, a neat fusing of spirit and substance. One difficulty of situating stating against materiality, for example, is that it is not the coin or what it bears that states, but stating is instead *located* on both sides of the coin. Turn this over, and the bearing of the 'head of the Statue of Liberty' might be understood to fall on the side of materiality, not only because the head is borne by the gold disc, but because it is precisely 'the head' and thus neither sign nor representation. The head is subject to repetition, however, in so far it is 'they'—the two discs—that bear it. In being cited in this way, the head can never fully be *there*. From this reading, we can conclude that stating is opposed to the materiality of bearing, but it is also a matter of location, whilst bearing is opposed to stating, yet falls short of material presence. If bearing calls upon material certainty, and resistance to interpretation, the danger in such a position is a fall into meaningless-ness. Stating helps here, in so far as it can be understood as articulation. As linguistic, however, the once avoided danger of misinterpretation is introduced. But this is fine, because, in a spiralling move, the stating is not understood to require a subject position, but is instead a spatial loca-tion, caught up in the materiality from which it must differ: stating that is no more than bearing, bearing that attains the status of stating.

4   '[…] ITS COAT-OF-ARMS, ITS TRADEMARK, ITS BEACON'

To state and to bear: if both can be understood as actions that make public, the latter has a countersense of carrying. If the discs, as coins, make known and give out, they also frame or hold. To help think a little more about what might be at stake in this tension, let us return to the sign made of solid gold, and the claim that what this sign hangs *as* is other than what it *is*: 'a dollar sign three feet tall, made of solid gold […] hung in space above the town, as its coat-of-arms, its trademark, its beacon'. Here, the sign can be understood to have a function, this troubling some-what the notion of suspension, that sense, introduced previously, of the sign hanging outside the circulation of money. In hanging as a 'trade-mark', the 'dollar sign […] made of solid gold' is other than money, nonetheless, like money, that is, the natural money of the gold standard, it is necessarily more than a trademark. We are back to something like the division between the gold coins and the authority they bear, only now it is that authority that enjoys the materiality of gold. In one sense, gold has gone up in the world since its time as coin, as it is now in the position of the guarantee rather than the guaranteed. It is an elevation that comes at a price, however. Thus, gold is still the excessive material condition of a sign; it falls outside of a given identity, rather than being its necessary condition. Moreover, it is not a hallmark exactly, as it only hangs as one; again, gold falls short of the intimate and irreducible connection between sign and meaning. Finally, the town is not itself gold, and thus the hallmark once more loosens what we might term the fixing of the sign, that is, we are not in the realm of binary signs, of materiality and meaning, but instead of a material aspect that is removed from identity. The result is that gold is not essential and all-of-a-piece, but the material condition of a hallmark that applies to something other than coin.

This supplementary status can be given a further ironic twist, as the sign also hangs as the collectively owned trademark of a town founded on the strictest principles of the sanctity and ubiquity of private property: d'Anconia 'gave that sign as an anniversary present to the owner of this place. [Mulligan] And then we all adopted it as our particular emblem' (Rand 1957, 706). The hallmark does not secure the economic identity of the valley, but instead introduces tensions: the possibility of non-contractual exchange, of collective ownership and identity, of gold that is something other than money.

I would suggest that a further connection can be read between the joke, the sign, the emblem and the hallmark, one that brings us back to the problematic relationship between the public and private. *Atlas Shrugged* is a book more prone to comedy than might be imagined, but this particular joke does not circulate. It is unclear whether the privacy *extends*: is Galt in on the joke, or does he simply identify it? In a sense it does not matter, because there is no joke here to which one might be privy: this is indeed a perspective on, rather than a retelling of, a joke. The absence or occlusion of the joke *is* its integrity. The joke is private and public, private precisely because of a frame that exceeds the private, private only through a wider authority. The private joke is not known as such from the site of privacy, in other words.

Division can also be understood to constitute the joke in the sense of a split in meaning. It could be argued that what allows, or even necessitates, 'the sign' also to be d'Anconia's 'private joke' is precisely the acceptance of this discrepancy. As introduced previously, in the Objectivist utopia, everything is claimed to be out in the open, ethics are rooted in competence, the economy in gold, and 'A' is most definitely 'A'. As Hugh Akston, the valley's philosopher, declares, 'we do not claim – we *show*', while Taggart 'wondered at the joyous, proud comfort to be found in a sense of the finite' (716, 735). Yet what hangs as a hallmark for this town is one thing and another, and thus set against immediacy, revelation, clarity. It is the kind of disruption that had better be kept private. Identified as a joke, the shifting identities of the sign can be separated from the daylight world of objectivity and stability. But the joke does not keep to its proper place, and disruptive divisions spread out into the world of certainty. This is, after all, a place in which the private joke that can never be brought to light is also a sign *that hangs as a beacon*. What shines out, and draws in, is obscured. The obscurity I read here is the impossibility of a constitutive tension—that is the deferral of meaning—ever coming simply to light.

5 ' [...] THE MOONLIGHT DRAINING ITS COLOR [...]'

It is a wonder that the sign made of gold sticks out so, as so much of the metal can be found in Galt's Gulch. On first arrival, Taggart sees a 'long, flat stretch of greenish gold at the foot of a canyon', the wheat fields of Midas Mulligan, later when she meets the great and the good of the valley they are illuminated by a 'golden sunburst of rays filling the great windows', and finally she finds herself enraptured by 'the golden patches of light on the wood of the table, on the buttered crust of the rolls, on the copper coffee pot, on Galt's hair' (717, 735, 763).

What are we to make of this profusion of gold? The most straightforward answer, perhaps, is that the accumulation of gold currency in the valley from Mulligan's mint leads to a world that shares its qualities of clarity and solidity. Such a reading is particularly suited to an Objectivist understanding of the gold standard. For the Objectivist, gold enables a perfect exchange or substitution, situating its various others within an economy of value, while remaining untouched by the process. This is comparable to the way what we might term a 'primary' meaning within language can be understood to enable figurative expression, thus 'real' gold can lend itself to the colour of a beloved's hair, or the shining of the sun. When gold is in this way taken to be the primary or literal meaning, the Objectivist might think they are on especially safe ground, as gold is embodying the literary function it is asked to fulfil: for the Randian, gold is exemplarily non-figurative. The objectivity of its value is what enables substitution.

To understand what might be difficult about such a line of thinking, we might follow Paul de Man in his reading of gold in the work of

David Hume, the theorist of gold whose shaping influence can be read in Greenspan's formulations as quoted previously. According to de Man, Hume, perhaps despite himself, understands the human predicament as one in which the 'proper' cannot be separated from the 'figural': we are like children for whom the colour in a peacock's tale is 'properly' gold, much as the same way gold in *Atlas Shrugged* is located in hair and sunshine (de Man 1978, 18–19). One of the challenges de Man reads in Hume's formulations is that gold is displaced within them, caught between substance and its properties, occupying the secondary, 'figural' position as well as that 'proper' to it. In this way, gold lacks the integrity that is understood to allow it the sliding of meaning in the first place.

There are added difficulties in *Atlas Shrugged*, however, as gold can be read as secondary in another, specific sense. Here we can turn once more to the 'sign made of solid gold' which is 'like some transmitter of energy', catching the sunrays, sending on what is comparable to energy, but not creating anything itself. Neither the dollar sign, nor the gold it is made of, is a first cause. It is the sun that is the originator of what is likened to energy.[10] As read previously, the sunrays in the valley are also gold at one stage. Thus gold, which as 'solid gold' is constitutive of, yet supplementary to, the sign, also, as the sunrays, precedes both sign and supplement. Gold is divided. The supplementary 'solid gold' of the sign cannot be transmitted. Only the sunrays can achieve this.[11]

Elsewhere, the sense that gold is other than substance is, perhaps, even clearer. When lit by the moon, d'Anconia's sign is understood to be made of a lesser metal:

> He [Richard Halley, a composer and resident of Galt's Gulch] looked at the darkness beyond the window, at a spot where, in a clearing of the branches, with the moonlight draining its color, leaving only its metallic luster, the sign of the dollar hung like a curve of shining steel engraved in the sky. (Rand 1957, 782)

It is a kind of naturalised, nocturnal deflation, the sign hanging now like steel in the night. Because colour is drained by the moonlight, gold can be read as property only, a supplement to the persistence of a metallic 'luster'. Gold is not the standard here, neither a natural category, but prone to the touch of nature, the influence of another. What the sign is made of is not only other than what it is, but this substance can be siphoned off, leaving something else that was always there. This is not simply metal, however, as metal is now, in one sense, a quality of a 'luster' that itself lacks substance.

It is, then, moonlight that determines, not the persistent, natural substance 'gold'. Here, moonlight can be compared and contrasted with the sunrays. If we return the 'gold' of the sunburst rays to the scene of the sign and the sun, the rays are not framed as figurative, but a first thing. Quality trumps substance, and figuration is the 'proper' sense of the word.

The solid gold and the sunrays do not keep even to these problematically shifting positions, however. When discussing the 'dollar sign made of solid gold', the narrator claims that Taggart is 'blinded by its glare', and this glare is thus not that of the sunrays, but belongs to what we have been understanding as the 'secondary' dollar sign. Moreover, when the sunrays are caught, it is like they are sent by 'some transmitter of energy [.. .] to stretch horizontally through the air above the roofs', and earlier Taggart is narrated as claiming that 'the straight line is the badge of man': the geometry of nature is said to be circular, the line is the mark of human intervention and invention (603). Thus the sunrays stretching 'horizontally' are not only to be taken as an original, natural phenomenon, caught and sent but otherwise untouched by the dollar sign made of solid gold. In such a reading, the glare really is that of the dollar sign. Nature recedes. Rather than gold as originating and primary, we have a privileging of invention and intervention; the shaping influence of the human. In this opposition a tension can be read, one tentatively introduced within my initial discussion of the theory of gold, and one familiar too from established accounts of the gold standard in literature. Gold is taken to be in want of nothing, an objective value because of its materiality. Equally, gold is a medium of exchange that moves beyond primitive barter, thus beyond also base materiality. Gold as substance is set against gold as money.[12]

To further think through this contradiction, it may help to turn to Taggart's first encounter with Galt, as he might seem to offer a way of understanding the relationship between nature and culture that allows us, in Rand's well-known phrase, to 'check our premises' (*Atlas Society* 2010). Within *Atlas Shrugged*, Galt is the great inventor and transformer, but all he achieves is rooted in an understanding of the fundamental laws of existence. He follows nature, but is not its slave. As previously indicated, what Taggart picks out as Galt's most distinguishing feature is the gold in his hair, a feature noted from this first meeting (Rand 1957,

701). Certainly, we could think about this gold in terms of readings offered already, and ask whether Galt is understood to embody objective value, or whether the appearance of gold here displaces the metal from its enabling position. Considering Galt more generally, the assumption is that this gold indicates harmony between the certainties of nature and the transformative potential of a morality that is on the gold standard. I am interested in the following quotation, however, also from Taggart's first meeting with Galt:

> It was as if he were a single whole, grasped by her first glance at him, like some irreducible absolute, like an axiom not to be explained any further, as if she knew everything about him by direct perception, and what awaited her now was only the process of identifying her knowledge. (704)

Everything to be known is directly perceived, in the moment, and this is irreducible. Nothing else is needed: Galt is wholly present to Taggart, or at least she is taken to understand their encounter 'as if' this were the case. According to the narration, at this point Galt appears to Taggart as a man of metal, his hair 'shaded from brown to gold in the sun' (701). As I read it, this gold shading cannot easily call upon material gold. If all is indeed to be grasped immediately, there can be no displacement or deferral of meaning and thus the precious metal gold is irrelevant to the shaded gold of the hair. Substance therefore falls outside of understanding.

What Taggart (perhaps) grasps can also be read as a fetishisation of gold, in Adorno's terms; seemingly shorn of its constitutive excesses, a law unto itself. One of those excesses is the gold associated with another resident of the gulch: Ragnar Danneskjöld, a pirate who sinks boats carrying gold gained through taxation, is noted for his golden hair, and, when in the outside world at least, has other connections to gold: his 'face seemed less revealing than the surface of the metal' (573). Rather than available all at once, this gold withholds. In a repetition of the gold that is a beacon and a private joke, gold can be read to be split between the two scenes; the most and least forthcoming of substances. In one sense, however, the gold that is grasped in an instance is as enigmatic as that compared to Danneskjöld, as the knowledge of it is yet to be 'identified', and is thus knowledge in want. The totality of knowledge is achieved through a loss placed beyond its bounds.

6   FAMILY VALUES

To think the above problematisation of the stability of gold will simply suffice as a critique of Randian philosophy is to fail to appreciate its arguments. Despite being premised on the unshakeable foundation of the real, Objectivism is rooted also in a resistance to reductive materialism. Immediate, bonded knowledge is never enough, and thus it is entirely right for Rand that Taggart must wait to identify what she knows.

The most sustained formulation of this understanding can be read in *The Romantic Manifesto*, in which Rand sets out her aesthetic theory and account of cognition. According to Rand, we sense the world in an immediate fashion, with these sensations available to us as 'units', which are then substituted for words that are, by a process of combination, integrated into ever-larger word concepts, which allow us to move beyond the limits of our immediate perceptions. The sum of these concepts is so great that it makes it difficult for the individual to gain a 'comprehensive view of existence to integrate his values, to choose his goals, to plan his future to maintain the unity and coherence of his life' (Rand 1975, 7). This is where art comes in, as it is claimed to be a 'selective recreation' of reality that *'brings man's concepts to the perceptual level of his consciousness and allows him to grasp them directly as if they were percepts'* (8). The problem, of course, is that the inadequacy of such grasping was the reason the whole chain of cognition needed to be forged in the first place, and Rand makes clear that we have to finally 'retranslate all the abstractions into the perceptual concretes for which they stand—i.e., reconnect them to reality' (9). *The Romantic Manifesto* might be understood to argue for a self-supporting notion of cognition, where the inadequacy of one part of a process is made up for in another. Instead, I read it to offer a narrative of displacement, an endless supplementation where the final moment of completion is always deferred. At every stage, something is lacking.[13]

Taggart's time in the valley thus repeats an account of cognition that is forwarded as part of a larger commitment to balancing rooted materialism with conceptual rigor and transformative invention, an account that I understand to be finally inadequate to the task. This commitment can be located also, for example, in the sense in which Rand's heroes, although focused on the materially achievable, are not primarily motivated by vulgar materialism. Take Hank Rearden, the last productive member of society to join Galt in his valley:

[the destroyers] prescribe my ends. I, who took pride in my ability to achieve the satisfaction of my desires, let them prescribe the code of values by which I judged my desires. I, who shaped matter to serve my purpose, was left with a pile of steel and gold, but with my every purpose defeated, my every desire betrayed, my every attempt at happiness frustrated. (858)

Rearden gets rich, but the looters get richer, and his dream of self-determination remains unfulfilled. Gold, for Rearden, is not an end in itself, and materiality is not the sure guarantee of value. In the context of a world run by 'looters', and shorn of the glamour of desire, the substance of gold is indeed detritus. A comparable dismissal of gold can be read in this limited celebration of the substance from Midas Mulligan: 'Gold is a fuel that will perform wonders, but no fuel can work where there is no motor' (737). Rather than a circulating, permanent means of exchange, a store of value, gold as fuel is there to be used up, and although vital for motion, it is not a first cause. Gold is not its own motor. If one were to think that Galt's motor stands against gold thus understood, Taggart is there to offer correction: 'there was no meaning in motors or factories or trains, [the] only meaning was in man's enjoyment of life' (ibid., 731). In what does this enjoyment consist? Ellis Wyatt, the valley's fracking king, answers with another question:

What's wealth but the means of expanding one's life? [...] It used to take me five hours to fill that tank. It now takes three. The two I save are mine – as precisely mine as if I moved my grave two further hours away for every five I've got. It's two more hours in which to work, to grow, to move forward. That's the savings account I'm hoarding. (722)

Wealth is important, but this is not to be confused with what Rearden finds himself left, the gold that is elsewhere described as 'the keystone supporting all the keystones' (728). Instead, wealth is time, the purpose of which is to forestall death. Wyatt's capitalism does not end with anything as solid as gold, but instead propels him towards an ever-receding grave: as Wyatt's ultimate end is postponed, the advantage he gains is that of moving forward. For Wyatt, this is the way of the world: '"Every living thing must grow. It can't stand still. It must grow or perish. Look – " He pointed at a plant fighting upward from under the weight of a rock – a long, gnarled stem, contorted by an unnatural struggle [...]' (ibid., 722). The difficulty in this is as much the naturalisation of the movement upwards as the notion that rocks create unnatural situations: stasis is to be avoided at all costs, but the result is an expansion that is pointless. Nature is not the site of plenitude, but of deferral. Here, gold is no first cause, nor any end, and neither is a motor. Instead it is desire and happiness that matter most, but these really are nothing but drive, the forestalling of death, the endless growth that seems to me implicated in the very struggle and stasis it is tasked with combating.[14]

Wyatt's investment in a boundless, meaningless expansion can, I think, be located in the destruction and misery required for 'the road' to be 'cleared'. It is also at home in the glamour and cruelty of the city, its skyscrapers, its uncompromising businessmen, its delight in pleasure, raw and refined, and rejection of social convention, most obviously that of marriage. Galt's Gulch is something else. For sure, we know that friends do put each other out of business there, and everyone is focused on making more, but when Taggart arrives it is a place of frontier cabins and light agriculture. All is stable, sunlit, and small.[15] To enter the valley is to encounter the bleeding edge of radical capitalism, but also to return to the past: as read above, when Taggart first encounters the currency Mulligan has introduced, she likens it to the gold coins of her forefathers. Entwined with the notion of gold, as oil, being constantly used up, that is, of being subject to one of capitalism's non-reversible reactions, there is an offer of another kind of continuity, that of family.

Here we might also introduce the valley's most beautiful residents, Danneskjöld and the Hollywood icon Kay Ludlow. Despite marriage being questioned in the novel, the figures of harmony and aesthetic perfection have tied the knot, the ceremony taking place in the valley officiated by Hugh Akston.[16] As introduced previously, Danneskjöld is likened in the narration to the gold he liberates, a quality Ludlow shares. They are a golden-haired golden couple (784).

Gold is not always so securely placed within marriage, however. Take the valley's baker: she took the vow necessary to join utopia independently of her husband. She is understood to be separate and equal. Moreover, she takes her role as a mother to be as much a 'profession' as her baking of bread: her children 'represent my particular career' (785). It is unclear, however, how she is financially reimbursed for this labour: there is no mention of gold coins. Thus even as motherhood is placed on a level footing with any other work, the contracts and payment that for Rand are the defining feature of such work are obscure. Childcare is granted a problematically exceptional status, and as such we should be cautious

about endorsing Rand's utopia as a liberation from conventional structures, including those of gender. Once again, there is in the valley a lack
necessary to presence, its perfection and plenitude relying on shadowy
labour. Here we might introduce Melinda Cooper's recent work on the
history of the American family:

> Yes, neoliberals persistently exhort individuals to take responsibility for
> their own fate, and yet the imperative of personal responsibility slides
> ineluctably into that of family responsibility when it comes to managing
> the inevitable problems of economic dependence (the care of children, the
> disabled, the elderly, or the unwaged). (Cooper 2017, 71)

Cooper's interest is in charting the relationship between conservative,
often Christian, commitments to family values, and neoliberalism, with its
potentially anti-normative championing of individual choice and responsibility. Often the former is taken to be window-dressing for the realpolitik
of the latter, but Cooper convincingly argues that each requires the other,
and that whether the family is understood to act in opposition to hedo-
nistic liberty, or as a counter to individuals failing to fully privatise the
cost of their sexual freedom, it is taken to be key to the functioning of a
just society. In the valley, individual liberty and the disappearance of the
state require the slack to be taken up somewhere: 'freedom of contract
cannot exist without the ostensibly natural, noncontractual obligations of
family' (117).

For the Randian, learning cannot easily be outsourced to schools, as
previous chapters have established, and it is thus not a surprise to learn
that the baker has chosen to come to the valley, as she can take the education of her children wholly upon herself within its confines. The work of
a mother is not simply rooted in a contract with her children, or herself,
however, as it calls upon other agreements. Here we might turn to an incident in *Atlas Shrugged* where the familial contract could be understood
to come to light. Galt is explaining to Taggart her living arrangements at
the gulch:

> I shall charge you for your room and board – it is against our rules to
> provide the unearned sustenance of another human being. Some of us
> have wives and children, but there is a mutual trade involved in that, and
> a mutual payment – he glanced at her – of a kind I am not entitled to
> collect. (760)

Firstly, of course, for Galt the 'us' does not include those who have husbands, and thus, within what by all accounts is a heterosexual society, women somehow are not included amongst those who can claim relationships of 'mutual' trade. The trade described is of a 'kind' that does not involve payment in gold, as is the case for all other trade. What, then, is involved? The mutual pleasure from sex, perhaps? The mutual trade is, however, in the 'hav[ing]' of a wife and children, and the payment is for Galt, not Taggart to collect. Could it be, then, that the danger in the 'having' of the wife and the children gaining 'unearned sustenance' is countered by the payment of sex by the wife? Or that, more subtly, the trade involves sustenance exchanged for sex, but the payment is mutual: both husband and wife gain pleasure? The uncertainty is significant: there is, it might seem, an economy outside the gold economy, a profession unlike any other, and if we cannot be wholly sure, it is because the whole operation does not belong to daylight world of the gold standard. This is not, after all, sexual payment, but rather that of a 'kind' that is never defined. Just as the vaunted material presence of gold is secured by all manners of occlusions and deferrals, so the general economy has its points of obscurity, and in these we can identify some of the inequalities utopia requires.

Anomalous as it may be in terms of the wider economy, marriage is no rarity in the gulch: although there is one large-eyed novelist who is said to worship Galt, and d'Anconia is still in love with Taggart after a past affair, all other desire is located in marital relationships. Indeed, marriage and the family return as the ordering structure of the most radically brilliant of the individualists: Galt, d'Anconia and Danneskjöld are understood to be the adopted 'sons' of Dr. Akston, and when Taggart joins them, it is as Galt's 'wife' (799). The family seemingly arise spontaneously when individuals return to an economy based not on the illusion of paper, but the materialised value of gold; to the age of our ancestors; and to lost youth, with Taggart repeatedly finding 'the recaptured sense of her childhood kept coming back to her' (784).[17]

This central family takes a step beyond even the baker household, where the work of mothers resists being placed within the transparent economy, as within it there is no place for mothers at all. Taggart marries into a family made up only of men, led by a favoured son, watched over by a patriarch. It is not, then, that the spontaneously arising structure grounds the lack that the open-ended capitalism of drive requires, but that such structures are less than fully present from the first. That is to say, we are not working even with the myth, critiqued by Cooper, of the subversive power of neoliberalism being grounded in the conservative doctrine of the family. The family, too, can be read in terms of lack. And not just the problematic notion of a mother being necessary in general to a notion of family, and hence identifiable as missing in this instance, but instead a construction of women in *Atlas Shrugged* as the necessity around which the logic of individualism fails. It is a difficulty that can also, of course, be read in the novel's wider investments in materiality and presence. Take, for example, its appeal to the return to a state of nature; this is as much a journey back to the incompletion of a childhood of immediate, unidentified experience as it is the ancient point of achieved success whose repetition in the present produces the notion of family; that sense in which Taggart is finding in the valley now a continuation of the work of her ancestors. Natural abundance is not all good news, in other words. It is a repeated tension. Thus, the substance of gold is to be praised because it carries its own value, just as immediate perception situates one within reality, and natural structures liberate one from the social, yet, for all that, gold requires money, immediate perception awaits identification, and familial bonds return to the authority of contract.

I would like to bring this concluding chapter to a close by reading the challenge of such divisions to the philosophy of *Atlas Shrugged* in the scene in which Taggart is made aware of her marital status. In response to a question from her, Hugh Akston offers a prolonged reply, ending as follows:

> You asked me whether I was proud of the way my three sons had turned out. I am more proud than I ever hoped to be. I am proud of their every action, of their every goal – and of every *value* they've chosen. And *this*, Dagny, is my full answer.

> The sudden sound of her first name was pronounced in the tone of a father; he spoke his last two sentences, looking, not at her, but at Galt. She saw Galt answering him by an open glance held steady for an instant, like a signal of affirmation. Then Galt's eyes moved to hers. She saw him looking at her as if she bore the title that hung in the silence between them, the title Dr Akston had granted her, but had not pronounced and none of the others had caught – she saw, in Galt's eyes, a glance of amusement at her shock, of support and, incredibly, of tenderness. (791)

Later, when alone: 'His wife – she thought, letting herself hear consciously the word Dr Akston had not pronounced [...]' (799). Knowledge does not come at once. Something is perceived, seen, and understood, but the narration only identifies what has been left unspoken after the event. This is not the only deferral or absence to be read, however. Indeed, as a scene of revelation, this has a remarkable opacity. We might begin a reading with a return to the concerns with the framing effects of narrative perspective engaged in my previous chapter. Take Galt's 'open glance': it has this status precisely through being viewed by another. Galt's thoughts are never narrated, and there is thus no internal division to him, but that means there is something closed about his openness. Like the 'private joke' as read above, his integrity requires a supplement. Even Taggart, whose thoughts are known by the narrating third, is, because of this, never available on her own terms, or, perhaps, it is that her own terms require another. Just as the pure substance of gold requires something other than itself to be an objective value, so too the radical independence of the Randian hero calls upon another. It is this framing narration that produces the notion of a truth withheld, the idea that an understanding has been reached that is so immediate that it does not have to be shared: the silence does not have to be spoken, as it is known for what it is by one who falls outside the circle. And what Akston has granted Taggart, what hangs in the silence between them, and what she sees (perhaps) in Galt's seeing of her, is 'title', at this stage, not 'wife'.

With this understanding, we might begin to situate the scene within the displacements read thus far. That is, how might this scene be read in terms of gold? As the 'title' is not pronounced, it can be understood to oppose gold: a withheld language that consequently lacks substance. The title is also, for the same reason, constructed as free from secondary articulation, remaining what it is and nothing more: gold as withheld. It also 'hangs', and thus repeats the dollar sign made of solid gold, although the hanging is 'in the silence between them', rather than 'space'. In both, however, I read a hanging that is in one sense free from context or structure—in space; in silence—yet also organises relationships, establishing a community; acting as the between that situates Galt in relation to Taggart. In both, what hangs is in some sense out of circulation, but, as we can now read in the 'title', it is also like a certain fantasy of money; a featureless medium for enabling human exchange, separable from other, formative relations.[18] The 'title' can be read in terms of gold in a further sense, as although it is not borne by Taggart, when Galt looks at her, within the narration's perspective on Taggart's perspective, it is 'as if' this was the case. I am thinking here of the head and the words borne by the gold coins, of course, but in the case of the 'title', there is not the play between the articulation of statement and the materiality of location. The 'title' is uncertainly placed. If it is borne by Taggart, it is also hanging in the silence between her and Galt. Certainly, we have the same, displacing, alienating sense of the relationship between a thing and what it bears, a relationship that is concerned with the excessive yet constitutive, but the 'title' is unrealised, absent at every turn: unpronounced; contentless; only seeming to be borne, with this established through a sequence of perspectives on perspectives.

From this we might claim, of course, that neither 'title' nor 'wife' have anything to do with gold. There is no mention of the substance. From the readings offered already in this chapter, however, it can be argued that the absence of gold is not a sure sign of gold's absence, and not only because gold's exchangeability means that it can be other than itself. Here we might return to the displacements of absence within this chapter: purity without supplement; futurity; death drive; repression of what is necessary to nature; the past; understanding bereft of identification.

To read gold, I am suggesting, is to follow the displacement of gold, of gold's displacement as absence, and thus also the displacements of absence.[19] Without a reading of these shifts, Rand is, at any one time, in a position to fix gold as certainty: materially present; absent truth; a hard-impacted value that extends. But this, I would argue, is to fetishize gold, repressing contradictions, and forestalling an engagement with the divisions and deferrals that it calls upon in any one moment. Gold, like utopia, is elsewhere, but not recoverably so: elsewhere is always elsewhere. To my mind, this state of affairs does not necessitate interpretive anarchy, but rather a need to take responsibility for one's reading. That is, I would call on Objectivist readers to move beyond a blithe acceptance of the substitutive power of gold, its presence in absence, and commit to a working through, however provisional, of its altarity within Rand's philosophy, its strange resistance to her arguments at their every turn. At the very least, this would question an all too easy avoidance of the family values in which the novel is invested; not that there is a liberation from family, neither that family is the sure base of Randian ideology, but, instead, like gold, it is the uncanny nature of the family, its shifts and deadlocks, that enables the mobilisation of Randian politics.

One final turn, then. Hugh Akston pronounces the sound of Taggart's first name in the tone of a father, whilst looking at Galt. A tone of a father is thus not Akston's alone, and perhaps indeed not his at all. I read a subtle distinction here, however. If the emphasis falls on the tone belonging to the father being pronounced by another, then the father is not secured as discrete. If the sense instead is Akston pronouncing in borrowed tones, then I take the father to be stabilised, with Akston produced as contingent and derivative. In the latter reading, the ability to pronounce in the tones of the father might provoke concern in the self-orientated Objectivist, yet this is countered by the assurance that there is no father here, and the familial identity has therefore not compromised Akston's individuality. From all of this we might conclude that if the tone of the father confirms the relationship between Galt and Akston, granting a value conferred only to subjects structured in this way, it suggests also in this the inapplicability of such structures. We are back to that central difficulty of gold: it is secure enough to resist cooption, yet because of this, it has the mobility required to enable universal exchange.

Rand's precise formulation can be understood to further challenge the certainty of the bond between Galt and his mentor, even as it is announced. Akston is looking at Galt, and pronouncing in the tones of the father, but whatever relationship is produced cannot be kept to the binary. Thus the sound is sudden, and, as I read it, this is so for a perspective on Taggart's perspective, not Galt's, while, for the narration, it is an unqualified fact that the pronouncing of the sound is in the tone of the father. Of course, it might be claimed that the tone of the father will be recognised by all in the room, because, as governed by rationality, their individualism finds its support in a shared understanding, but there is, despite this, something that is not caught. This is what is not pronounced. Kept private, this can be understood to establish the familial bonds that work against what I have been terming the daylight world of the gulch. One aspect of this achievement, however, is that what fails to be caught by some is entirely unconcerned with the father: as unpronounced, *there is no paternal tone*. The paternal relationship is thus the most obvious and the most lacking, requiring recognitions and structures that exceed individual subjectivity, yet dividing up the social, burrowing out spaces of intimacy. My argument is that an engagement with the politics of Objectivism necessitates also an engagement with this familial uncanny, that is, what is required of critics of Objectivism is not simply a celebration of impossibility against Randian rationality, but a working through of impossibility's violence, its disappearances and dangers.

Acknowledgements My thanks to Grant Cocks, Stephen Thomson, Kristina West, and Karin Lesnik-Oberstein for their help in the research, writing, and editing of this chapter.

Notes

1. This was almost twenty years before Greenspan became Chairman of the Federal Reserve and temporarily abandoned his own commitment to the gold standard. Post-crash, gold is very much back in vogue, both in right-wing economic discourse, now supported by Greenspan, and, for example, the promotion of Bitcoin (Golumbia 2016). The connection is made by Murname (2018).

2. Hume's essay is collected in Eichengreen (1997), along with other major essays, including P. B. Whale's 'The working of the prewar gold standard'. Rather than seeing these various accounts to be in conflict, Eichengreen argues that they represent a range of perspectives on the standard that it is the task of the contemporary theorist and historian to connect.

3. Such questions direct me to Derrida (1972). This text is the subject of critique for many New Historicist works, including Michaels (1987), as introduced below. The interest in this present chapter in reading the figurative, citation, and constitutive absence points to the influence of Derrida's text, and suggests differences between my own approach and that of critics such as Michaels.

4. Hence also, I think, the need to offer something other than, or in addition to, a historicist account. Historicist accounts of gold do not always work through the extent to which they are caught up in a discourse of 'index'.

5. For a more thorough reading of the history of the shock doctrine as it relates to Rand, see Tucker-Abramson (2018).

6. In terms of the notion of gold as constructed by the text here as that which it cannot contain, see the discussion of textuality, happiness, and the future in Lesnik-Oberstein (2010).

7. For a discussion of material production and gold, and the difficulties it poses for utopian accounts such as that offered by Rand, see Eichengreen (1997), Bott (2013). For an additional discussion of the problems of bitmetalism, see, for example, Thomas (1991).

8. For the link between such a notion, and Rand's imperialist project, see Duggan (2019). Rand does discuss how the residents of the gulch are to

follow Mulligan's example and turn their assets into gold prior to arrival, but gold is always imported. The question of its production is missed.

9. Or it has been spent on being removed from circulation. For more, see Michaels (1987). It is worth pointing out that a great deal of gold is at stake, as the dollar sign made of solid gold is three foot high.

10. For a comparable reading, see Derrida (1974) and see also Harrison (1999).

11. Or, more precisely, transmission is what the catching of rays is 'like'.

12. This is the starting point for Walter Benn Michaels reading of the gold standard in nineteenth century American literature (Michaels 1987).

13. It is difficult to give a sense of just how convoluted and inconsistent these arguments are, but take the following as just one example: 'With the exception of proper names, every word we use is a concept that stands for an unlimited number of concretes of a certain kind', yet 'Language is a code of visual-auditory symbols that serves the psycho-epistemolgical function of converting abstractions into concretes', where '*conceptual*' understanding is achieved 'by means of *abstractions*' (Rand 1975, 5–6). For Rand, language is and is not conceptual, and it stands in for concretes even as it produces them.

14. See Tucker-Abramson for an alternative reading of death drive in the novel: the ideology of *Atlas Shrugged* is critiqued, as within this the looters are taken to be wedded to an outlook defined by literary naturalism, so they cannot understand the logic of what is occurring around them, and their own part in it, mistaking 'opportunities' for demonic, unaccountable repetitions (Tucker-Abramson 2018, 96–100).

15. Hoberek (2005) and Tucker-Abramson (2018) convincingly read the gulch in terms of a binding of frontier and suburban imagery, with Tucker-Abramson offering an extended working through of the racial politics upon which the frontier calls: '*Atlas Shrugged* doesn't need to mention race because Rand's description of the decaying and economically blighted urban core—contrasted with the well-organized and affluent suburban development that Atlantis represents—is already coded with the new segregationist language of white flight' (Tucker-Abramson 2018, 91).

16. The collapse of Rearden's socially sanctioned marriage, and that of Taggart's 'looter' brother can, I think, be included in Duggan's (2019) list of those aspects of *Atlas Shrugged* that help it gain a queer following.

17. Again, my thoughts here turn to Barthes formulations as introduced above. My reading of Galt's Gulch differs markedly from Alan Clardy's productive account. For example, it is Clardy's contention that 'the domain of intimate, family relationships seems of minimal importance, if not irrelevant in Rand's utopia' (Clardy, 202, 242).

18. I am thinking of the following, for example, 'In its free or equilibrium state, money appears so neutral as to exert no power at all on the actual workings of economic exchange—money is merely a veil that permits the proper unfolding of contractual relations' (Cooper 2017, 58).

19. In what I would argue continues to be the greatest work on the literary gold standard, Walter Benn Micheals offers two stunningly brief comments that place the kind of reading offered here in this chapter within the logic of the gold standard. Addressing Michaels' critique in the form of a note seems appropriate, therefore, although I intend to engage this work in more detail at a later date. For Michaels, close textual reading is itself problematically on the gold standard because it adheres to a 'logic', wherein there is a split between natural materiality and meaning, with meaning nonetheless naturalised within materiality. Wide ranging and exacting criticism of this argument, and the dismissal of text-based or deconstructive criticism that results, have already been offered by Culler (2007) and Dean (1993). For a critique from a New Historicist position, see Thomas (1991). Suffice to argue here that I am reading the gold standard and its relationship to naturalism in terms of displacement and deferral, not, as Michaels does, the limited and always identifiable gap necessary to meaning. This is not, as Dean argues, the gap of the 'psychoanalytic conception of the subject as a subject originally divided against itself' (Dean, 253). As Dean contends, it is a resistance to such constitutive division, and the related complexities of subjecthood and society, that underwrites Michaels' wider political project of replacing the politics of difference and diversity on the left with one concerned only with 'class' (Michaels 2006). Cooper (2017), as introduced above, forwards a counter-'logic' that I understand to demonstrate how the kind of framing of this conflict offered by Michaels itself has a history, one that sees figures on the left enter into alliances with both neoliberal and neoconservative forces to protect what are taken to be broad class interests. I would suggest any reading of Michaels might do well to begin with *Family Values: Between Neoliberalism and the New Social Conservatism*. But that is a project for another time.

Bibliography

Adorno. 1974 [1951]. *Minima moralia: Refelections from a damaged life*, trans. E.F.N. Jephcott. London: Verso.

Atlas Society. 2010. Check your premises. Atlascoiety.org/commentary/commentary-blog/4229-check-your-premises. Accessed 12 February 2019.

Barthes, Roland. 1991 [1970]. *S/Z.*, trans. Richard Miller. New York: Hill and Wang.

Bott, Sandra (ed.). 2013. *The global gold market and the international monetary system from the late nineteenth century to the present: Actors, networks, power.* Basingstoke: Palgrave Macmillan.

Chatham House. 2012. *Gold and the international monetary system.* Royal Institute for International Affairs.

Clardy, Alan. 2012. Galt's Gulch: Ayn Rand's utopian delusion. *Utopian Studies* 23 (1): 238–262.

Cooper, Melinda. 2017. *Family values: Between neoliberalism and social conservatism.* New York: Zone Books.

Culler, Jonathan. 2007. *The literary in theory.* Standford: Standford University Press.

Dean, Tim. 1993. Wanting Paul de Man: A critique of the 'logic' of new historicism in American studies. *Texas Studies in Literature and Language* 35 (2): 251–277.

De Man, Paul. 1978. The epistemology of metaphor. *Critical Inquiry* 5: 13–30.

Derrida, Jacques. 1972. *Limited Inc*, trans. Samuel Weber and Jeffrey Mehlman. Evanston: Northwestern University Press.

———. 1974. White mythology: Metaphor in the text of philosophy, trans. F.C.T. Moore. *New Literary History* 6 (1): 5–74.

———. 1992. *Given time: I. counterfeit money*, trans. Peggy Kamuf. Chicago and London: The University of Chicago Press.

Duggan, Lisa. 2019. *Mean girl: Ayn Rand and the culture of greed.* Oakland, CA: University of California Press.

Eichengreen, Barry and Flandreu, Marc (eds.). 1992. *Golden fetters: The gold standard and the great depression, 1919–1939.* New York: Oxford: Oxford University Press.

———. 1997 [1985]. *The gold standard in theory and history*, 2nd ed. London: Routledge.

Frisch, Helmut. 1983. *Theories of inflation.* Cambridge: Cambridge University Press.

Golumbia, David. 2016. *The politics of bitcoin: Software as right-wing extremism.* Minneapolis: University of Minnesota Press.

Greenspan, Alan. 1966. Gold and economic freedom. In *Ayn Rand, capitalism: The unknown ideal*, ed. Ayn Rand, 101–107. New York: Signet.

Harrison, Bernard. 1999. 'White mythology' revisited: Derrida and his critics of reason and rhetoric. *Critical Inquiry* 25 (3): 505–534.

Hoberek, Andrew. 2005. *The twilight of the middle class: Post world war II American fiction and white collar work.* Princeton: Princeton University Press.

Klein, Naomi. 2007. *The shock doctrine: The rise of disaster capitalism.* London: Allen Lane.

Lesnik-Oberstein, Karin. 2010. *Oliver Twist*, the narrators tale. *Textual Practice* 15 (1): 87–100.

Michaels, Walter Benn. 1987. *The gold standard and the logic of naturalism.* Berekely, Los Angeles, London: University of California Press.

———. 2006. *The trouble with diversity: How we learned to love identity and ignore inequality.* New York: Metropolitan Books.

Mises Institute. 2017. Alan Greenspan admits Ron Paul was right about gold. mises.org/wire/alan-greenspan-admits-ron-paul-was-right-about-gold. Accessed 1 February 2020.

Murname, Ben. 2018. *Ayn Rand and the posthuman; the mind-made future.* Basingstoke: Palgrave Macmillan.

Rand, Ayn. 1957. *Atlas shrugged.* New York: Random House.

———. 1966. *Capitalism: The unknown ideal.* New York: Signet.

———. 1975. *The romantic manifesto.* New York: Signet.

Thomas, Brook. 1991. Walter Benn Michaels and the new historicism: Where's the difference? *Boundary 2* 18 (1): 18–59.

Tucker-Abramson, Myka. 2018. *Novel shocks: Urban renewal and the origins of neoliberalism.* New York: Fordham University Press.

Wilt, Judith. 1999. The romances of Ayn Rand. In *Feminist interpretations of Ayn Rand*, ed. Mimi Gladstein and Chris Matthew Sciabarra, 173–198. University Park: Pennsylvania State University.

INDEX

Lightning Source UK Ltd.
Milton Keynes UK
UKHW020800310119
336352UK00002B/20/P

9 780368 142437